BASIC

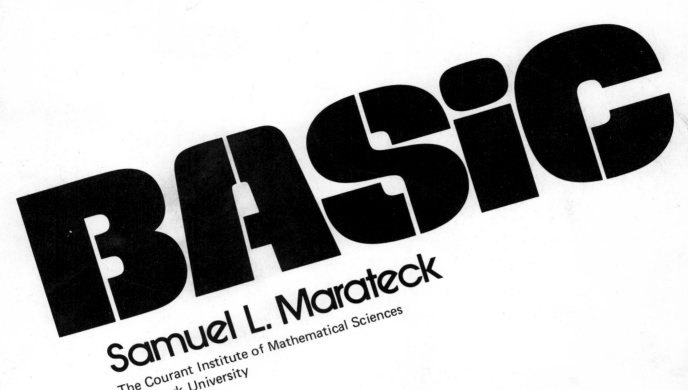

Samuel L. Marateck

The Courant Institute of Mathematical Sciences
New York University

NEW YORK   SAN FRANCISCO   LONDON

 ACADEMIC PRESS

A Subsidiary of Harcourt Brace Jovanovich, Publishers

ACADEMIC PRESS, INC.
111 Fifth Avenue, New York, New York 10003

United Kingdom Edition published by
ACADEMIC PRESS, INC. (LONDON) LTD.
24/28 Oval Road, London NW1

Library of Congress Cataloging in Publication Data

Marateck, Samuel.
    BASIC.

    Bibliography: p.
    Includes index.
    1.   Basic (Computer program language)   I.   Title.
QA76.73.B3M37   001.6'424   74-27787
ISBN 0–12–470450–6

To my parents Harold and Rita

Contents

1

Introduction to Computers and Programming

2

Introduction to BASIC

3

The Various System Commands and Their Uses

4

READ, DATA, GO TO, IF, **and** INPUT **Statements**

5

The FOR–NEXT **Loop**

6

Strings and Library Functions

7

The STOP, **Multiple Assignment, and** ON–GO TO **Statements and Subscripted Variables**

8

Subscripted String Variables, Subroutines and User-Defined Functions

9

Doubly Subscripted Variables and Matrices

10

PRINT USING and Files

Preface

This book is an outgrowth of notes the author uses in a course in BASIC that he teaches to undergraduates at New York University. Its purpose is to teach the student how to program using the BASIC language, and it has been written for students who have no prior knowledge of computers or programming. In order to make the book easier for such students to understand, the author in most cases has introduced only one new programming concept per program. Thus, many of the programs in the book are first written as a series of smaller programs, each of which serves as a step in understanding the entire larger program. The author has found this to be an effective teaching technique.

Simple programs have been used to illustrate the various programming techniques discussed in this book. These programs are the solutions to problems drawn from various disciplines, and they are of a nature such that students, whatever their major field, should understand them without difficulty.

The author has also included in the book examples of common programming mistakes made by beginning students when they are not explicit enough in translating their thoughts into programming instructions. The author has found this type of example to be another effective teaching technique. Now a word on why BASIC is the ideal language to use in an introductory course.

The vast majority of BASIC programs are typed and run in an interactive environment; that is, the student and computer can interact with each other while the student is typing and running his program. For instance, the computer informs the student that he has made an error almost as soon as he has made it. The student can then correct his mistakes and rerun his program without delay. This immediate feedback enables students to learn the elements of programming quite easily. In order to make this task even easier, the author has designed the book in the following way: the right-hand pages contain pictorial material on programming, which should be easily digestible; this is described in detail in "To the Reader" (page xi). The left-hand pages contain the text. You will see that strict adherence to this design has resulted in a number of partially filled pages. It has been the author's experience that, in many cases, students who have sat down at the teletypewriter without having previously gone to class, and have used only the right-hand pages of preliminary versions of this book, have been able to write programs in their first session at the teletypewriter. In order for the student to understand all the ramifications of the programming techniques described he should also read the text on the left-hand facing page. We now make some remarks about BASIC itself.

The BASIC language was developed under the direction of J. Kemeny and T. Kurtz at Dartmouth College in the 1960s. Since then, the various manufacturers of computers in developing their own versions of BASIC have added programming instructions to the original Dartmouth version. Fortunately, the significant additions incorporated in these various versions of BASIC for the most part have been quite similar. Therefore, the reader should encounter no difficulty in running on any computer that supports BASIC the overwhelming majority of the programs presented in this book. This includes the programs involving matrix operations.

The format of the matrix statements is such that one general form can be used on all computers. However, depending on the version of BASIC you are using, you may have options on how and where in the program you can dimension matrices other than in a DIM statement. Therefore, in order to enable you to run the programs that involve matrices on any computer, we have written these programs without using any of the available dimension options. However, we have described all the possible dimension options in a table that appears at the end of the chapter on matrices.

Perhaps the only way that your interaction with the computer may differ somewhat from what we describe here is how you instruct the computer to process your program. We have described the processing instructions—called system commands—that are in most general use, i.e., those used in Dartmouth BASIC [GE, DEC(PDP), CDC, UNIVAC, and RTB]; however, we have detailed in the footnotes how the system on another popular system, the one used on the Hewlett-Packard 2000 series, differs from what we describe in the text. In the other chapters we have described in the footnotes how some aspects of the instructions used on other systems—especially the Hewlett-Packard but also the XDS Sigma series, IBM 360, IBM 370, and CDC 6600—differ from what we describe in the text.

The chapters in this book, with the exception of the one on system commands (Chapter 3), should be read in sequential order. The reader may want to defer reading Chapter 3 until some later time. Chapter 3 was placed toward the beginning of the book because it was felt that the knowledge of system commands would enable the reader to write and correct programs more easily and effectively.

The programs shown in this book were checked out and run on one or more of the following computers: Hewlett-Packard 2000C, CDC 6600, XDS Sigma 7, IBM 370, and UNIVAC 1108.

It is a pleasure to thank Professor J. T. Schwartz and Professor Max Goldstein for their kindness to me while I was writing this book, and Jeffrey Akner and Martin Mathiot for granting me free time on their machines.

To the Reader

This book has been written with the premise that it is at times easier to learn a subject from pictorial representations supported by text than from text supported by pictorial representations. With this in mind, beginning with Chapter 2 we have used a double-page format for our presentation. On the left-hand page (we call it the text page) appears the text, and on the right-hand page (we call it the picture page) appears the pictorial representation, consisting mostly of programs and tables.

Each picture page was written to be as self-contained as possible, so that the reader, if he so desires, may read that page first and absorb the essence of the contents of the entire double page before going on to read the text. The text page consists of a very thorough discussion of the programming techniques presented on the picture page. It refers to parts of the programs and tables on the picture page; when reference is made on the text page to a given line of print on the picture page, that line—whenever it is feasible to do so—is reproduced in the text to promote readability. Students who have a previous background in programming languages and others who understand the picture page completely may find that in some chapters they can skip the text (left-hand) pages and concentrate on the picture pages.

The following techniques are used as aids in making the picture page self-contained.

1. As many as possible of the ideas discussed in the text are illustrated in the programs and tables. The captions beneath these capsulate much of what is said in the text.

2. Words underlined in the captions describe lines underlined in the figures. To illustrate this, Fig. 2.1a is reproduced below.

```
10      LET A=21.2
20      LET B=30.1
30      END
```

Figure 2.1a. A simple BASIC program illustrating the use of the assignment statement.

The statements 10 LET A = 21.2 and 20 LET B = 30.1 are underlined to show that they are described by the words underlined in the caption. Thus they are both assignment statements.

3. To the right of most programs appears a table that describes what effect certain lines in the program have on the computer's memory. For instance, the following table describes the effect that the line of programming to its left has on the memory:

		Line no.	A
10	LET A=21.2	10	21.2

We see from the table that line number 10 of the program causes the number 21.2 to be associated with A in the computer's memory. The line-by-line analysis afforded by these tables should aid the reader in understanding the program.

1

Introduction to Computers and Programming

1.1. General Remarks

Most of you reading this book have had very little previous experience with computers. You therefore may think of a computer as an electronic brain that makes important decisions for astronauts or predicts the outcome of political elections. A computer is certainly this, and more. However, it is not a machine that does things of its own volition, independent of what man orders it to do. At the present stage of their development, computers only follow the instructions that people give them. These instructions are called programs, and the people who write programs are called programmers.

The form that these instructions take depends on the programming language the programmer uses. Some of these languages are hard to learn whereas others are relatively easy. It is the purpose of this book to teach you how to write programs in the language that is the easiest to learn. It is called BASIC, an acronym for Beginner's All-purpose Symbolic Instruction Code. First, a few comments on computers and programming languages in general.

One way of picturing a computer is as a maze of on–off electrical switches connected by wires. Thus, you might imagine that, if a programmer wished to instruct a computer to do something, he would have to feed it a program composed of a series of on–off types of instructions. As a matter of fact, the first programs written were like this. The type of language that uses this form of instruction is called "machine language," and it is, to a limited extent, still used today by certain categories of expert programmers. Writing programs in machine language is very tedious. For this reason, computer languages closer in form to English and algebra have been devised. The easiest of these to learn is BASIC.

A program written in BASIC cannot be directly understood by the computer; it must first be translated into machine language. A special program, called a compiler, which is already present in the computer, does this. BASIC has grammatical rules that must be followed by the programmer. These rules are similar to those in English which govern the sequence of words in a sentence, punctuation, and spelling—we shall learn these rules in later chapters. Before the compiler translates your program, it checks whether you have written your program instructions according to the grammatical rules. If you make grammatical errors in writing an instruction, don't worry; the compiler has been written so that it will inform you of these. You must correct the errors before the compiler will translate your program. Do not be surprised if your programs are full of errors—it is a rare person who can write a program without making them.

Now, we give a more detailed view of the computer. Essentially, the computer consists of an *input unit,* a *memory unit,* an *arithmetic unit,* an *output* unit, and a *control unit.* We communicate our program to the computer through the *input unit.* All the mathematics and decisions in the program are done in the *arithmetic unit.* Numbers are stored in the *memory,* which consists of thousands of memory locations. We shall speak about these memory locations in more detail later in this chapter. The computer communicates the results of our program to us through the *output unit.* Finally the *control unit* directs the activities of the other four units.

The word hardware is used to describe the physical components of the computer, such as these units, whereas the word software is used to describe the programs. We shall use the word system to describe the programs, such as the compiler, that process the programs you write.

In general, the system used on one make of computer will differ somewhat from the system used on another make. In fact, it is possible to implement more than one system on a given computer. Therefore, when we describe the differences—most of them minor—that one may encounter when running the same BASIC program on different computers, we shall, for the most part, attribute these differences to the system employed.

We now describe that piece of hardware which, for most of you, will be the only part of the computer you will ever encounter: the teletypewriter.

1.2.   The Teletypewriter

The teletypewriter is both an input and an output device. Basically, it is a typewriter that is electrically connected to the rest of the computer. From now on we will follow the common practice of using the word *computer* to refer to the rest of the computer as opposed to the teletypewriter. The programmer types his program on the teletypewriter, and the computer types the results on it. The part of the teletypewriter that comes into actual contact with the teletypewriter paper while doing the printing is called the printing head. In Fig. 1.1 we show a typical teletypewriter.

Figure 1.1. Teletype Model 33 unit. (Courtesy of Teletype Corporation.)

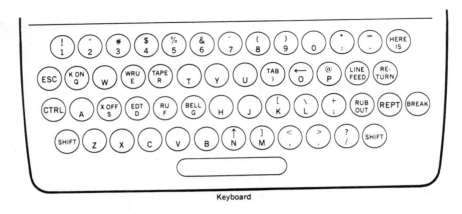

Keyboard

Figure 1.2. Teletypewriter keyboard. (Courtesy of Teletype Corporation.)

The teletypewriter keyboard—the one shown in Fig. 1.2 is for the Teletype Corporation teletypewriter—differs somewhat from the typewriter keyboard. Although you can type lowercase letters—for example, a—on a typewriter, you cannot type them on the teletypewriter; when you depress the teletypewriter key marked A, a capital letter A appears on the teletypewriter paper. If you simultaneously depress the SHIFT key and one of the keys on which there is both a letter of the alphabet and above it a symbol—for example,

the ↑, but not a capital N, will be printed. On the other hand, if you try to depress simultaneously the SHIFT key and one of the keys on which there is both a letter and above it a group of letters—for example,

nothing will be typed. These groups of letters, in almost all cases, are not used to communicate with the computer. If they are used, they must be depressed simultaneously with the CTRL key.

We now briefly describe the function of the other keys. Some of these functions will be described in greater detail in the appropriate places later in the book.

LINE FEED: This key advances the paper in the teletypewriter one line.

RETURN: This key returns the typing head to the beginning of the next line, signaling the computer that you have finished typing a line. The information on that line is then recorded by the computer.

RUB OUT: In some systems, if this key is depressed before RETURN, it deletes the line just typed so that the line is not recorded by the computer. It is also used in punching a paper tape.

BREAK: This key is used on some systems to stop your program or the automatic retyping of your program.

ALT MODE or, on some teletypewriters, ESC: If this key is depressed before RETURN, it deletes the line just typed so that the line is not recorded by the computer.

CTRL: In some systems, when this key is depressed simultaneously with some other key, it has the same effect as BREAK.

REPT: This key, when depressed simultaneously with another key, causes the action of that key to be repeated.

HERE IS: This key is used in the process of punching a paper tape to produce holes in the tape for a leader or trailer.

The operation of the remaining keys is the same as on a typewriter. If the key is depressed, the lower symbol appearing on the key is typed. If the key is depressed together with the SHIFT key, the upper symbol is typed. We shall explain the function of the symbols that are neither numeric nor alphabetic as we encounter them in the book. For the remainder of the book we shall refer to the symbols on the keyboard—except for the groups of letters—as characters.

1.3. Solving a Problem

We now describe the solution of a problem, which will give us a further insight into computers and programming. The problem is to determine the regional distribution of people standing in line in a certain city. That is, we wish to determine how many people come from the north, south, east, and west sides of the city.

We begin by drawing on a piece of paper four boxes, which we label N, S, E, and W, as shown in Fig. 1.3a. These letters represent north, south, east, and west, respectively. We shall place in the appropriate box a number indicating the number of people we have encountered from the north, south, east, and west sides of the city, as we question the people in line.

The composition of the line is shown in Fig. 1.3a. The fact that the first letter on the line is a W means that the first person comes from the west; the same type of correspondence is applied to the rest of the line. The arrow indicates which person we are questioning. Before reading the next paragraph, please study all of Fig. 1.3.

We first place a zero in each of the four boxes, as shown in Fig. 1.3a. This indicates that we have not as yet encountered anyone from any section of the city. We ask the first person in line which part of the city he is from. We are told "the west." We record this by adding 1 to the 0 which is in the box marked W, obtaining 1. In order to record this result, we erase the zero that was originally in this box and replace it by the digit 1. The box for the west now contains 1, and the other three boxes still contain 0, as shown in Fig. 1.3b. We ask the second person where he is from; he answers, "the north." We thus add 1 to the 0 which is in the box marked N, obtaining 1. To record this we erase the 0 in this box and replace it by a 1, as shown in Fig. 1.3c. We see here that the rest of the boxes still contain the numbers they contained in Fig. 1.3b. We ask the third person where he is from; he answers, "the west." We now add 1 to the 1 already in the box marked W, obtaining 2. We then erase 1, the previous entry in the box, and replace it with 2, as shown in Fig. 1.3d. We continue to the end of the line, applying this same procedure to each person we question. After the last person has told us where he is from and the information has been recorded, the boxes contain the numbers shown in Fig. 1.3e.

If this problem were to be programmed and run on a computer, the function of the boxes—that is, to contain or "store" the numbers—would be played by the computer's memory locations. Like the boxes, a memory location can store only one number at a time; moreover, when the computer places a number in a memory location, it automatically erases the location's previous contents—that is, the number that was previously stored there. The placing of zeros in all the boxes at the beginning of the problem and the addition of 1s to the correct boxes would be done by the computer's arithmetic unit. The people standing in line are called the *data* or *input* to the program. We would type on the teletypewriter both the program that solves the problem and the data for the program, thus transmitting them to the computer. After the program was done—if we wanted—the computer would type the results of the program on the teletypewriter. The control unit would supervise the activities of the other four units as they did this problem.

Indeed, all the power of the computer is not exhibited in our example. For instance, the computer can multiply many numbers together and get the results almost immediately. It can do a multitude of complex calculations that man, without the aid of a computer, would hesitate to undertake. In the following chapters we shall give many examples of what computers can do.

SOLVING A PROBLEM

Problem: Determining the regional distribution of people standing in line in a certain city. The letter N denotes north, S denotes south, E denotes east, W denotes west. The arrow indicates which person is being questioned.

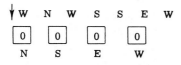

Figure 1.3a. Composition of the line and the contents of the boxes before questioning begins. The arrow is at left of line, indicating that questioning has not begun.

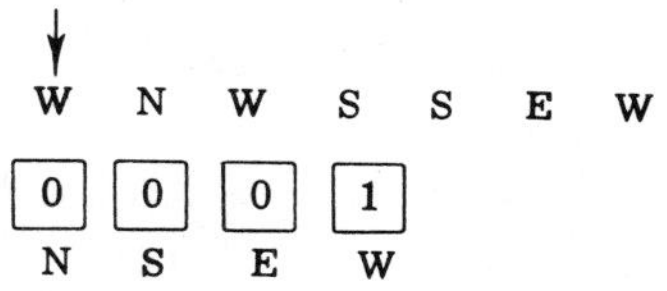

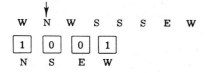

Figure 1.3b. We add 1 to the box for west after questioning the first person.

Figure 1.3c. We add 1 to the box for north after questioning the second person.

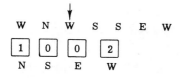

Figure 1.3d. We add 1 to the box for west after questioning the third person. It now contains 2.

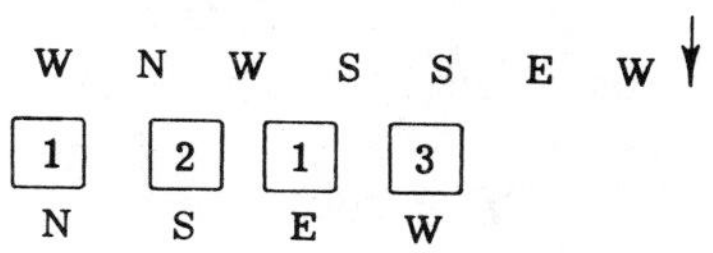

Figure 1.3e. The contents of all boxes after we have questioned each person in the line.

1.4. Time-Sharing

Most BASIC programs are processed by what is called a time-sharing system. On most of these systems, the programmer types his program on the teletypewriter while it is connected to the computer. When a programmer makes a grammatical error in an instruction, he is informed by the computer what and where his error is. This is done either as soon as he has finished typing a line and depressed the RETURN key, or after he has finished typing the entire program, depending on the system used. Also, after he has finished typing his program, he receives the results almost immediately. If the programmer so desires, he can write his program so that he can interact with the computer while it is processing his program.

The power of this system is that many programmers can communicate with the computer simultaneously and thus share a given period of time on the computer; hence the term time-sharing. The teletypewriters connected to the computer are called time-sharing terminals. Even when many programmers are using the time-sharing system, the computer responds very quickly to anything typed on an individual teletypewriter.

1.5. Getting on the Computer

The first thing you do is to turn the teletypewriter ON–OFF switch to LINE. Then you must identify yourself to the computer. This process of identifying yourself is called "logging in." Essentially it involves typing your identification number and password, both of which have been assigned to you by the computer center. After you log in, the system on most computers responds in one of the following ways.

If the system can accept more than one language, it will first request what language you will be using. We now describe a procedure that is followed on many versions of BASIC. The computer requests the language you want to use, by typing

```
SYSTEM--
```

Since you want to write a program in BASIC, you type BASIC and then hit the RETURN key. The computer then asks whether you are writing a new program by typing

```
NEW OR OLD--
```

If you are writing your first program or a new program, type NEW after this and then hit the RETURN key (the meaning of OLD will be explained in Chapter 3). The computer then requests the name of the new program by typing

```
NEW PROGRAM NAME--
```

You then type the name you have selected for your program. For instance, you might type

```
PROG1
```

On most systems, the program name can consist of up to 6 characters.

After you have typed the name of your program, you hit the RETURN key. The computer then types READY, signifying that it is ready to receive BASIC instructions. You then type your program. This sequence of the questions the computer asks and the answers you supply are given in Table 1.1.

GETTING ON THE COMPUTER

Line no.	Computer types	You type	Then you
1	`SYSTEM--`	`BASIC`	Depress the RETURN key
2	`NEW OR OLD--`	`NEW`	Depress the RETURN key
3	`NEW PROGRAM NAME--`	`PROG1`	Depress the RETURN key
4	`READY`	Your program	

Table 1.1. After you have successfully identified yourself to the computer, you must inform the computer that you: wish to use the BASIC language (line 1); wish to write a NEW program (line 2); wish the name of this program to be PROG1 (line 3). The computer signals that it is ready to receive your next instruction by typing READY (line 4). You then type your program. On some systems, BASIC is the only language available for teletypewriter; in this case, line 1 is omitted. You log out by typing BYE.

Some systems that accept only BASIC programs from the teletypewriter will type the sequence of questions we have just discussed but will omit—as you might expect—typing SYSTEM. Thus, the first question it types is NEW OR OLD. The procedure you should then follow is the same as the one just discussed.

On other computers that accept only BASIC programs on the teletypewriter, after you sign in the computer will immediately be ready to accept BASIC instructions. It will type some appropriate welcoming message or simply type the word READY. You then type your program.

Time-sharing users are usually assigned a specific amount of time. Thus, you should inform the computer when you have finished using the teletypewriter so that no one else can use your alloted time after you have left. The process is called logging out. You log out by typing BYE or some other message prescribed for the computer you use. We describe the time you spend on the teletypewriter between logging in and logging out as a session. After you have typed BYE, the computer types a response; this usually informs you how much time you used at your session on the teletypewriter.

2

Introduction to BASIC

2.1. General Remarks

A BASIC program is a series of statements, which are instructions to the computer. Each statement appears on one line, and each line must be given a different line number (sometimes called a statement number). Thus, no two statements can have the same line number. The line numbers are whole numbers and can vary between 1 and, on most systems, 99999.

In Fig. 2.1a we see a simple BASIC program consisting of three statements, which appear on the lines numbered 10, 20, and 30. The END statement appearing in line 30 signals the computer that we wish the program to end. Every BASIC program must have an END appearing as the highest-numbered statement.* We shall now explain the meaning of the other statements appearing in Fig. 2.1a.

2.2. The Assignment and PRINT Statements; RUN; Add and Multiply

In order to store a number in a location in the computer's memory, we give these locations names, which are called variables, and assign numbers to them in the program. The assignment of numbers to the variables is made by a statement beginning with the word LET, as shown in the program in Fig. 2.1a. Here A and B are the variables. Thus, in line 10 of Fig. 2.1a we assign the number 21.2 to A by typing †

$$10 \quad LET \ A=21.2$$

This is a direction to place the number 21.2 in the memory location named A. In a similar way, in line 20 we assign the number 30.1 to B by typing

$$20 \quad LET \ B=30.1$$

This is a direction to place the number 30.1 in the memory location called B. Another way of describing what has happened in these two statements is to say that A has been given the value 21.1, and B the value 30.1.

* On the XDS Sigma series, you do not need an END statement.

† On some teletypewriters the digit zero is printed with a slash drawn through it, i.e., Ø .

A SIMPLE PROGRAM

```
10   LET A=21.2
20   LET B=30.1
30   END
```

Figure 2.1a. A simple BASIC program showing the use of the assignment statement. The number 21.2 is assigned to variable A and 30.1 to B. Each line in the program has a different line number, and the program must end with the word END.

We have now written a program but have not as yet told the computer what to do with it. Obviously, we wish the computer to follow the instructions in the statements of the program. When the computer does this, we say it "executes" the statements. We tell the computer to execute the statements in our program by typing the word RUN as shown in Fig. 2.1b. We note here that RUN is not a statement in the program but an order to the computer concerning the processing of the program itself and is called a "system command." Since any instruction with a line number is considered to be a statement, we must type system commands without line numbers; this we have done, as is shown for the system command RUN in Fig. 2.1b.

After we type RUN, assuming that we have made no errors, the computer executes each line of our simple program—beginning with the lowest-numbered statement and then executing the next sequentially numbered statement until it reaches the highest-numbered one. It follows this order unless we specifically instruct it in the program to follow a different order. We shall described how to change the order in a later chapter.

We now follow the execution of the program in Fig. 2.1a with the help of the table for Fig. 2.1a. This table shows the value of the variables as each line number of the program is executed (the table is meant to be used as a learning aid; it is not part of the program).

Line no.	A	B
10	21.2	Undef
20	21.2	30.1

We see from this table that at line 10 the value associated with A in the computer's memory is 21.2, and at line 20 the value associated with B is 30.1. We also note that at line 10 of the program the variable B has not yet been assigned a number. In such a case, we say that the variable is undefined. This is reflected in the table by the entry "Undef" in the position corresponding to line 10 and the variable B. When a variable has been assigned a number, we say that the variable is defined.

Once a variable is assigned a given number, it retains that assignment until the end of the program unless we assign it a new number. Thus, we see from the table for Fig. 2.1a that at line 20

Line no.	A	B
20	21.2	30.1

the computer remembers that the number 21.2 was assigned to the variable A.

When the computer encounters the END statement, it finishes execution. It usually signifies this by typing a message on the teletypewriter. Depending on the system used by the computer, it may type READY, DONE, END, or some other appropriate message. In this book we shall follow the most common convention and use the word READY to signify the end of execution.

The results of the execution are shown in Fig. 2.1b. We note, to our disappointment, that the computer has printed nothing in Fig. 2.1b but the word READY.

Only the word READY was typed by the computer because the computer executed the two assignment statements, encountered the END statement, and then stopped, "ready" to receive another instruction (as we shall see, this instruction could be either a new statement

RUNNING A PROGRAM

```
1Ø    LET  A=21.2
2Ø    LET  B=3Ø.1
3Ø    END
```

Figure 2.1a. The figure is reproduced for the reader's convenience.

Line no.	A	B
10	21.2	Undef
20	21.2	30.1

Table for Fig. 2.1a. Status of the variable assignments in Fig. 2.1a, given by line number. At line 10 the value of B has not yet been defined. At line 20 the computer remembers that 21.2 was assigned to A.

```
RUN
READY
```

Figure 2.1b. Running the program shown in Fig. 2.1a. RUN is a command to the computer to process the program and thus does not have a line number. READY signifies that the computer has finished processing the program and is "ready" to receive another program or command. Nothing else was typed here because we did not instruct the computer to do so.

in the program or a system command). Since we did not instruct the program to communicate the assignments to us during the execution of the program, it did not do so.

To remedy this situation, we have rewritten our original program and have added a PRINT statement,

```
30    PRINT A,B
```

as shown in Fig. 2.2a. This statement tells the computer to print on the teletypwriter first the number assigned to the variable A and then, on the same line, the number assigned to the variable B. The order in which the numbers assigned to A and B will be printed by the computer is determined by the order in which A and B appear in the PRINT statement. The variables in the PRINT statement must be separated by a comma, as is shown in Fig. 2.2a, or by a semicolon.

If we want to determine how the results of the program in Fig. 2.2a will appear on the teletypwriter we instruct the computer to execute the program. As mentioned before, this is done by typing the word RUN on the teletypewriter. The computer then prints the results:

```
21.2                30.1
```

where 21.2 is the value of A, and 30.1 is the value of B. It then prints the word **READY**. All this is shown in Fig. 2.2b.

We see from the table for Fig. 2.2a that, during execution, by the time the PRINT statement in line 30 is reached

Line no.	A	B
30	21.2	30.1

both A and B have been defined. The computer (as we have mentioned before) remembers the numbers assigned to both variables and will have no difficulty in printing them. However, if either A or B has not been defined by the time the PRINT statement in line 30 is executed, depending on the type of computer * we use, an error may occur in the running of the program. We shall discuss this below.

If, after the program has been run, we wish to reverse the order in which the numbers assigned to the variables A and B are printed, we have to reverse the order of the variables in the PRINT statement. Thus, line 30 of Fig. 2.2a should now be written

```
30    PRINT B,A
```

We retype the program with this change as shown in Fig. 2.2c. When the program is executed, the computer prints

```
30.1                21.2
```

where 30.1 is the value of B, and 21.2 is the value of A. It then prints the word **READY**. This is shown in Fig. 2.2d.

If we had wanted to print only one variable—for example, A—then we would have typed statement 30 as

```
30      PRINT A
```

and would not have typed a comma after A. We shall discuss the PRINT statement in more detail in Section 2.6.

---

* For instance, the use of an undefined variable in a program will produce an error if the program is run on the Hewlett-Packard HP 2000C.

USING THE PRINT STATEMENT

```
10   LET A=21.2
20   LET B=30.1
30   PRINT A,B
40   END
```

Figure 2.2a. A BASIC program with a PRINT statement (which prints the results on the teletypewriter). The variables A and B must be separated by a comma or a semicolon.

Line no.	A	B
10	21.2	Undef
20	21.2	30.1
30	21.2	30.1

Table for Fig. 2.2a. Status of the variable assignments for Fig. 2.2a given by line number. Note: Both variables must be (and have been) assigned values before they are printed in line 30.

```
RUN

21.2            30.1
```
Value of A   *Value of* B
```
READY
```

Figure 2.2b. Running the program of Fig. 2.2a. The order in which the variables appear in the PRINT statement determines the order in which their values will be printed.

```
10   LET A=21.2
20   LET B=30.1
30   PRINT B,A
40   END
```

Figure 2.2c. Line 30 in this program replaces line 30 in the previous program (Fig. 2.2a) and thus changes the order in which A and B are printed as shown in Fig. 2.2d.

```
RUN

30.1            21.2
```
Value of B   *Value of* A
```
READY
```

Figure 2.2d. Running the program of Fig. 2.2c.

We now alter our program so that it will add the value of A to the value of B and assign the result to C. We do this by including

40   LET C=A+B

in the program. The plus sign, as you might expect, is the symbol for addition. Since we want the computer to print the result of this addition, we also add

50   PRINT C

to the program. The altered program is shown in Fig. 2.3a. Note that the line number of the END statement must be changed so that it is still the highest-numbered statement in the program.

The table for Fig. 2.3a shows the status of each of the variables at each line of the program, as they are executed by the computer. We see that at line 30

Line no.	A	B	C
30	21.2	30.1	Undef

the variable C is yet undefined. Consequently, at this line in the program

30   PRINT A,B

we have instructed the computer to print only those variables that have been assigned numbers, namely, A and B, but not C. If we do not wish to, we do not have to insert a PRINT statement in the program here. We have done this only for instructional purposes. It is important to observe that, after values of A and B have been printed here, the computer still remembers them. Thus, when the computer prints something, it simply copies a number from a memory location to the teletypewriter—the computer does not erase the number from the memory location. The computer can thus perform the calculation in 40 LET C $=$ A $+$ B.

We explain this statement with the help of line 40 of the table:

Line no.	A	B	C
40	21.2	30.1	51.3

The computer is instructed to take the value of A (which we see is 21.2) add it to the value of B (which we see is 30.1), and assign the result (which is 51.3) to C.

We obtain the results of this program by typing the command RUN. We see in Fig. 2.3b that each PRINT produces a separate line of results.

21.2   30.1

are the results of the PRINT statement in line 30 and are thus the values of A and B,

51.3

is the result of the PRINT statement in line 50. It is the value of the sum of A and B.

PERFORMING AN ADDITION

```
10        LET A=21.2
20        LET B=30.1
30        PRINT A,B
40        LET C=A+B
50        PRINT C
60        END
```

Figure 2.3a. We have altered the program of Fig. 2.2a so that in line 40, we now instruct the computer to add the value of A to the value of B and then to assign the result to C. In line 50 we print this result. The symbol for addition is the plus sign.

Line no.	A	B	C
10	21.2	Undef	Undef
20	21.2	30.1	Undef
30	21.2	30.1	Undef
40	21.2	30.1	51.3
50	21.2	30.1	51.3

Table for Fig. 2.3a. Status of the variable assignments for Fig. 2.3a, given by line number. We see from line 40 that after A and B have been printed their values are still stored in the computer's memory. Thus in line 40, the computer has no difficulty in calculating A+B; it assigns the result—which we see is 51.3—to C.

```
RUN
21.2            30.1 ← Printed by line 30
51.3 ←               Printed by line 50
READY.
```

Figure 2.3b. The results of Fig. 2.3a. Each PRINT statement produces a new line of results.

The symbol for multiplication in BASIC is the asterisk, *. We use it in the program of Fig. 2.4a. Here we have altered the preceding program so that it calculates the product A*B, i.e., multiples the value of A by the value of B; then assigns the results to C. This is done in

40   LET C=A*B

We see from the table for Fig. 2.4a that when line 40 is executed

Line no.	A	B	C
40	21.2	30.1	638.12

the product 638.12 is assigned to C. The printed results obtained when the program is run are shown in Fig. 2.4b.

21.2   30.1

These numbers are the result of the PRINT statement in line 30 and are the values of A and B, respectively.

638.12

is the result of the PRINT statement in line 50. It is the value of the product A*B.

A calculation involving only numbers can also be done in an assignment statement. Thus we can rewrite the program of Fig. 2.4a, so as to eliminate the assignment statements in lines 10 and 20 and simply write

40   LET C=21.2*30.1

as we have shown in Fig. 2.4c (we have also eliminated the PRINT statement in line 30 since there is no need for it). The result of running this program is shown in Fig. 2.4d. As to be expected, 638.12, the result of the calculation, is the same as the result of the calculation for the previous program. In Section 2.7, we will describe all the operations available in BASIC and their use.

PERFORMING A MULTIPLICATION

```
10        LET A=21.2
20        LET B=30.1
30        PRINT A,B
40        LET C=A*B
50        PRINT C
60        END
```

Figure 2.4a. We have altered the preceding program (Fig. 2.3a) so that in line 40, we now instruct the computer to multiply the value of A by the value of B and then to assign the result to C. The symbol for multiplication is the asterisk, *.

Line no.	A	B	C
10	21.2	Undef	Undef
20	21.2	30.1	Undef
30	21.2	30.1	Undef
40	21.2	30.1	638.12
50	21.2	30.1	638.12

Table for Fig. 2.4a. Status of the variable assignments for Fig. 2.4a given by line number. In line 40 the product A*B is calculated and the result (which is 638.12) is assigned to C.

```
RUN
21.2                  30.1  ←-Printed by line 30
638.12 ←——————————— Printed by line 50
READY.
```

Figure 2.4b. The results of Fig. 2.4a.

```
40        LET C=21.2*30.1
50        PRINT C
60        END
```

Figure 2.4c. We rewrite the preceding program (Fig. 2.4a) so that the calculation in the assignment statement (line 40) is in terms of numbers only. We have thus eliminated lines 10 to 30 because now there is no need for them.

```
RUN
638.12
READY.
```

Figure 2.4d. The result of running the program of Fig. 2.4c. The result of the calculation is the same as in Fig. 2.4b.

We now investigate what happens when we assign a new number to a variable that has already been defined. For example, the variable B, which is originally assigned the value 30.1 in line 20 of Fig. 2.5a.

$$20 \quad \text{LET} \quad B=30.1$$

is redefined in line 40:

$$40 \quad \text{LET} \quad B=25.6$$

We observe the consequence of this in line 40 of the table for Fig. 2.5a:

Line no.	A	B
40	21.2	25.6

i.e., the number assigned to B is no longer the previous one, 30.1, but the new number 25.6. When the computer executes line 50 of the program:

$$50 \quad \text{PRINT} \quad A,B$$

it will thus print 25.6 as the value of B. To check this, we run the program. The results are as we expect and are shown in Fig. 2.5b; because there are two PRINT statements, we again get two lines of results:

$$21.2 \qquad\qquad 30.1$$

which is printed by line 30, and

$$21.2 \qquad\qquad 25.6$$

which is printed by line 50. Note that the number 25.6 printed by line 50 is the one that was most recently assigned to B in the program. We can summarize this by saying that we can place only one number at a time in the memory location, and the number that remains is the one placed there last.

We now discuss the form of the two types of statements we have learned so far: the assignment statement and the PRINT statement.

ASSIGNMENT

The form of the assignment statement must be: statement number, followed by the word LET, followed by a variable, followed by an equals sign, followed by what we want to assign to the variable. Examples of assignment statements we could write at this point are:

```
 20    LET  R=A
300    LET  Z=-19536.7
 80    LET  W=X
 40    LET  T=A+D
 50    LET  W=R*Y
160    LET  U=1*2*3
100    LET  A=13.2+B
```

GIVING A VARIABLE A NEW VALUE (REDEFINING IT)

```
10   LET A=21.2
20   LET B=30.1
30   PRINT A,B
40   LET B=25.6
50   PRINT A,B
60   END
```

Figure 2.5a. A program in which one of the variables—in this case B—is redefined (given a new value).

Line no.	A	B
10	21.2	Undef
20	21.2	30.1
30	21.2	30.1
40	21.2	25.6
50	21.2	25.6

Table for Fig. 2.5a. Status of the variable assignments in Fig. 2.5a, given by line number. The value of B changes at line 40 since B is redefined there in the program.

```
RUN
 21.2          30.1 ←— Original value of B
 21.2          25.6 ←— Redefined value of B
READY
```

Figure 2.5b. The results of running the program in Fig. 2.5a. The value of B printed in the second line is the most recently defined value.

In the assignment statements as in any other statement, we are allowed to place blanks between any of the characters. In most systems, one may omit the word **LET** from the assignment statement. Thus on these systems

```
50      W=R*Y
```

would be a valid assignment statement.

In the assignment statement, as well as in the other types of statements we will learn if we do not follow the form prescribed for the statement (e.g., if we misspell **LET** or omit the equals sign) a grammatical error will result. An example of an incorrect assignment statement is

```
20   LET  4=R
```

The statement is incorrect because a number (here 4), and not a variable, follows **LET**.

PRINT

> The form of the **PRINT** statement is: statement number, followed by the word **PRINT**, followed by the items to be printed (so far, we have seen that these items * can be variables.) If there is more than one item in the **PRINT** statement, the items must be separated by commas, as we have shown, or by semicolons. Ordinarily, each **PRINT** statement instructs the computer to start a new line of typing on the teletypewriter. Examples of **PRINT** statements we could write at this point are:
>
> ```
> 30   PRINT A,B,C
> 40   PRINT D;A,X
> ```

2.3. The Naming of Variables

The BASIC programmer has very little freedom in naming variables. A variable name may be composed of one or two characters. The first character must be a letter. If the variable name is composed of two characters, the second must be one of the digits from 0 to 9. An example of a valid variable name is A9; A10 is an illegal variable name because it contains three characters. In Fig. 2.6 we show some examples of legal variable names, and in the table for Fig. 2.6 illegal variable names with the reasons for their illegality. If you use an illegal variable in a program, a grammatical error will result.

---

* We will see that these items can also be numbers, calculations, and strings (defined in Section 2.6).

NAMING VARIABLES

A1	A2	C6	H7
R	S6	B9	A2
T	U	V	W

Figure 2.6. Legal BASIC variable names: They consist of at most two characters, the first of which must be a letter. The letter may be followed by a second character, which must be a digit from 0 to 9.

Illegal variable name	Reason for illegality
AA	Second character not a digit
4F	First character not a letter
A2B	More than 2 characters
$1	Illegal character for first character

Table for Fig. 2.6. Illegal BASIC variable names with explanation of why they are illegal.

2.4. The Computer's Response to Grammatical Errors

We now discuss what happens when we run a program that contains grammatical errors. Such a program is shown in Fig. 2.7a.

```
10        WET  A=10.2
20        LET  ANS=31
30        LET  C=A*ANS
40        PRINT  C
50        END
```

Before executing this program, the computer checks every line of it for grammatical errors. The results are shown in Fig. 2.7b. The error message

```
        ILLEGAL  INSTRUCTION  IN  10
```

refers to the fact that **LET** is misspelled in

```
10        WET  A=10.2
```

The error message

```
        ILLEGAL  VARIABLE  IN  20
```

refers to the fact that the variable ANS in

```
20        LET  ANS=31
```

is an illegal variable. The error message

```
        ILLEGAL  VARIABLE  IN  30
```

refers to the fact that the illegal variable ANS is used in

```
30        LET  C=A*ANS
```

After the computer has found all the grammatical errors, it signals that it is ready to receive another instruction. On most systems, it does this by typing **READY**. In Fig. 2.7c we rewrite the program and correct all the mistakes. We then run it (Fig. 2.7d) and obtain the proper results.*

You will no doubt agree that the technique we have just discussed for correcting a program is tedious, since it involves retyping the entire program. We now discuss a more efficient way of altering programs, using the editing feature of the time-sharing BASIC system.

---

* On some versions of BASIC, the computer detects a grammatical error as soon as you finish typing the line on which you made the error. You must correct the error before you type the next line. In the next section we will give a full description on how to correct errors, including the correction of a given line in your program.

CORRECTION OF GRAMMATICAL ERRORS—A SIMPLE-MINDED APPROACH

```
10        WET  A=10.2
20        LET  ANS=31
30        LET  C=A*ANS
40        PRINT C
50        END
```

Figure 2.7a. A program in which errors are made: we misspell LET in line 10, and use the illegal variable ANS in lines 20 and 30.

```
RUN
ILLEGAL INSTRUCTION IN 10
ILLEGAL VARIABLE IN 20
ILLEGAL VARIABLE IN 30
READY
```

Figure 2.7b. Running the program of Fig. 2.7a. The computer finds all the grammatical errors we made.

```
10        LET  A=10.2
20        LET  A1=31
30        LET  C=A*A1
40        PRINT C
50        END
```

Figure 2.7c. We rewrite the program of Fig. 2.7a, correcting the errors. We now spell LET correctly and use the variable A1 in place of the illegal variable ANS.

```
RUN
 316.2
READY.
```

Figure 2.7d. Running the program of Fig. 2.7c. We now get error-free results.

2.5. Editing BASIC Programs Using Time-Sharing; LIST and SCRATCH

We will assume throughout this book that the teletypewriter is always connected to the computer. (When this is the case, the teletypewriter is said to be on-line.) As soon as the the RETURN key is depressed, the line just typed is recorded by the computer.

First we will discuss the correction of typing errors. We give as an example a PRINT statement in which we have mistakenly typed a Y instead of a T, as shown in Fig. 2.8a.

30 PRINY

and have caught the error before typing another character. We can delete the Y by typing an arrow (←) after it. We then type a T and proceed as usual, typing the variables we want printed

30 PRINY←T A,B

as is shown in Fig. 2.8b. When we depress the RETURN key, the corrected statement

30   PRINT A,B

will be recorded by the computer.

If we had discovered the error after we typed the A, e.g.,

30 PRINY A

as shown in Fig. 2.8c, we would have to delete the Y, the A, and the blank between them. We would thus type three ← s and would follow this by the proper characters

30 PRINY A←←←T A,B

as shown in Fig. 2.8d.

Again, after we hit the RETURN key, the corrected statement 30 PRINT A,B, is recorded by the computer. This method can be used for correcting statements and also system commands.

If we discover the mistake after we have finished typing the entire line but before we hit the RETURN key, and it is too cumbersome to use many arrows to correct it, we can hit the ESC key. Hitting the ESC key eliminates the entire line before it is recorded by the computer. On some types of teletypewriters the ALT MODE key or RUB OUT key will delete the line. After we have hit the ESC key, the computer returns the printing head to the beginning of the next line, and we can type the correct version of the previous line.

USING THE EDITING FEATURE TO REPLACE INCORRECT CHARACTERS IN A GIVEN LINE

```
30 PRINY
```

Figure 2.8a. A statement in which we discover an <u>error</u> immediately after we have made it. The correct statement should be: 30 PRINT A,B.

```
30 PRINY←T A,B
```

Figure 2.8b. We delete the <u>incorrect character,</u> Y, by typing an ← after it. Then we type T, the character by which we want to replace Y. Next we type the variables whose values we want printed by the program. When we hit the RETURN key, the corrected statement 30 PRINT A,B is transmitted to the computer.

```
30 PRINY A
```

Figure 2.8c. A statement in which the <u>error</u> is not discovered directly after it is made.

```
30 PRINY A←←←T A,B
```

Figure 2.8d. We delete the Y and the A and the <u>blank between them</u> with three consecutive arrows. We then type the desired characters.

If we discover the mistake after depressing the RETURN key, we can correct the error simply by retyping the entire line, including the line number as well. Since two statements cannot have the same line number, this procedure replaces the original incorrect statement with the retyped corrected one.* The reason for this is that any statement typed on the tele-typewriter—except during the execution of that program—under ordinary conditions will be included as part of the previous program. Thus statements can be included either before or after a program is run.

Armed with this knowledge we can now much more efficiently correct the program (originally shown in Fig. 2.7a) that contained grammatical errors. In Fig. 2.9a we again present this program and the errors detected by the computer after we had typed RUN. All we have to do to correct the program is retype correctly those lines that were incorrect in Fig. 2.9a. We correctly retype these lines as shown in Fig. 2.9b.

As soon as this is done, the retyped statements become part of the program shown in Fig. 2.9a, thus replacing the original statements that were incorrect. When we run the program, as is shown in Fig. 2.9c, we get an error-free result. Thus when the computer informs us that we have made errors, all we have to do to correct them is type the incorrect statement correctly and type RUN. We do not have to retype the entire program as we did previously. This technique of typing statements after the original version of the program is finished can be used also to add statements to, or delete statements from, a program. Hence we will refer to it as an editing technique. Using this editing technique we will now repeat the first few changes we made to the first program we discussed in this chapter.

---

* If the version of BASIC you are using detects an error in a line immediately after you have typed the line, this procedure will not stop the computer from typing an error message. After the computer has typed the error message, you should retype the entire line correctly. This new line replaces the original incorrect statement.

USING THE EDITING TECHNIQUE TO REPLACE INCORRECT LINES IN A PROGRAM

```
10      WET A=10.2
20      LET ANS=31
30      LET C=A*ANS
40      PRINT C
50      END
RUN
ILLEGAL INSTRUCTION IN 10
ILLEGAL VARIABLE IN 20
ILLEGAL VARIABLE IN 30
READY
```

Figure 2.9a. Running the incorrect program we presented in Fig. 2.7a.

```
10 LET A=10.2
20 LET A1=31
30 LET C=A*A1
```

Figure 2.9b. All we have to do to correct the program is correctly retype the incorrect lines, including the line numbers. The correctly typed lines replace the incorrect lines in Fig. 2.9a. Thus, we do not have to retype the entire program.

```
RUN
316.2
READY.
```

Figure 2.9c. Running the program of Fig. 2.9a as corrected in Fig. 2.9b. We see that we get an error-free result.

The first program that appeared in Section 2.1 is the one now shown in Fig. 2.10a. After running that program, we decided to add a PRINT statement to it. We will now number this statement as line 28:

```
28   PRINT A,B
```

We can now add it to the program of Fig. 2.10a simply by typing it after the last statement in that program or after the program has been run. As shown in Fig. 2.10b, we choose to type this statement after the last statement in the original program. After we type this statement, as soon as we hit the RETURN key the statement is included as part of the program. During execution of the altered program, line 28 will be executed after line 20 but before line 30. In order to see this, we type RUN. The results also are shown in Fig. 2.10b.

```
21.2              30.1
```

We would have obtained the same results if we had included statement 28 in the original program.

We now employ another feature of the time-sharing system to see how the program presently looks. By using the system command LIST, we tell the computer to type all the statements that we have typed, but which have not been erased, since we logged in. The statements will be typed with the line numbers in numerical order regardless of the order in which we typed them. This system command and the ensuing printing of our program is shown in Fig. 2.10c. After the program is typed, on many makes of computers the message READY will also be typed. LIST is a system command, just as RUN is, since it is an instruction to the computer concerning the processing of a program. It is thus typed without a line number. When the computer types a program, we say that the computer lists the program.

In Section 2.2 we reversed the order in which A and B were typed. Using the editing feature, we make the same alteration to the program of Fig. 2.10c by typing

```
28   PRINT B,A
```

after the listing of that program is finished. The alteration is shown in Fig. 2.10d. Since no two instructions can have the same statement number, this last procedure deletes the statement in line 28 in the preceding program and replaces it with the statement just typed. We can check to see that this was in fact done by typing the command LIST. This, with the ensuing listing of the present program, is shown in Fig. 2.10d.

USING THE EDITING TECHNIQUE TO ADD LINES TO, AND CHANGE LINES OF, A PROGRAM

```
10    LET A=21.2
20    LET B=30.1
30    END
```

Figure 2.10a. This is Fig. 2.1a reproduced for the reader's convenience.

```
28   PRINT A,B
RUN

21.2              30.1

READY
```

Figure 2.10b. We add a statement to the program of Fig. 2.10a simply by typing it after that program (or we may type it after running the program). Thus the statement of line 28 has become part of the previous program (Fig. 2.10a). This editing procedure eliminates the necessity of retyping the entire program. The running of the program is also shown here.

```
LIST

10    LET A=21.2
20    LET B=30.1
28    PRINT A,B
30    END

READY
```

Figure 2.10c. By typing the system command LIST, we instruct the computer to print all the statements we typed, but did not erase, since we logged in. Note: Although chronologically we typed statement 28 after 30, all the statements are printed here in numerical order. The running of the program is also shown here.

```
28   PRINT B,A
LIST

10    LET A=21.2
20    LET B=30.1
28    PRINT B,A
30    END

READY
```

Figure 2.10d. We change the statement in line 28 shown in the previous program (Fig. 2.10c) simply by typing 28 followed by the changed statement. We verify that it has replaced statement 28 in the previous program by typing LIST, whereupon the computer types the program.

In writing a program, sometimes we wish to delete a statement without replacing it with another. For instance, in the program which added the values of A and B (originally shown in Fig. 2.3a, now repeated in Fig. 2.11a), we might want to omit 30 PRINT A,B from the program after running it the first time. We can do this by simply typing the line number,

30

without any statement following the line number, as shown in Fig. 2.11b. We see the effect this has on the program when we type LIST—now statement 30 has been deleted. When we run the program, as is shown in Fig. 2.11c, we see that only one line of results is produced—the number that represents the sum of the value of A and the value of B

51.3

We conclude this section by discussing an "unexpected" result of using the editing system: During a given session at the teletypewriter, those statements that are not deleted from a previous program will automatically be incorporated in the present program and will "haunt" the programmer. For example, if, after running the program shown in Fig. 2.11b, we typed the program

```
10 LET A=13.2
20 PRINT A
30 END
```

as shown in Fig. 2.11d and then listed it, as shown in Fig. 2.11e, we would find in our program the "extra" statements:

```
40      LET C=A+B
50      PRINT C
60      END
```

These, of course, are the statements of the previous program that were not replaced. How then do we erase all of the previous program? Simply by typing the command SCRATCH before we type the present program, as shown in Fig. 2.11f. Then, when we list our program, we obtain only those statements that we typed after the command SCRATCH, as shown in Fig. 2.11g.

USING THE EDITING TECHNIQUE TO DELETE A LINE FROM A PROGRAM

```
10        LET  A=21.2
20        LET  B= 30.1
30        PRINT A,B
40        LET  C=A+B
50        PRINT C
60        END
```

Figure 2.11a. We will delete line 30 from this program.

```
30
LIST
10        LET  A=21.2
20        LET  B= 30.1
40        LET  C=A+B
50        PRINT C
60        END
READY
```

Figure 2.11b. We can delete a line from a program simply by typing the line number without anything following it. Thus, since we want to delete line 30 from the preceding program (Fig. 2.11a), we type "30" as is shown here. When we list the program, we see that line 30 has been deleted.

```
RUN
51.3
READY
```

Figure 2.11c. Running the program in Fig. 2.11b.

"UNEXPECTED" CONSEQUENCES OF THE EDITING TECHNIQUE

```
10 LET A=13.2
20 PRINT A
30 END
```

Figure 2.11d. Typing a new program after running the previous program (Fig. 2.11c).

```
LIST
10        LET  A=13.2
20        PRINT A
30        END
40        LET  C=A+B
50        PRINT C
60        END
READY
```

Figure 2.11e. When we list our program, we find that those statements from the previous program which were not replaced by our current statement numbers, are also included.

```
SCRATCH
READY
10 LET A=13.2
20 PRINT A
30 END
```

Figure 2.11f. The command SCRATCH deletes all previous statements. Thus, we should type SCRATCH before we type a new program.

```
LIST
10        LET  A=13.2
20        PRINT A
30        END
READY
```

Figure 2.11g. Now when we type LIST, only the program we just typed is printed.

2.6   **More on the** PRINT **Instruction**

As we have seen, we instruct the computer what variables to print, and in what order, by typing these variables after the word PRINT with commas or semicolons separating them; for example, in Fig. 2.12a

$$40 \quad \text{PRINT B2,C1,A}$$

we instruct the computer to print the values assigned to B2, C1, and A in that order. We can check this order by typing the command RUN. The results are shown in Fig. 2.12b.

It is important to note that the order in which the assignments are made to each variable does not affect the order in which they are printed. This can clearly be seen from the table for Fig. 2.12a. By looking only at line 40

Line no.	A	B2	C1
40	376.2	−26.2	936

we cannot determine in what order the variables were assigned values; we do see, however, that all the variables are defined. Thus, for the printing order, the computer relies on the order in which the variables appear in the PRINT instruction:

$$40 \quad \text{PRINT B2,C1,A}$$

In order to portray this more strikingly, we show in Fig. 2.13a a program in which the PRINT instruction is the same as in the previous program. However, although the assignment of the variables is also the same, the order in which the assignments are made is reversed as compared to the order in Fig. 2.12a; i.e., C1 is assigned first (in line no. 10) and A last (in line no. 30).

We see, as we expect, that line 40 of the table for Fig. 2.12a is identical to line 40 of the table for Fig.2.13a. Thus, since the PRINT statements are also the same, results of the two programs of Figs. 2.12a and 2.12b should be identical. We see that they are by comparing Fig. 2.12b with Fig. 2.13b.

MORE ON THE PRINT STATEMENT

```
10    LET A=376.2
20    LET B2=-26.2
30    LET C1=936
40    PRINT B2,C1,A
50    END
```

Figure 2.12a. A program that prints the values of three variables. The order in which the variables appear in the PRINT instruction determines the order in which their values will be printed.

Line no.	A	B2	C1
10	376.2	Undef	Undef
20	376.2	−26.2	Undef
30	376.2	−26.2	936
40	376.2	−26.2	936

Table for Fig. 2.12a. Status of the assignments of variables in Fig. 2.12a given by line number.

```
RUN
-26.2          936                      376.2
         Value of B2     Value of C1           Value of A
READY
```

Figure 2.12b. The results of the program shown in Fig. 2.12a.

```
10    LET C1=936
20    LET B2=-26.2
30    LET A=376.2
40    PRINT B2,C1,A
50    END
```

Figure 2.13a. Same as the program of Fig. 2.12a, but the variables are assigned their values in a different order.

Line no.	A	B2	C1
10	Undef	Undef	936
20	Undef	−26.2	936
30	376.2	−26.2	936
40	376.2	−26.2	936

Table for Fig. 2.13a. Status of the assignments of variables in Fig. 2.13a, given by line number. Line 40 in this table is identical to line 40 in the table for Fig. 2.12a. Thus the results of the PRINT instructions in Fig. 2.12a and Fig. 2.13a are identical.

```
RUN
-26.2                936                   376.2
         Value of B2       Value of C1           Value of A
READY
```

Figure 2.13b. Results of running the program of Fig. 2.13a. We see that the order in which the variables are assigned values prior to the PRINT instruction, does not affect the order in which they are printed. Thus the results shown in Figs. 2.13b and 2.12b are identical.

We note that in line 40 of the preceding program

```
40    PRINT B2,C1,A
```

commas are used to separate the variables in the PRINT instruction. Since, ordinarily, each PRINT instruction produces a new line of results, the comma separates the variables whose values are typed on a given line. It would thus be a mistake to type a comma between the PRINT and the variable B2.

The reader might well ask what happens if the programmer types a comma after the last variable in the PRINT instruction

```
40    PRINT B2,C1,
```

as shown in line 40 of Fig. 2.14a. According to our previous explanation of the comma as a separator, we would expect another variable to be printed following C1 on the same line of results. This is exactly what happens; the results printed by the next PRINT instruction

```
50    PRINT A,C1
```

appears on the same line (see Fig. 2.14b) as the results printed by line 40:

```
-26.2          936          376.2          936
```

As a reminder of what happens if no comma appears after the last variable in a PRINT instruction, we show a program in Fig. 2.15a and, in Fig. 2.15b, the results of running it. We see, as we expect, that we now get two lines of results

```
-26.2          936
376.2          936
```

If we so desire, we can place the numbers we want printed in the PRINT statement itself, for example,

```
10    PRINT -376.2,-26.2,936
20    END
```

as is shown in Fig. 2.16a. As in the case of variables in a PRINT statement, the numbers must be separated by commas, as we have shown, or by semicolons. The results of running this program are shown in Fig. 2.16b.

HOW TO MAKE TWO PRINT STATEMENTS PRODUCE THEIR RESULTS ON ONE LINE

```
10    LET A=376.2
20    LET B2=-26.2
30    LET C1=936
40    PRINT B2,C1,
50    PRINT A,C1
60    END
```

Figure 2.14a. A program in which a comma follows the last variable in a PRINT instruction (here, line 40). As a consequence, the results of the next PRINT instruction (here, line 50) also will appear on the same line of results, as shown in Fig. 2.14b.

```
RUN
-26.2          936
READY
```

```
376.2              936
```

Figure 2.14b. Running the program shown in Fig. 2.14a; two PRINT instructions have produced one line of results because of the last comma in line 40.

```
10    LET A=376.2
20    LET B2=-26.2
30    LET C1=936
40    PRINT B2,C1
50    PRINT A,C1
60    END
```

Figure 2.15a. A program in which no comma follows the last variable in a PRINT instruction; consequently two lines of results are produced as shown in Fig. 2.15b.

```
RUN
-26.2          936
 376.2         936
READY
```

Figure 2.15b. Running the program shown in Fig. 2.15a shows that each PRINT instruction produces a separate line of results.

PLACING NUMBERS IN A PRINT STATEMENT

Figure 2.16a. A program that prints the numbers given in the PRINT statement. Note: It is not necessary to first assign these numbers to variables and then place the variables in the PRINT statement.

```
10    PRINT -376.2,-26.2,936
20    END
```

```
RUN
-376.2          -26.2          936
READY
```

Figure 2.16b. Running the program of Fig. 2.16a.

The results of the programs we have previously discussed have been printed simply as numbers. Unless we read the program that produced the results, we have no way of knowing what these numbers represent. This situation can easily be rectified by adding to the PRINT instruction any descriptive information we want printed. The information must appear between quotation marks. Any group of characters that appears between quotation marks is called a string and is printed on the teletypewriter exactly as it appears in the PRINT instruction.

We now present a program, shown in Fig. 2.17a, that multiplies the value of B2 by the value of C1 and assigns the answer to A. In line 40 we use strings to label the results

> 40   PRINT "B2=",B2,"C1=",C1,"ANS=",A

Thus B2=, C1=, and ANS= are three examples of strings. Just as variables are separated from each other in PRINT instructions by commas or semicolons, so too are strings separated from variables and from each other by commas or semicolons. The result of the PRINT instruction is shown in Fig. 2.17b. We see that when there is not enough room to print all the information on one line of the teletype page, the computer prints the remaining information—here 3414.4—on the next line.

A string does not have to have any relationship to what follows it in the PRINT instruction. The only connection it has to what follows it is that which you, the programmer, make when you write the PRINT instruction. Thus, the computer interprets

> 40   PRINT "B2=",B2,"C1=",C1,"ANS=",A

as follows: Print the following information:
1. the characters in the first string (in this case B2=) followed by
2. the value assigned to B2, followed by
3. the characters in the second string (in this case C1=) followed by
4. the value assigned to C1, followed by
5. the characters in the third string (in this case ANS=), followed by
6. the value assigned to A, which in this case is the product of the value of B2 multiplied by the value of C1.

Line 40 could conceivably have been written so that the strings incorrectly label the results

> 40   PRINT "C1=",B2,"B2=",C1,"B2=",A

as we see in Fig. 2.18a. The computer would interpret this line step by step in the order prescribed in line 40 and would produce the incorrectly labeled results shown in Fig. 2.18b. This is not signaled as an error by the computer since it cannot check whether or not the characters in the string correctly describe the variables in the PRINT statement that the programmer wants them to describe. We conclude this section by noting that when a PRINT statement with nothing following the word PRINT (e.g., 10   PRINT) is executed, the computer skips a line without typing anything on it.

USING STRINGS IN A PRINT STATEMENT

```
10        LET  B2=194
20        LET  C1=17.6
30        LET  A=B2*C1
40        PRINT  "B2=",B2,"C1=",C1,"ANS=",A
50        END
```

Figure 2.17a. A program in which strings are used to label the results. The characters between the quotation marks will be reproduced in the results exactly as they appear in the PRINT instruction. The program performs a simple multiplication.

```
RUN
B2=                    194            C1=              17.6           ANS=
   3414.4
READY
```

Figure 2.17b. Results of running the program of Fig. 2.17a. The strings, e.g., B2=, do not have to have any connection with what follows in the printed results. The computer printed the value of A (3414.4) on the second line because there was not enough space for this number on the first line.

```
10        LET  B2=194
20        LET  C1=17.6
30        LET  A=B2*C1
40        PRINT  "C1=",B2,"B2=",C1,"B2=",A
50        END
```

Figure 2.18a. The program of Fig. 2.17a rewritten so that the strings in line 40 incorrectly label the results.

```
RUN
C1=                    194            B2=              17.6           B2=
   3414.4
READY
```

Figure 2.18b. Running the program of Fig. 2.18a. The results are incorrectly labeled, but the computer cannot detect this error.

2.7. Performing Calculations in BASIC

Mathematical expressions, as they appear printed in books, in general occupy more than one line of print. As an example, it takes three lines of print to write the expression appearing in the following equation:

$$y = \frac{(x+3)^2 \cdot (A+4)}{R+3.1}$$

The expression is that entity which appears to the right of the equals sign.

One line is required for the exponent 2, one line for $(x+3) \cdot (A+4)$, and one line for the divisor $R+3.1$. Since in BASIC, the program is executed line by line, the programmer cannot write mathematical expressions on many lines simultaneously—as he would normally do—but must use one line at a time. For this reason, some of the symbols used to express mathematical operations in BASIC and some of the conventions used, differ from those in algebra. The operations available in BASIC are tabulated below:

Operation	Symbol used in BASIC
Addition	+
Subtraction	−
Multiplication	*
Division	/
Exponentiation	↑

We note that BASIC symbols for multiplication, division, and exponentiation differ from their algebraic equivalents.

We begin by discussing the operation of addition, which (as we have seen in Section 2.2) is the same in BASIC as in algebra. Figure 2.19a shows an example of the use of the addition operator in a BASIC program:

```
20    LET Y=A+4
```

This instructs the computer to take the value assigned to A, add the number 4 to it and assign the resulting sum to Y. We see from line 20 of the table for Fig. 2.19a:

Line no.	A	Y
20	3.2	7.2

that the number 7.2 assigned to Y, is just the sum of 4 and 3.2, the value of A. To check this, we run the program as shown in Fig. 2.19b and obtain the expected results. This last program could have been written so that the calculation would have been done in the PRINT statement, as we see in line 20 of Fig. 2.20a:

```
20    PRINT "Y=";A+4
```

In this program the variable Y is not used at all. When we run this program we see that the results, as shown in Fig. 2.20b,

```
Y= 7.2
```

are the same as those of the preceding program (see Fig. 2.19b).

The program of Fig. 2.20a can be simplified even further by eliminating the assignment instruction in line 10 and writing the PRINT statement as

```
10    PRINT "Y=";3.2+4
```

as shown in Fig. 2.20c. The results of running this program, shown in Fig. 2.20d, are the same as those produced by the two preceding programs.

ADDITION REVISITED

```
10    LET A=3.2
20    LET Y=A+4
30    PRINT "Y=";Y
40    END
```

Figure 2.19a. A program that shows an example of the mathematical operation addition. In line 20, Y is assigned the value of A plus the number 4.

Line no.	A	Y
10	3.2	Undef
20	3.2	7.2
30	3.2	7.2

Table for Fig. 2.19a. Status of the variable assignments in Fig. 2.19a, given by line number.

```
RUN
Y= 7.2
READY
```

Figure 2.19b. The results of running the addition program in Fig. 2.19a.

PERFORMING THE ADDITION IN THE PRINT STATEMENT

```
10    LET A=3.2
20    PRINT "Y=";A+4
30    END
```

Figure 2.20a. A program in which an addition is done in the PRINT instruction.

Line no.	A
10	3.2
20	3.2

Table for Fig. 2.20a. Status of the variable assignments in Fig. 2.20a. Since Y is not now used in this program, it does not appear in the table.

```
RUN
Y= 7.2
READY
```

Figure 2.20b. The result of running the program in Fig. 2.20a.

```
10    PRINT "Y=";3.2+4
20    END
```

Figure 2.20c. We shorten the program of Fig. 2.20a by eliminating 10 LET A = 3.2 and doing the addition of the two numbers in the PRINT statement.

```
READY
Y= 7.2
RUN
```

Figure 2.20d. The result of running the program in Fig. 2.20c.

Although you can perform a calculation in a PRINT statement, you cannot make an assignment there. Thus,

20   PRINT Y=3.2+4

in which an attempt is made to assign the sum of 3.2+4 to Y, will not produce the desired results.*

A variation on the last three programs is one that calculates the current balance in your checking account. Such a program is shown in Fig. 2.21a. In line 20 the number 36 representing a new deposit is added to the variable B1, which represents the original balance; the resulting sum is again assigned to B1. Thus:

20   LET B1=B1+36

Note that this would not make sense algebraically. In BASIC, the literal meaning of this instruction is: Let the value that will be assigned to B1 be the sum of the previous value assigned to B1 plus the number 36. When a variable has its value increased this way it is called an accumulator. From line 10 of the table for Fig. 2.21a, we see that the value assigned to B1 in the computer's memory before the deposit, was 114.23.

Line no.	B1
10	114.23

From line 30 we see that the number assigned to B1 after the deposit is made, is the sum of the old balance, 114.23, plus the deposit, 36.00, and thus equals 150.23:

Line no.	B1
30	150.23

We check this by running the program, as shown in Fig. 2.21b. The result as typed on the teletypewriter is

CURRENT BALANCE $ 150.23

The dollar sign in the results is obtained by including it as the last character in the string in line 30.

Writing a program to print both the deposit and the current balance is not much more difficult. In writing such a program (see Fig. 2.22a) all we have to do is alter line 30 (the printing line) to

30   PRINT "CURRENT BALANCE $";B1;"DEPOSIT $";36

by adding the string DEPOSIT $ and then the number 36. The results are shown in Fig. 2.22b. Line 30 could also be written with the 36 included in the second string in the PRINT statement, thus

30   PRINT "CURRENT BALANCE $";B1;"DEPOSIT $36"

---

* On most systems this is considered illegal. However, on some systems, like the HP2000C, the computer will determine whether Y has previously been assigned the value 3.2 + 4 or 7.2 in the program. If it has been assigned this value, the computer prints a 1 when it executes this statement. This indicates that Y = 7.2 is true. If Y has not been assigned this value, the computer prints a zero when it executes this statement, thus indicating that Y = 7.2 is false.

USING AN ACCUMULATOR

```
10   LET B1=114.23
20   LET B1=B1+36
30   PRINT "CURRENT BALANCE $";B1
40   END
```

Figure 2.21a. A program that calculates the current balance, B1, of a checking account. In line 20, the value assigned to B1 is increased by 36 (the value of the deposit) and the result is again assigned to B1. When a variable like B1 has its value increased by adding a number to its original value, it is called accumulator.

Line no.	B1
10	114.23
20	150.23
30	150.23

Table for Fig. 2.21a. Status of the variable assignments made in Fig. 2.21a by line number. The value of B1 is changed by line number 20 of the program, and thus line number 30 prints the most recently assigned value.

```
RUN

CURRENT BALANCE $ 150.23

READY
```

Figure 2.21b. The results of the program in Fig. 2.21a. Note that the dollar sign must be written as the last character in the quoted string.

```
10   LET B1=114.23
20   LET B1=B1+36
30   PRINT "CURRENT BALANCE $";B1;"DEPOSIT $";36
40   END
```

Figure 2.22a. Same as the preceding program (Fig. 2.21a), but this program prints both the balance and deposit.

```
RUN

CURRENT BALANCE $ 150.23      DEPOSIT $ 36

READY
```

Figure 2.22b. Running the program of Fig. 2.22a.

We next discuss mathematical expressions that contain more than one mathematical operation. In order to enable the program to execute such mathematical expressions, a priority has been assigned to each operation, as shown in Table 2.1. In other words, the computer does not perform all the operations in an expression simultaneously. The first one it does is exponentiation, then it does multiplication and division, and finally addition and subtraction. We now explain this in more detail. The computer reads the part of the expression to the right of the equals sign as we would read an English sentence—from left to right. It first searches for an exponentiation and if it finds it, performs that operation. If there is more than one exponentiation, the computer performs them as it encounters them—from left to right. It then returns to the equals sign and searches from left to right for multiplications and divisions and performs them as it encounters them. Finally, it returns to the equals sign and searches from left to right for additions and subtractions and performs them, again, as it encounters them.

As an example of how a mathematical expression is calculated in BASIC, we now discuss the evaluation of the expression $A*B + C/D - 2$ in

$$\text{LET } Y = A*B+C/D-2$$

where for didactic purposes we have assigned $A = 1$, $B = 2$, $C = 3$, and $D = 4$. We see that in this expression the multiplication and the division have the highest priority. Since the multiplication is to the left of the division, $A*B$ is evaluated first and yields the intermediate result, 2. Then C/D is evaluated and gives 0.75 as another intermediate result. The operations that are performed next are the additions and subtractions. Since the addition is to the left of the subtraction, the addition in $A*B + C/D$ is performed next, and we obtain $2 + 0.75$, which equals 2.75, as our next intermediate result. Finally, the subtraction is performed, i.e., 2 is subtracted from 2.75, and we obtain 0.75 as our final answer. All of this is expressed in tabular form in Table 2.2.

PRIORITY OF MATHEMATICAL OPERATIONS

Priority	Operation	Symbol
First	Exponentiation	↑
Second	Multiplication	*
	Division	/
Third	Addition	+
	Subtraction	−

Table 2.1. Priority of the mathematical operations. Exponentiations are done first, followed by multiplications and divisions, followed by additions and subtractions.

Example 1. Evaluating $Y = A*B + C/D − 2$ where $A = 1$, $B = 2$, $C = 3$, and $D = 4$

Step	Part of expression evaluated	Value
1	A*B	2
2	C/D	0.75
3	A*B + C/D	2 + 0.75 = 2.75
4	A*B + C/D − 2	2.75 − 2 = 0.75

Table 2.2. The evaluation of a mathematical expression in BASIC where $A = 1$, $B = 2$, $C = 3$, and $D = 4$. The steps are given in sequential order. If more than one operation in an expression have the same priority, the left-hand one is evaluated first.

By now the reader may have guessed that the BASIC expression A*B+C/D−2 we have just evaluated would be written in an algebra book as:

$$Y = A \cdot B + \frac{C}{D} - 2$$

not as

$$Y = \frac{A \cdot B + C}{D - 2}$$

The reader might now ask: How then is an expression like the one appearing in

$$Y = \frac{A \cdot B + C}{D - 2}$$

written in BASIC? The reader may be tempted to write the latter expression as we show in the following assignment statement

LET Y=A*B+C/D-2

However, we have just shown that this is wrong, since it is the BASIC equivalent of $Y = A \cdot B + \frac{C}{D} - 2$. In order to write the expression in question correctly in BASIC, we use parentheses. In an expression, the operations enclosed in parentheses are performed before any of the operations outside the parentheses. The operations within the parentheses are performed from left to right with the priorities we previously discussed. If there are parentheses around more than one part of an expression, the parenthesized parts are performed from left to right.

Knowing this, we should now see why $Y = \frac{A \cdot B + C}{D - 2}$ is written in BASIC as

LET Y=(A*B+C)/(D-2)

We now show how this is evaluated. Again for didactic purposes, we take A = 1, B = 2, C = 3, and D = 4. Since there are two parenthesized parts, the leftmost one is evaluated first: the computer first calculates A*B, which yields 2, then it evaluates the addition in A*B+C and obtains 5. Then it moves to the next parenthesized part and evaluates D−2, which yields 2. Having finished evaluating the parenthesized parts, it divides (A*B+C) by (D−2), obtaining (5/2), which equals 2.5. Table 2.3 shows the steps in the calculation and the results of each operation. A commonly made error is to omit the parentheses. If this is done, the expression is evaluated as we have shown in Table 2.2.

For future reference, note that in BASIC the word "expression" does not have to mean a group of numbers and/or variables used with mathematical operations in a calculation; it can also mean simply a number or a variable. Thus the following are all valid BASIC expressions: 13.62, A2, A1*(4+B).

Example 2. Evaluating $Y = (A*B+C)/(D-2)$ where $A=1$, $B=2$, $C=3$, $D=4$

Step	Part of expression evaluated	Value
1	A*B	2
2	A*B+C	5
3	(D−2)	2
4	(A*B+C)/(D−2)	5/2=2.5

Table 2.3. Evaluating the BASIC equivalent of

$$Y = \frac{A*B+C}{D-2}$$

The steps are given in sequential order. The parts of an expression which are parenthesized are evaluated first. If the parentheses are omitted, the expression is evaluated as we have shown in Table 2.2.

We conclude this section with a discussion of a program shown in Fig. 2.23a, which calculates the principal, or the amount of money in a bank account, at the end of a given number of years. The algebraic formula used is

$$P = D(1+R)^N$$

where D is the deposit, R is the rate of interest, N is the number of years, and P is the principal. As with any other formula you wish to use in a program, you do not have to understand the derivation of this formula in order to write a program that will give you the correct answer. What you do have to know, however, is how to write this formula in BASIC. The operations involved in this formula are an addition, $(1+R)$, which is written the same way in BASIC; an exponentiation, $(1+R)^N$, which is written in BASIC as $(1+R) \uparrow N$; and a multiplication, $D(1+R)^N$, which is written in BASIC as D*(1+R) $\uparrow$ N. Thus the whole formula is written in BASIC as it appears in line 40 of Fig. 2.23a:

```
40        LET P=D*(1+R)↑N
```

We calculate the principal for a deposit, D, of 1000; interest rate, R, of 5%, which must be written as .05; and a number of years, N, equal to 4. When we run the program, as shown in Fig. 2.23b we obtain $1215.51 as the answer.

The present program can be written so that the entire calculation is done in the PRINT statement. Thus:

```
10        PRINT "PRINCIPAL = $";1000*(1+.05)↑4
```

as is shown in Fig. 2.23c. The results of running this program are shown in Fig. 2.23d. As we expect, they are the same as those shown in Fig. 2.23b.

Although the multiplication sign is usually omitted in the writing of an algebraic formula in a book, one cannot omit the multiplication sign in BASIC. Thus

```
40    LET P=D(1+R)↑N
```

would not be the BASIC equivalent of the interest formula. Another mistake that is sometimes made in writing such formulas is to omit the parentheses, thus producing the following

```
40    LET P=D*1+R↑N
```

Because of the priorities of the different operations, this would be evaluated as follows: the first one to be done would be R $\uparrow$ N giving .05 $\uparrow$ 4 or .00000625. The second operation would be D*1, giving 1000. The last operation to be done would be the addition in D*1 + R $\uparrow$ N giving 1000+.00000625 or 1000.00000625, which is not the correct result. This error would not be detected by the compiler. The program would thus produce the wrong result. Another commonly made error is to forget one of the parentheses, thus writing the formula as

```
40    LET P=D(1+R↑N
```

This is an illegal statement and would be detected as such by the compiler. It is illegal because there is no closing parenthesis at the right to match the left parenthesis in the expression. The rule governing the use of parentheses is that parentheses must be used in pairs. The three errors we just discussed are shown in tabular form in Table 2.24.

We note, in concluding this section, that two arithmetic operations cannot directly follow each other. Thus 20 LET A=B*−10 is illegal. It would have to be written as 20 LET A=B*(−10).

PROGRAMMING THE INTEREST FORMULA

```
10      LET  D=1000
20      LET  R=.05
30      LET  N=4
40      LET  P=D*(1+R)↑N
50      PRINT "PRINCIPAL =$";P
60      END
```

Figure 2.23a. A program which determines the principal, P, for a deposit, D, at a rate of interest, R, for N years. The algebraic formula used is $P = D (1+R)^N$.

```
RUN
PRINCIPAL =$ 1215.51
READY
```

Figure 2.23b. Running the program of Fig. 2.23a.

```
10      PRINT "PRINCIPAL = $";1000*(1+.05)↑4
20      END
```

Figure 2.23c. The preceding program (Fig. 2.23a) rewritten so that the entire calculation is now done in the PRINT statement.

```
RUN
PRINCIPAL = $ 1215.51
READY
```

Figure 2.23d. Running the program of Fig. 2.23c. As we expect, the results are the same as the ones shown in Fig. 2.23b.

Incorrect statement	Reason
40 LET P = D(1+R) ↑ N	Multiplication sign omitted
40 LET P = D* 1+R ↑ N	Parentheses omitted
40 LET P = D*(1+R ↑ N	Right-hand parenthesis omitted

Table 2.4. Common errors made in writing the formula shown in line 40 of Fig. 2.23a.

2.8. How Commas and Semicolons Affect the Printed Results

We now discuss with the aid of Fig. 2.24a what affects the positioning of the results of a program. Initially, the numbers 10.1, 20.2, and -7 are assigned to the variables X, Y, and Z, respectively. They are then printed by three PRINT instructions that are identical except for the interchanging of commas and semicolons. Depending on the BASIC system one uses, the computer will be able to print the results on lines that are 70, 72, or 75 columns * wide. These columns are numbered from left to right. The value of the first variable appearing in a PRINT statement is printed starting in the first column on the teletypewriter page. Thus the value of X in all PRINT statements of Fig. 2.24a will be printed starting in the first column on the page.

If a comma precedes a variable in a PRINT statement, the computer will print the value of that variable starting in one of the following columns.† These columns (on most systems) are the 16th, 31st, 46th, and 61st columns. The column which the computer chooses is the lowest-numbered one that does not yet contain any printed results (if a result has been printed starting in the 61st column, the computer will print the value of the next variable starting in the 1st column on the next line). As an example, when the computer encounters the first comma in

$$40 \quad PRINT \ X,Y,Z$$

it will print the value of Y starting in the 16th column since it has not yet printed anything there. When the computer encounters the second comma, it cannot print the value of Z starting in the 16th column, since it has already printed something there. Consequently, it prints it starting in the 31st column. This property of the comma makes it a useful tool for aligning columns of numbers in a table. In order to show which columns the results are printed in, we have included line 5 in the program to label the results. When the program is run, as shown in Fig. 2.24b, the first two lines we obtain are

```
123456789-123456789-123456789-123456789-
 10.1           20.2           -7
```

We note here that when the value of a variable is printed the first space is reserved for the sign of the value. If the value is positive, that space is left blank. If the value is negative, a minus sign is printed before the number. Thus when line 40 is executed, since 10.1 and 20.2 are both positive, they are printed starting in columns 2 and 17, respectively. Since -7 is a negative number, it is printed starting in column 31, as we have seen in Fig. 2.24b.

In the next PRINT statement, the variables are separated by semicolons: 50   PRINT X;Y;Z. It produces the result

```
 10.1          20.2          -7
```

We see that the results are spaced more closely together. For our purposes it will suffice to say that the rule in effect here is as follows: When two variables are separated by a semicolon, their values will be printed more closely together than when the variables are separated by a comma.

---

* Each column is defined by two imaginary vertical lines on the teletypewriter paper. Its width is the width of one teletypewriter character.

† As we will see, this also applies when a comma precedes a string, a number or any type of expression in a PRINT statement. Please note that on almost all systems, a comma cannot immediately follow the word PRINT in a PRINT statement.

HOW COMMAS AND SEMICOLONS AFFECT THE PRINTED RESULTS

```
5    PRINT "123456789-123456789-123456789-123456789-"
10   LET X=10.1
20   LET Y=20.2
30   LET Z=-7
40   PRINT X,Y,Z
50   PRINT X;Y;Z
60   PRINT X;Y,Z
70   END
```

Figure 2.24a. A program that shows the effect of commas and semicolons on the printing. The three PRINT instructions are identical except for the commas and semicolons. Both of these punctuation marks determine in which column the value of the variables following it in a PRINT statement will be printed.

```
RUN
123456789-123456789-123456789-123456789-
   10.1             20.2             -7
   10.1        20.2        -7
   10.1        20.2             -7
READY
DONE
```

Figure 2.24b. Result of program in Fig. 2.24a. When a comma precedes a variable, its value will be printed starting in the 16th, 31st, 46th, or 61st column. When a semicolon, as opposed to a comma is used in a PRINT instruction, the results are printed more closely together.

The final PRINT instruction has one semicolon and one comma separating the variables: 60 PRINT X;Y,Z. This produces the following spacing.

```
10.1            20.2                      -7
```

The spacing between 10.1 and 20.2 is the same as it is in the results of line 50 since a semicolon separates X and Y in both statements. Since a comma precedes Z, its value (−7) will be printed starting in the 16th, 31st, 46th, or 61st column. Since nothing yet has been printed starting in the 31st column (the second lowest numbered of these four columns), the −7 is printed there.

We now discuss the effect of commas and semicolons in a PRINT statement on the printing of strings. A comma used in a PRINT statement has the same effect on where a string following it will be printed as it has on where a variable following it will be printed. To show this, we study the program of Fig. 2.25a, in which commas separate three strings in one PRINT statement

```
40    PRINT "X VALUE","Y VALUE","Z VALUE"
```

and three variables in another

```
50    PRINT X,Y,Z
```

When the program is run as shown in Fig. 2.25b, the string X VALUE (the first string in the PRINT statement in line 40) will be printed beginning in the first column of the teletypewriter page. Similarly, the value of the first variable, X, in the PRINT statement in line 50 will also be printed starting in the first column on the next line. Note, however, that 10.1 begins one space to the right, in column 2, because the number is positive, and the plus sign is not printed.

The string Y VALUE and the value of the variable Y, will both be printed starting in the 16th column because they are both preceded by commas and nothing has been printed starting in this column. Finally the string Z VALUE and the value of Z will both be printed starting in the 31st column because they are both preceded by commas and nothing has been printed starting in that column. In order to show which columns the results are printed in, we have included line 5 of the program to label the results. The results are:

```
123456789-123456789-123456789-123456789-
X VALUE         Y VALUE        Z VALUE
   10.1            20.2         -7
```

as is shown in Fig. 2.25b.

USING COMMAS TO PRODUCE RESULTS IN TABULAR FORM

```
 5   PRINT "123456789-123456789-123456789-123456789-"
10   LET X=10.1
20   LET Y=20.2
30   LET Z=-7
40   PRINT "X VALUE","Y VALUE","Z VALUE"
50   PRINT X,Y,Z
60   END
```

Figure 2.25a. A program in which commas are used in the PRINT statements so that the strings X VALUE, Y VALUE, Z VALUE will be printed beginning in the same columns as the variables X, Y, and Z. Thus the commas in a PRINT statement have the same effect on the positioning of the printing of strings as they do on the positioning of the printing of variables.

```
RUN
123456789-123456789-123456789-123456789-
X VALUE              Y VALUE             Z VALUE
  10.1                 20.2                -7
READY
```

Figure 2.25b. Running the program of Fig. 2.25a. The numbers 10.1 and 20.2 begin one space to the right of the place that the strings above them begin because the first space in the printing of numbers is reserved for the number's sign. Since −7 is negative, it begins in the same column as the string above it.

The effect that semicolons have on strings in a PRINT statement is as follows. If a semicolon *follows* a string in a PRINT statement, whatever follows that semicolon will be printed right next to the string. For example, in line 10 of Fig. 2.26a

10   PRINT "X=";10.1

since a semicolon follows the string, X=, the results will be printed as

X= 10.1

as we see in the running of the program shown in Fig. 2.26b. One intervening space was left in the results because the sign of 10.1 is positive. As another example, since in line 20

20   PRINT "STRING ONE";"STRING TWO"

a semicolon follows STRING ONE, the results will be printed as

STRING ONESTRING TWO

Thus when a semicolon separates two strings, they will be printed without any space between them.

Recalling the fact that the placement of a comma or a semicolon at the end of a PRINT statement causes the results of the next PRINT statement to be printed on the same line, we see that

30   PRINT "STRING ONE";
40   PRINT "STRING TWO"

in Fig. 2.26a will produce the result (Fig. 2.26b)

STRING ONESTRING TWO

Thus, the two strings in two different PRINT statements will be printed on one line without any space between them. When a semicolon separates a variable from a string and precedes the string, as in 50   PRINT 10.1;"X", the spacing in the results will be the same as if the semicolon separated two variables. Thus a few spaces will separate the value of the variable from the string when the results are printed

10.1   X

as we see in Fig. 2.26b. Finally, if one is not particularly interested in the spacing of the results, on most systems one can eliminate the punctuation marks—commas and semicolons—which separate strings from variables or numbers in a PRINT statement. Thus in Fig. 2.26a

60   PRINT "X="10.1"END"

is permissible and produces the results

X= 10.1   END

as we see in Fig. 2.26b.

THE EFFECT OF SEMICOLONS ON STRINGS

```
10    PRINT "X=";10.1
20    PRINT "STRING ONE";"STRING TWO"
30    PRINT "STRING ONE";
40    PRINT "STRING TWO"
50    PRINT 10.1;"X"
60    PRINT "X="10.1"END"
70    END
```

Figure 2.26a. A program which shows that when a semicolon follows a string (as in lines 10, 20, and 30), what follows the semicolon is printed next to the string. When a semicolon separates a variable from a string and precedes the string as in line 50, a few spaces will separate the value of the variable from the string when the results are printed.

```
RUN
X= 10.1
STRING ONESTRING TWO   ⟵ Printed by line 20
STRING ONESTRING TWO   ⟵ Printed by lines 30 and 40
 10.1          X
X= 10.1             END
READY
```

Figure 2.26b. The running of the program in Fig. 2.26a. Note: the semicolon which ends line 30, causes the strings appearing in lines 30 and 40 to be produced on one line without any space. On most computers one can eliminate the semicolons or commas that separate strings from variables and from numbers in a PRINT statement. We see this in line 60.

2.9. Using Undefined Variables in a Program

We now discuss what happens when we use an undefined variable in a program. In Fig. 2.27a we present a program written to calculate the product of 37 times 63. We start by assigning 37 to A in 10 LET A=37; however, we forgot to define B. Thus in line 20

$$20 \qquad \text{LET} \quad \text{C=A*B}$$

we are instructing the computer to multiply A by an undefined variable, B, and then assign the result to C. The computer will respond to this in one of two ways, depending on the version of BASIC we are using:

1. Most types of systems will assign zero to all undefined variables. Thus in line 20, the computer will assign zero to B. Consequently, the value of C will also be zero. When we run the program on such computers, we obtain results such as that shown in Fig. 2.27b

$$\text{C= } \quad 0$$

This is not the result we intended to obtain when we wrote the program. The computer, however, has no way of knowing our intentions. It simply follows the instructions in the program. We note here that on such computers the use of an undefined variable is not considered an error.

2. Other types of computers will type an error message when line 30 is executed as shown in Fig. 2.27c. The message tells us how we erred: namely, we used an undefined variable in line 20. As soon as the computer has typed this message, it has gone as far as it is going to in terms of executing the program. It is thus ready to receive another instruction, be it the first statement in another program or a system command.

We also see from Fig. 2.27c how the computer responds to an error that it discovers during the execution of the program. This type of error is called on "execution error." As soon as the computer discovers an execution error, it stops executing the program. It then prints a message describing the error and where it occurred in the program. The computer is then ready to receive another instruction.

THE EFFECT OF USING AN UNDEFINED VARIABLE IN A PROGRAM

```
10   LET A=37
20   LET C=A*B
30   PRINT "C=";C
40   END
```

Figure 2.27a. The variable B is undefined in line 20.

```
RUN
C= 0
READY
```

Figure 2.27b. Running the program of Fig. 2.27a. Most computers assign zero to undefined variables. The value of B therefore is zero. Consequently, the value of C—as we see here—is also zero.

```
10       LET A=37
20       LET C=A*B
30       PRINT "C=";C
40       END
RUN
UNDEFINED VALUE ACCESSED IN LINE 20
READY
```

Figure 2.27c. Running the program of Fig. 2.27a on a different computer. On some computers—like the one this program was run on—the use of an undefined variable is considered an error. The computer prints the error message. It is then ready to receive another instruction from the programmer.

2.10. Writing and Reading Paper Tape

If you are using a teletypewriter equipped with a paper tape punch, you can disconnect the teletypewriter from the computer and type your program on paper tape; this is called typing your program off-line. Then if the BASIC system you are using can read paper tape, you can reconnect the teletypewriter to the computer and then instruct the computer to read your program from the paper tape.

Here are the steps you must follow to type a paper tape off-line.

1. Turn the ON–OFF switch to LOCAL.

2. Depress the ON button on the paper tape punch.

3. Depress the combination of the "REPT" and "RUB OUT" keys on the teletypewriter for about 10 seconds. This produces a leader on the paper tape that will enable you to position the paper tape on the paper tape reader.

4. Type each line of your program. Each time you hit a key, the teletypewriter will punch holes in the tape corresponding to the character you want typed or the function (RETURN, LINE FEED, etc.) you want performed. At the end of each line press the RETURN key, the LINE FEED key, and then the RUB OUT key. To correct errors, follow the procedure discussed in Section 2.5.

5. At the end of your program, depress the HERE IS key. This produces a line of holes on the tape that will serve as a trailer. These holes are smaller than the ones we just discussed, which are used to represent the different characters and functions on the teletypewriter keys. If you examine the paper tape, you will see that these small holes run along the entire length of the paper tape. They are called tape-feed holes and will enable the paper tape reader to move the paper tape and therefore read it.

6. Tear off the paper tape by pulling the paper tape up. This will create a V-shaped cut at the end of the tape. Thus the end of the tape will look like the tail of an arrow, and the beginning of the tape will look like the point of an arrow.

In order to read a paper tape, proceed according to the following steps:

1. Turn the ON–OFF switch to LINE.

2. The paper tape reader is directly below the paper tape punch. It is covered by a plastic gate shaped like an arrow. Press the latch that is to the right of the gate, and the gate will swing open. Place the leader in the paper tape reader so that the tape-feed holes engage the pointed wheel; then snap the gate shut.

3. Log in, then follow the usual procedure for requesting BASIC, including naming your new program.

4. Type TAPE and then hit the RETURN key. The computer will respond by typing READY.

5. Turn on the paper tape reader by moving the lever on the reader to START. Your program will then be read.

6. After your program has been read, type KEY. This will enable you to enter instructions from the teletypewriter keyboard.

PROBLEMS

1. What type of statement must the highest-numbered one in a BASIC program be?

2. Write a program to multiply 26.2 by 497.23.

3. What are the results of the following program?
   ```
   10    LET  A=16
   20    LET  B=3
   30    PRINT A*B
   40    LET  A=7
   50    PRINT A*B
   60    END
   ```

4. Which of the following are illegal BASIC variable names?

   ANS, A1, A10, 2R, Z3

5. What, if anything, is wrong with the following lines?
   a. 40   PRINT "ANSWER=R/2
   b. PRINT "THINK"
   c. 15   PRINT "THINK"
   d. 10   RUN

6. What results does each of the following statements produce?
   ```
   10    PRINT 2+3
   10    PRINT "2+3"
   ```

7. What, if anything, is the difference between the following statements?
   ```
   10    LET X=Y↑2
   10    LET X=Y2
   ```

8. What, if anything, is the difference between these statements?
   ```
   10    LET X=Y↑3
   10    LET X=Y*Y*Y
   ```

9. What are the results of the following program?
   ```
   10    PRINT 1*2*3*4;
   20    PRINT 1+2+3+4
   30    END
   ```

10. What value is calculated for each of the following statements?
    a. 10   LET A=4-2↑2
    b. 10   LET B=(4+2)/4-3
    c. 10   LET C=4+2/(4-3)
    d. 10   LET D=(4+2)/(4-3)
    e. 10   LET E=4*3+2

11. What is wrong with each of the following BASIC statements?
    a. 10 LET A10=B+C
    b. 10 LET A+D=2/F
    c. 10 LET R=C+*D
    d. 10 LET L=A1(L+2)
    e. 10 LET C↑2=A↑2+B↑2

12. Write the BASIC equivalent of the following algebraic equations.

$$\text{a.} \quad A = \frac{3+B}{B+2}$$

$$\text{b.} \quad R = \frac{(A+B)^2 - R}{3}$$

$$\text{c.} \quad C2 = A^2 + B^2$$

13. Write a program to add the following numbers:
    13.26, 27.2, 183.2, 16.4, 98.92

14. Write a program that averages the numbers in problem 13.

15. What is produced by the following three programs?

```
10  PRINT "E";        10  PRINT "E",        10  PRINT "E"
20  PRINT "N";        20  PRINT "N",        20  PRINT "N"
30  PRINT "D"         30  PRINT "D"         30  PRINT "D"
40  END               40  END               40  END
```

16. Describe the difference between typing a system command and a BASIC instruction.

17. Explain the function of RUN, LIST, and SCRATCH. Can these commands be preceded by a statement number?

18. What is printed by the following programs?

```
10  LET A=2           10  LET A=2
20  LET B=A↑2+3       20  LET B=A↑2+3
30  PRINT A+B         30  PRINT B*C
40  END               40  END
```

3

The Various System Commands
and Their Uses

3.1. System Commands

We have so far discussed three system commands: RUN, LIST, and SCRATCH. You may remember that these are instructions to the computer concerning the processing of a program, and therefore they appear without a line number preceding them. The program shown in Fig. 3.1a will be used to demonstrate the use of system commands.*

On most systems, the programmer need use only the first three letters of the command. Thus, if you type LIS, your program will be printed (see Fig. 3.1b); on some computers, the listing begins with the name of your program. Similarly, if you type SCR, your program will be erased (the name of the program, however, is not erased).

If you so desire, you can have only part of the program listed. Thus, if you type a line number after the LIST command, only those lines in your program from that line number on are printed. Thus, when we typed LIS 10† in Fig. 3.1c, we obtained

```
10 LET Y=(X+3)/5
19 PRINT X,Y
20 END
```

Line 9 was not printed. If we type a number, a comma, and another number after the LIST command, only those statements having line numbers from the first number typed to the second number typed will be printed. Thus LIS 9,19 instructs the computer to print

```
9 LET X=3
10 LET Y=(X+3)/5
19 PRINT X,Y
```

The computer does not print line 20.

These features of the LIST command make it convenient to examine parts of a large program. It is important to note that none of these LIST commands destroy the statements that were not printed. If at the end of a partial listing we typed LIS, the entire program would be printed.

* The system commands we described here are used on GE, DEC (PDP), CDC, UNIVAC, and RTB (Real Time Basis) systems in the form we describe here or in a slightly modified form. The commands for Hewlett Packard systems are given in the footnotes to this chapter.

† On the HP 2000C, we would type this as LIST-10.

PROGRAM ON WHICH SYSTEM COMMANDS WILL BE DEMONSTRATED

```
SYSTEM--BASIC
NEW OR OLD--NEW
NEW PROGRAM NAME--PROG1
READY
9 LET X=3
10 LET Y=(X+3)/5
19 PRINT X,Y
20 END
```

Figure 3.1a. A simple program, written in BASIC and named PROG1, which we wrote after we had requested—as is shown here—the BASIC system.

ABBREVIATING THE LIST COMMAND

```
LIS
9 LET X=3
10 LET Y=(X+3)/5
19 PRINT X,Y
20 END
READY
```

Figure 3.1b. On many systems any system command may be represented by its first three letters. Thus, when we type LIS, the program we just typed (shown in Fig. 3.1a) is printed.

LISTING PART OF PROGRAM

```
LIS 10
10 LET Y=(X+3)/5
19 PRINT X,Y
20 END
READY
```

Figure 3.1c. When we type a line number after LIS, the program is printed from that line number on. If, for the program of Fig. 3.1a, we had written LIS 9,19, then only the line numbers 9 through 19 would have been printed.

After we have written a program, we may want the sequencing of the line numbers to be uniform. The system command RENUMBER (or REN) accomplishes this. It instructs the computer to renumber the first statement as 10, the second as 20, and the third as 30, etc., so that the intervals between the line numbers is 10. In Fig. 3.1d we typed RENUMBER. The computer then renumbers the line numbers of the program we typed in Fig. 3.1a. After renumbering the program, it types READY. In order to see how the program was renumbered, we type LIST (see Fig. 3.1d) and we obtain:

```
10 LET X=3
20 LET Y=(X+3)/5
30 PRINT X,Y
40 END
```

The line numbers in the program have now been permanently changed. On some systems, the command RESEQUENCE is used instead of RENUMBER.

We may wish to erase sections of our program. We can do this by using the system command DELETE (or DEL). We instruct the computer which group of statements we wish to erase by typing DELETE followed by the first line number of that group, a comma, and then the last line number of that group. Thus when we type* DELETE 20,40 as is shown in Fig. 3.1e, we erase lines 20 through 40 of the preceding program (shown in Fig. 3.1d). When we type LIST, as shown in Fig. 3.1e, line 10—the only line that was not erased—is printed. If we wished to erase only one line, we would type DELETE followed by the number of that line. Thus DELETE 20 would erase only line 20. In all cases, as soon as the computer has erased the appropriate line or lines, it types READY. On some systems, the word EDIT must precede DELETE and RENUMBER (RESEQUENCE).

If at this point we decided to write an entirely new program having a new name, we would wish to erase all the statements that remain from the previous program, including the program name. The system command NEW erases the previous program and its name. Therefore, when we type NEW, as is shown in Fig. 3.2a, the computer erases the remaining statements from the previous program (PROG1). It then responds by typing

NEW PROGRAM NAME--

Since we wish to name our new program PROG2, we type this new name and then hit the RETURN key. The computer responds by typing READY. All of this is also shown in Fig. 3.2a. On some systems, in order to change the name of the program after we have erased it, we must use the system command NAME, followed by the new name.[†]

In Fig. 3.2b, we write the program we have just named PROG2

```
10 PRINT "PRODUCT=";3*(4+7)
20 END
```

We run it as shown in Fig. 3.2c and obtain the result

PRODUCT= 33

At the end of the program, the computer prints READY and we type the comman BYE signaling that we are logging out. In order for you to understand the significance of this and the other system commands we have learned, we now describe an area in the computer's memory called the working area.

---

* On the HP 2000C, we would type DELETE-20,40.

† For instance on the HP 2000C we would first type SCRATCH and then on the next line NAME— PROG2.

RENUMBERING THE STATEMENTS IN A PROGRAM

```
RENUMBER
READY
LIST
10 LET X=3
20 LET Y=(X+3)/5
30 PRINT X,Y
40 END
READY
```

Figure 3.1d. The system command RENUMBER (or REN), renumbers the program you have just typed (Fig. 3.1a), starting at line number 10, in intervals of 10.

DELETING STATEMENTS IN A PROGRAM

```
DELETE 20,40
READY
LIST
10 LET X=3
READY
```

Figure 3.1e. We instruct the computer to erase a group of statements in the preceding program by typing DELETE or (DEL) followed by the first line number of that group, a comma, and then the last line number of the group. Thus DELETE 20,40 erases line numbers 20 through 40 of the program shown in Fig. 3.1d. On some systems, if only one line number follows DELETE, only that line is erased. We see the effect of DELETE when we LIST the program.

INFORMING THE COMPUTER THAT YOU WANT TO WRITE A NEW PROGRAM

```
NEW
NEW PROGRAM NAME--PROG2
READY
```

Figure 3.2a. If we wish to write a new program with a new name, we type the system command NEW. The computer erases the previous program and then responds as shown. On some systems in order to write a new program having a new name, we must first use the system command SCRATCH, then the system command NAME followed by the name of the program.

```
10 PRINT "PRODUCT=";3*(4+7)
20 END
```

Figure 3.2b. The second program we have written since we signed in (see Fig. 3.1a).

USING BYE

```
RUN
PRODUCT= 33
READY
BYE
```

Figure 3.2c. Running the program of Fig. 3.2b and then logging out by using the command BYE. All the system commands that we have learned so far operate on the working area of the computer's memory. All the program statements we write are also placed there. When we log in, a working area is assigned to us. When we log out, it is destroyed. Thus the program we wrote in Fig. 3.2b is destroyed.

A working area is automatically assigned to you when you log in. In it are placed your program statements. The command LIST prints all the statements in your working area. The command DELETE removes statements from your working area. The command SCRATCH removes from your working area everything but the program name. The command NEW removes from your working area everything including the program name. The command RUN executes the statements in your working area. The command BYE logs you out and erases your entire working area.

In the next session at the teletypewriter, we will learn (see Fig. 3.3a) that we cannot retrieve the last program we wrote; this is to be expected since the command BYE erased it.

We proceed as usual by logging in and then requesting the BASIC language, Then, since we wish to obtain * PROG2, the last program we wrote at the previous session, we respond to

NEW OR OLD--

by typing OLD. The computer responds by typing

OLD PROGRAM NAME--

We type PROG2. The computer searches for the program but cannot find it. So it responds with

PROGRAM NAME NOT FOUND

and then READY. Our only alternative now is to retype the program, as shown in Fig. 3.3b. We thus type NEW. The computer responds by typing NEW PROGRAM NAME --. We type PROG2. The computer types READY, then we type our program:

```
10 PRINT "PRODUCT=";3*(4+7)
20 END
```

In order to store this program permanently in the computer's memory, we next type the system command SAVE.

So that you may understand the significance of this command, we now describe a second area in the computer' memory, called the storage area. A storage area is assigned to a person, usually for a semester. Any program that person stores there remains there for the period assigned unless he deliberately erases it. The command SAVE instructs the computer to copy a program from the working area to the storage area and to store it there. When it does this, it does not erase the program from the working area.

After we type SAVE, as shown in Fig. 3.3b, the computer types READY, indicating that it has saved program PROG2 in the storage area. We then type BYE and end our session at the teletypewriter. The number of programs we can store in the storage area depends on the size of the storage area allotted.

---

* On the HP 2000C, we would type GET—PROG2.

AN UNSUCCESSFUL ATTEMPT TO OBTAIN A PREVIOUS PROGRAM

```
SYSTEM--BASIC
NEW OR OLD--OLD
OLD PROGRAM NAME--PROG2
PROGRAM NAME NOT FOUND
READY
```

Figure 3.3a. In the beginning of the next session at the teletypewriter we try to obtain PROG2, the last program we wrote at the previous session. The computer informs us that it cannot be found. The reason is that we destroyed PROG2 which we typed BYE at the end of the previous session. Our only alternative is to use the command NEW and rewrite the program; this is shown in Fig. 3.3b.

SAVING A PROGRAM FOR FUTURE USE

```
NEW
NEW PROGRAM NAME--PROG2
READY
10 PRINT "PRODUCT=";3*(4+7)
20 END
SAVE
READY
BYE
```

Figure 3.3b. The system command SAVE takes the program you have just written in the working area and copies it into a part of the computer's memory called the storage area. The storage area is assigned to a student, usually for a term. Any program placed there by the student remains there for that time unless the student deliberately erases it.

At our next session at the teletype, we request PROG2 by typing OLD. The computer responds with

OLD PROGRAM NAME-

and we type PROG2. The computer copies PROG2 from the storage area and places it in the working area; it then types READY. We can now run the program by typing RUN. We do this, as is shown in Fig. 3.3c. The computer runs the program and then prints the results:

PRODUCT= 33

and then types READY. Since the program now is in the working area, we can list the program. We do this, as shown in Fig. 3.3d, and obtain a listing of the program.

```
10  PRINT "PRODUCT=";3*(4+7)
20  END
```

We need not keep a record of the programs we have saved in the storage area. The system command CATALOG (or CAT) instructs the computer to print all the names of the programs * we have saved. The use of this command is shown in Fig. 3.3e. Since we have saved only one program, PROG2, the computer prints only this program name. Had we saved many programs, the computer would have printed them all here. We then type BYE and end our session at the teletypewriter.

* The data files are also listed. See Chapter 10 for an explanation of data files.

A SUCCESSFUL ATTEMPT TO OBTAIN A PREVIOUS PROGRAM

```
SYSTEM--BASIC
NEW OR OLD--OLD
OLD PROGRAM NAME-PROG2
READY
RUN
PRODUCT= 33
READY
```

Figure 3.3c. The next session at the teletype-writer shows that once a program has been placed in the storage area it can be retrieved by using the command OLD. We then run the program and obtain the results.

```
LIST
10 PRINT "PRODUCT=";3*(4+7)
20 END
READY
```

Figure 3.3d. Listing the program which was brought from the storage area to the working area in Fig. 3.3c.

OBTAINING A CATALOG OF SAVED PROGRAMS

```
CATALOG
PROG2
READY
BYE
```

Figure 3.3e. The system command CATALOG (or CAT) instructs the computer to print all the names of the programs we have saved. Since we saved only PROG2, only this name is printed.

At our next session at the teletypewriter, in response to NEW OR OLD we inform the computer that we wish to write a new program. We name the program DIVIS. It consists of the statements:

```
10 PRINT "QUOTIENT=";36/(3+4+5)
20 END
```

We run it and obtain the results

```
QUOTIENT= 3
```

All of this is shown in Fig. 3.4a. The program, meanwhile, is stored in the working area. If we want to run the program named PROG2, which, as we remember is in the storage area, we type the command OLD (see Fig. 3.4b.) This command will enable the computer to copy the specified program from the storage area to the working area. The computer responds to this command by typing

```
OLD PROGRAM NAME--
```

We type PROG2. The computer first erases the previous program (here DIVIS) from the working area. It then copies PROG2 from the storage area and places it in the working area. Then it types READY. Since PROG2 is now in the working area, we can instruct the computer to list it by typing LIST. We do this, as shown in Fig. 3.4b, and obtain

```
10 PRINT "PRODUCT=";3*(4+7)
20 END
```

Sometimes we wish to alter a program that is already in the storage area. Let us see how we would alter PROG2. First, we must instruct the computer to copy the program from the storage area to the working area. We have already done this for PROG2 by typing OLD, as shown in Fig. 3.4b. We then alter the program as shown in Fig. 3.4c. Here we have added the statement:

```
5 PRINT "QUOTIENT=";36/(3+4+5)
```

to the program. If we then wish to, we can type LIST to check that the alteration was done correctly. This step is not required; however since it is preferable to use LIST, we have shown it in Fig. 3.4c. We then type

```
REPLACE
```

This erases the old version of PROG2 from the storage area and replaces it with the new version of PROG2 that we just wrote.*

---

* On the HP 2000C, we would first type KILL—PROG2 and then on the next line SAVE.

OBTAINING A PREVIOUS PROGRAM IN THE MIDDLE OF A SESSION

```
SYSTEM--BASIC
NEW OR OLD--NEW
NEW PROGRAM NAME--DIVIS
READY
10 PRINT "QUOTIENT=";36/(3+4+5)
20 END

RUN

QUOTIENT= 3

READY
```

Figure 3.4a. At the next session we write a new program. We have done this in order to show what happens to this program when we next request a program from the storage area. This is shown in Fig. 3.4b.

```
OLD
OLD PROGRAM NAME--PROG2

READY

LIST
10 PRINT "PRODUCT=";3*(4+7)
20 END
READY
```

Figure 3.4b. The command OLD enables the computer to copy a stored program from the storage area to the working area. Once we indicate the program's name (PROG2), the computer erases the previous program (DIVIS shown in Fig. 3.4a) from the working area and places the stored program (PROG2) there.

ALTERING A SAVED PROGRAM, THEN REPLACING IT WITH A NEW VERSION

```
5 PRINT "QUOTIENT=";36/(3+4+5)
LIST
5 PRINT "QUOTIENT=";36/(3+4+5)
10 PRINT "PRODUCT=";3*(4+7)
20 END
READY
REPLACE
READY
BYE
```

Figure 3.4c. Once a stored program has been placed in the working area, we can alter it if we wish. In this case we add the statement 5 PRINT "QUOTIENT = ";36/(3+4+5). We then list the program. Finally, we replace the old version of PROG2, which is in the storage area, with the altered version by typing the command REPLACE. The listing of the program here is convenient but not necessary.

At the next session at the teletypewriter, after we log in, we request the program PROG2, as shown in Fig. 3.5a. The program, which is now saved in the storage area under the name PROG2, is the revised version shown in Fig. 3.4c. After the computer has placed this program in the working area, it types READY. When we type LIST, the program printed by the computer is this revised version:

```
5 PRINT "QUOTIENT=";36/(3+4+5)
10 PRINT "PRODUCT=";3*(4+7)
20 END
```

We now investigate what happens when we wish to save a new program and have mistakenly called it by the same name as one that is already in the storage area. In Fig. 3.5b we write the new program but accidentally name it PROG2, the name of a saved program. When we attempt to save this new program, the computer responds by typing:

```
PROGRAM NAME HAS BEEN USED
READY
```

In order to rename the program, we use the system command RENAME followed by the new name, which in this case is PROD

```
RENAME PROD
```

The computer responds by typing READY. We can then successfully save the program.

If we want to erase a program from the storage area, we type the system command *
UNSAVE (or UNS). This command erases the program in the storage area whose name is the same as the one presently in the working area. If we want to erase PROG2, we must first use this as the new program name when the computer types

```
NEW PROGRAM NAME--
```

We thus type PROG2, as shown in Fig. 3.5c. We then type

```
UNSAVE
```

After we have typed UNSAVE, the program signifies that it has erased PROG2 from the storage area by typing READY. To check that this has in fact been done, we request PROG2 from the storage area by first typing OLD and then the program name. The computer responds as we expect by typing PROGRAM NAME NOT FOUND.

* On the HP 2000C, we would type KILL—PROG2.

REQUESTING AN ALTERED PROGRAM

```
SYSTEM--BASIC
NEW OR OLD--OLD
OLD PROGRAM NAME--PROG2
READY
LIST
5 PRINT "QUOTIENT=";36/(3+4+5)
10 PRINT "PRODUCT=";3*(4+7)
20 END
READY
```

Figure 3.5a. At the next session at the teletypewriter, when we request the stored program PROG2 we obtain the altered version we stored by the REPLACE instruction in Fig. 3.4c. We then list it.

RENAMING A PROGRAM

```
NEW
NEW PROGRAM NAME--PROG2
10 PRINT 1*2*3*4*5*6
20 END
SAVE
PROGRAM NAME HAS BEEN USED
READY
RENAME PROD
READY
SAVE
READY
```

Figure 3.5b. Shows what happens when we call a new program the same name as a saved program and then want to save the new program; the computer types PROGRAM NAME HAS BEEN USED. In order to rename our new program, we use RENAME followed by a new name. We then save the new program under the name PROD.

ERASING A SAVED PROGRAM

```
NEW
NEW PROGRAM NAME--PROG2
READY
UNSAVE
READY
OLD
OLD PROGRAM NAME--PROG2
PROGRAM NAME NOT FOUND
READY
BYE
```

Figure 3.5c. In order to erase a program from the storage area, we use the command UNSAVE. This erases the program in the storage area whose name is the same as the one in the working area. We then check whether in fact PROG2 was erased. When we request the program, the computer responds as we expect: PROGRAM NAME NOT FOUND.

In Table 3.1 we summarize the use of the different system commands. The sets of system commands we have described in this chapter are the ones most generally used. However, some of the system commands we have described may not be available on the version of BASIC you are using. For instance, in one version of BASIC,* the command GET is used in place of OLD; KILL is used in place of UNSAVE, and there is no equivalent of NEW—you must use the command NAME to name your programs. However the modifications in most cases are minor. With little practice, you can master the system commands for your system.

PROBLEMS

1. Given the following program
```
10   LET X=3
20   LET Y=(X+3)/5
30   PRINT X,Y
40   LET X=4
50   LET Y=(X+3)/5
60   PRINT X,Y
70   END
```
   write the system commands that instruct the computer to delete lines 10 to 30, then to renumber the statements in the altered program so that the line numbers begin at 10 and increase by 10, and finally to list the program.

2. Assume that the program in Problem 1 is named PROG. What would be printed after the following lines have been typed?
```
40
50
60
SAVE
READY
OLD
OLD PROGRAM NAME--PROG
READY
RENUMBER
READY
LIST
```

3. Write the set of commands that would enable you to eliminate statement number 40 from PROG1, which is currently being saved in the computer's memory, and to save the corrected version under the name PROG1.

* As we have seen, this is the case on the HP 2000C.

SUMMARY OF THE USE OF SYSTEM COMMANDS

Working area (W.A.)   Storage area (S.A.)

| Current program | ←—— OLD ——→
——— SAVE ———→
——— REPLACE —→ | Stored programs |

NEW—erases W.A. and gives program a new name
RUN—executes program
LIST—lists program
DELETE—erases specific lines in program
SCRATCH—erases program but not name
RENAME—renames program

OLD—erases W.A. and copies programs from S.A. to W.A.
SAVE—copies program from W.A. into S.A.
REPLACE—replaces program in S.A. with program of the same name currently in W.A.
UNSAVE—erases the program in S.A. which has the same name as the one in W.A.

Table 3.1. System commands used in working area (abbreviated W.A.) versus system commands that have an effect on the storage area (abbreviated S.A.). The arrows indicate the direction in which the program is copied. Thus OLD copies a stored program from the storage area to the working area.

4

READ, DATA, GO TO, IF, and INPUT Statements

4.1. READ and DATA Statements

The READ and DATA statements enable the programmer to assign values to variables in the program without having to use assignment statements. We see how this works by studying a program that contains a READ statement

```
10    READ D,R1,R2,R3
```

and a DATA statement

```
40    DATA 30,3.2,7.1,2.7
```

The program is shown in Fig. 4.1a. The purpose of the program is to calculate the average daily rainfall (in inches) over a 30-day period given the fact that it rained on only three days. The rainfall on these days was 3.2, 7.1, and 2.7 inches. We have placed the number 30, and these three numbers in the DATA statement of line 40.

During the execution of a program, the READ statement assigns the numbers in the DATA statement in the order in which they appear, to the variables in the READ statement in the order in which the variables appear. Thus 30 (the number of days), the first number appearing in the DATA statement is assigned to the first variable D in the READ statement. The second number, 3.2 (the rainfall on the first day it rained), is assigned to the second variable, R1. The third number, 7.1, is assigned to the third variable, R2, and finally, the fourth number, 2.7, is assigned to the fourth variable, R3. The variable assignments after the READ statement is executed are shown in line 10 of the table for Fig. 4.1a.

Line no.	D	R1	R2	R3
10	30	3.2	7.1	2.7

In line 30

```
30    PRINT "AVERAGE=";(R1+R2+R3)/D
```

the three rainfalls (the values of R1, R2, and R3) are added together, then divided by the number of days (the value of D), and the results are printed (Fig. 4.1b).

USING THE READ AND THE DATA STATEMENTS

```
10   READ D,R1,R2,R3
20   PRINT "D=";D;"R1=";R1;"R2=";R2;"R3=";R3
30   PRINT "AVERAGE=";(R1+R2+R3)/D
40   DATA 30,3.2,7.1,2.7
50   END
```

O.K

Figure 4.1a. A program which calculates (R1+R2+R3)/D using a DATA statement. During the execution of the program, the computer assigns the numbers in the DATA statement (line 40), in the order in which they are written, to the corresponding variables in the READ statement (line 10), as is shown in the table to Fig. 4.1a. Thus the number 30 is assigned to D, 3.2 to R1, 7.1 to R2, and 2.7 to R3.

Line no.	D	R1	R2	R3
10	30	3.2	7.1	2.7
20	30	3.2	7.1	2.7
30	30	3.2	7.1	2.7

Table for Fig. 4.1a. Status of the variable assignments for the program shown in Fig. 4.1a. The variables are assigned values when the READ statement (line 10) is executed.

```
RUN
D= 30    R1= 3.2           R2= 7.1          R3= 2.7
AVERAGE= .433333
READY
```

Figure 4.1b. Running the program of Fig. 4.1a.

The effect of the READ, DATA combination in this case is the same as the four assignment statements in Fig. 4.2a

```
10    LET D=30
20    LET R1=3.2
30    LET R2=7.1
40    LET R3=2.7
```

As proof of this, we run both programs and the results are the same for both of them, as shown in figures 4.1b and 4.2b.

```
D= 30    R1= 3.2        R2= 7.1        R3= 2.7
AVERAGE= .433333
```

READ

The form of the READ statement is: line number, followed by READ, followed by one or more variables. If more than one variable appears in the READ statement, the variables are separated by commas

```
10    READ D
10    READ D,R1,R2,R3
```

DATA

The form of the DATA statement is: line number followed by DATA, followed by one or more numbers. If there is more than one number, the numbers are separated by commas

```
10    DATA 2.7
20    DATA 30,3.2,7.1
```

If these forms for the DATA and READ statements are not followed, a grammatical error will result. The DATA and READ statements, unlike the PRINT statement, cannot end with a comma * or a semicolon; also semicolons cannot be used to separate the variables or numbers.

* On the CDC 6600, one can end a DATA statement with a comma.

```
10   LET D=30
20   LET R1=3.2
30   LET R2=7.1
40   LET R3=2.7
50   PRINT "D=";D;"R1=";R1;"R2=";R2;"R3=";R3
60   PRINT "AVERAGE=";(R1+R2+R3)/D
70   END
```

Figure 4.2a. The program calculates $(R1+R2+R3)/D$ and produces the same results as the program in Fig. 4.1a. Compare this program with the preceding one since it uses assignment statements instead of READ and DATA statements.

```
RUN
D= 30    R1= 3.2         R2= 7.1         R3= 2.7
AVERAGE= .433333
READY
```

Figure 4.2b. Running the program of Fig. 4.2a. Note that the results of this program are the same as those for the program of Fig. 4.1a.

The DATA statements, as opposed to other types of statements, is not executed as an instruction in the program. Rather, it is simply a visible means of storing numbers that will be assigned to variables by a READ statement at some point in the program. Since DATA statements are not executed, it does not matter where they appear in the program. In order to demonstrate this, we have written a program, shown in Fig. 4.3a, which is the same as the one we studied in Fig. 4.1 except that the DATA statement

```
10    DATA 30,3.2,7.1,2.7
```

is now the first statement in the program. Because the DATA statement is not executed—the numbers in it are not used until a READ statement is executed—the entry in line 10 of the table for Fig. 4.3a is: Not executed.

Once the READ statement

```
20    READ D,R1,R2,R3
```

is executed, the variables are defined as shown in line 20 of the table for Fig. 4.3a.

Line no.	D	R1	R2	R3
20	30	3.2	7.1	2.7

To check that this program produces the same results as the program of Fig. 4.1a, we run it. The results shown in Fig. 4.3b

```
D= 30    R1= 3.2        R2= 7.1        R3= 2.7
AVERAGE= .433333
```

are the same as the ones for Fig. 4.1a, which are shown in Fig. 4.1b.

THE DATA STATEMENT CAN BE PLACED ANYWHERE IN THE PROGRAM BEFORE THE END STATEMENT

O.K

```
10    DATA 30,3.2,7.1,2.7
·20   READ D,R1,R2,R3
30    PRINT "D=";D;"R1=";R1;"R2=";R2;"R3=";R3
40    PRINT "AVERAGE=";(R1+R2+R3)/D
50    END
```

Figure 4.3a. A third version of the program that calculates (R1+R2+R3)/D. This program is the same as the one in Fig. 4.1a except for the position of the DATA statement. It is now the first statement in the program. The results of the two programs are identical. Since a DATA statement is not executed, you can place it anywhere in the program before the END statement.

Line no.	D	R1	R2	R3
10	Not executed			
20	30	3.2	7.1	2.7
20	30	3.2	7.1	2.7
30	30	3.2	7.1	2.7
40	30	3.2	7.1	2.7

Table for Fig. 4.3a. Status of the variable assignments for the program shown in Fig. 4.3a. The variables are not assigned values until the READ statement (line 20) is executed, although the DATA statement is the first statement in the program.

```
RUN
D= 30    R1= 3.2        R2= 7.1        R3= 2.7
AVERAGE= .433333
READY
```

Figure 4.3b. Running the program of Fig. 4.3a. The results are identical to those of Fig. 4.1b.

We now investigate what happens when a DATA statement, for example

        10   DATA 30,3.2,7.1,2.7

from Fig. 4.3a, is written as two statements:

        10   DATA 30,3.2,7.1
        15   DATA 2.7

as shown in Fig. 4.4a. What happens during the execution of the programs is that the READ statement of Fig. 4.4a.

        20   READ D,R1,R2,R3

is originally paired with the DATA statement that has the lowest line number:

        10   DATA 30,3.2,7.1

Thus the computer assigns 30 to D, 3.2 to R1, and 7.1 to R2. A number is then needed to assign to R3. There are no more numbers available in line 10, so the number that will be assigned to D is obtained from the next-lowest-numbered DATA statement, no matter where it is in the program. In the program of Fig. 4.4a, the next-lowest-numbered statement happens also to be the next statement:

        15   DATA 2.7

The computer then assigns 2.7 the first number in that DATA statement, to R3. We see from line 20 of the table for Fig. 4.4a

Line no.	D	R1	R2	R3
20	30	3.2	7.1	2.7

that the numbers assigned to the variables are the same as would be assigned if all the numbers had appeared in one DATA statement. To check this we run the program. The results are shown in Fig. 4.4b

        D= 30   R1= 3.2   R2= 7.1   R3= 2.7
        AVERAGE= .433333

and we see that they are the same as those produced by the program of Fig. 4.3a.

DIVIDING THE NUMBERS IN A DATA STATEMENT INTO MORE THAN ONE DATA STATEMENT DOES NOT AFFECT THE RESULTS

```
10    DATA 30,3.2,7.1
15    DATA 2.7
20    READ D,R1,R2,R3
30    PRINT "D=";D;"R1=";R1;"R2=";R2;"R3=";R3
40    PRINT "AVERAGE=";(R1+R2+R3)/D
50    END
```

O.K
Imp.

Figure 4.4a. A fourth version of the program that calculates (R1+R2+R3)/D. This program shows that when a DATA statement is split into two DATA statements, the results are the same as though they had not been split. The number 30 is assigned to D, 3.2 to R1, 7.1 to R2, and 2.7 to R3.

Line no.	D	R1	R2	R3
10		Not executed		
15		Not executed		
20	30	3.2	7.1	2.7
30	30	3.2	7.1	2.7
40	30	3.2	7.1	2.7

Table for Fig. 4.4a. Status of the variable assignments in the program shown in Fig. 4.4a shown by line number.

```
RUN
D= 30    R1= 3.2        R2= 7.1        R3= 2.7
AVERAGE= .433333
READY
```

Figure 4.4b. The results of running the program of Fig. 4.4a.

We now investigate what would happen if we interchanged the order in which the two DATA statements appeared in the last program, so that they now appear as

```
10    DATA 2.7
20    DATA 30,3.2,7.1
```

as shown in Fig. 4.5a. As we mentioned before, the first READ statement in the program

```
30    READ D,R1,R2,R3
```

is first paired with the lowest-numbered DATA statement in the program; consequently, it is now paired with

```
10    DATA 2.7
```

The computer therefore assigns 2.7 to D. A number is then needed to assign to R1. Since there are no more numbers available in line 10, the required number is obtained from the next-lowest-numbered DATA statement

```
20    DATA 30,3.2,7.1
```

Thus the computer then assigns 30 to R1, 3.2 to R2, and finally 7.1 to R3. The result of the interchange has been that the numbers have been assigned to the wrong variables. This is shown in line 30 of the table for Fig. 4.5a.

Line no.	D	R1	R2	R3
30	2.7	30	3.2	7.1

To check this we run the program. The results are shown in Fig. 4.5b.

```
D= 2.7          R1= 30    R2= 3.2            R3= 7.1
AVERAGE= 14.9259
```

The results are wrong. We therefore see that although the DATA statements are not executed in the program, the order of their line numbers relative each other is important since it determines which number is assigned to which variable.

THE POSITIONS OF DATA STATEMENTS RELATIVE TO EACH OTHER IN A PROGRAM AFFECT THE RESULTS OF RUNNING THE PROGRAM

```
10    DATA 2.7
20    DATA 30,3.2,7.1
30    READ D,R1,R2,R3
40    PRINT "D=";D;"R1=";R1;"R2=";R2;"R3=";R3
50    PRINT "AVERAGE=";(R1+R2+R3)/D
60    END
```

O.K
Imp.

Figure 4.5a. An incorrect version of the program that calculates (R1+R2+R3)/D. In this program, the order that the two DATA statements appeared in the previous program is interchanged. The result is that the numbers are assigned to the wrong variables; i.e., now 2.7 is assigned to D, 30 to R1, 3.2 to R2, and 7.1 to R3.

Line no.	D	R1	R2	R3
10		Not executed		
20		Not executed		
30	2.7	30	3.2	7.1
40	2.7	30	3.2	7.1
50	2.7	30	3.2	7.1

Table for Fig. 4.5a. Status of the variable assignments in the program shown in Fig. 4.5a shown by line number. Because the two DATA statements have been interchanged in the program, the numbers have been assigned to the wrong variables.

```
RUN
D= 2.7          R1= 30    R2= 3.2          R3= 7.1
AVERAGE= 14.9259
READY
```

Figure 4.5b. Running the program of Fig. 4.5a. Because of the interchange of the DATA statements we get the wrong results.

In order to show that the DATA statements that are paired with a READ statement need not be consecutively numbered, we present the program shown in Fig. 4.6a. The two DATA statements, 10   DATA 30, 3.2, 7.1 and 25   DATA 2.7, are separated by another statement. The numbers assigned to the variables as shown in the table for Fig. 4.6a are the same as for the last correct program (Fig. 4.4a). We check this by running the program. The results are shown in Fig. 4.6b

```
D= 30    R1= 3.2        R2= 7.1            R3= 2.7
AVERAGE= .433333
```

A DATA STATEMENT DOES NOT HAVE TO FOLLOW IMMEDIATELY A PRECEDING DATA STATEMENT

```
10    DATA 30,3.2,7.1
20    READ D,R1,R2,R3
25    DATA 2.7
30    PRINT "D=";D;"R1=";R1;"R2=";R2;"R3=";R3
40    PRINT "AVERAGE=";(R1+R2+R3)/D
50    END
```

Imp.
O.K

Figure 4.6a. A sixth version of the program that calculates $(R1+R2+R3)/D$. This program shows that two DATA statements (lines 10 and 25) which will supply the numbers for one READ statement (line 20) need not be consecutively numbered.

Line no.	D	R1	R2	R3
10		Not executed		
20	30	3.2	7.1	2.7
25		Not executed		
30	30	3.2	7.1	2.7

Table for Fig. 4.6a. The status of the variable assignments in program of Fig. 4.6a shown by line number.

```
RUN
D= 30    R1= 3.2        R2= 7.1          R3= 2.7
AVERAGE= .433333
READY
```

Figure 4.6b. Running the program of Fig. 4.6a.

Next in our study of the operation of the DATA and READ statements, we investigate what happens when there is more than one READ statement in a program, as is shown in Fig. 4.7a. In this program we have two READ statements

```
30   READ D,R1,R2
40   READ R3
```

Again, as we have mentioned before, the first READ statement

```
30   READ D,R1,R2
```

is paired with the first DATA statement in the program

```
10   DATA 30
```

Thus the computer assigns 30 to D. A number must then be assigned to R1. Since there are no remaining numbers in line 10, the required number must be obtained from the next-lowest-numbered DATA statement

```
20   DATA 3.2,7.1,2.7
```

The computer then assigns 3.2 to R1 and 7.1 to R2. The assignments that have been made in the READ statement in line 30 are shown in line 30 of the table for Fig. 4.7a.

Line no.	D	R1	R2	R3
30	30	3.2	7.1	Undef

Note that R3 is still undefined since it did not appear as a variable in this READ statement.

The computer has now finished assigning numbers to the variables in the READ statement of line 30. It then goes on to execute the next statement in the program; in this case, it is another READ statement

```
40   READ R3
```

The computer must now assign a number to R3. It takes 2.7, the next available number in the DATA statement, and assigns it to R3. Now, all the variables appearing in the READ statements of the program have been defined, as is shown in line 40 of the table for Fig. 4.7a.

Line no.	D	R1	R2	R3
40	30	3.2	7.1	2.7

We then run the program. The results are shown in Fig. 4.7b.

MORE THAN ONE READ STATEMENT IN A PROGRAM

```
10    DATA 30
20    DATA 3.2,7.1,2.7
30    READ D,R1,R2
40    READ R3
50    PRINT "D=";D;"R1=";R1;"R2=";R2;"R3=";R3
60    PRINT "AVERAGE=";(R1+R2+R3)/D
70    END
```

Imp.

O.K

Figure 4.7a. Last (seventh) version of the program that calculates (R1+R2+R3)/D. In this program there is <u>more than one READ statement</u>. The number <u>30</u> is assigned to D, 3.2 to R1, 7.1 to R2, and 2.7 to R3.

Line no.	D	R1	R2	R3
10		Not executed		
20		Not executed		
30	30	3.2	7.1	Undef
40	30	3.2	7.1	2.7
50	30	3.2	7.1	2.7
60	30	3.2	7.1	2.7

Table for Fig. 4.7a. The table shows that the variables in the first READ statement (line 30) are matched with the numbers 30, 3.2, and 7.1 in the DATA statements. Then R3 in the next READ statement (line 40) is matched with 2.7, the next available number in the DATA statement.

```
RUN
D= 30    R1= 3.2        R2= 7.1        R3= 2.7
AVERAGE= .433333
READY
```

Figure 4.7b. Running the program of Fig. 4.7a.

We now discuss an aspect of the READ and DATA statements that will enable us to redefine variables in a program very easily. In Fig. 4.8a, we show a program that has two identical READ statements

```
30    READ L,W
50    READ L,W
```

The program calculates the area of a rectangle which has a length L and a width W. Again, during the execution of the program the first READ statement (line 30) is paired with the first DATA statement (line 10). Thus the computer first assigns 22.1 to L and then 30.3 to W. This is shown in line 30 of the table for Fig. 4.8a.

Line no.	L	W
30	22.1	30.3

The computer then executes the PRINT statement

```
40    PRINT L,W,L*W
```

Here, the area is calculated, and then the length, width, and area are all printed. The results are shown in Fig. 4.8b. When the computer executes

```
50    READ L,W
```

it takes 16.1, the next available number in the DATA statement and assigns it to L. It then assigns 17.41 to W. Thus L and W have been redefined in this statement. This is shown in line 50 of the table for Fig. 4.8a.

Line no.	L	W
50	16.1	17.41

When we run the program we obtain three lines of printing (Fig. 4.8b):

```
LENGTH          WIDTH           AREA
22.1            30.3            669.63
16.1            17.41           280.301
```

The first line is produced by line 20. The second line is produced by line 40, and the third by line 60. The numbers are lined up directly beneath the words LENGTH and WIDTH because commas separate the variables in lines 40 and 60 as well as the strings in line 20 (see Section 2.8).

USING A READ STATEMENT TO REDEFINE VARIABLES

```
10    DATA 22.1,30.3,16.1,17.41
20    PRINT "LENGTH","WIDTH","AREA"
30    READ L,W
40    PRINT L,W,L*W
50    READ L,W
60    PRINT L,W,L*W
70    END
```

Figure 4.8a. A program which calculates the area of a rectangle given the length L and the width W. The variables L and W are redefined in the second READ statement (line 50). The program calculates the area corresponding to a length L and a width W.

Line no.	L	W
10	Not executed	
20	Undef	Undef
30	22.1	30.3
40	22.1	30.3
50	16.1	17.41
60	16.1	17.41

Table for Fig. 4.8a. This shows how the numbers in the DATA statement are assigned to the variables in the READ statement. When the second READ statement in the program (line 50) is executed, 16.1 and 17.41 are assigned to L and W, respectively. Thus L and W have been redefined here.

```
RUN
LENGTH          WIDTH           AREA
   22.1            30.3            669.63
   16.1            17.41           280.301
READY
```

Figure 4.8b. Running the program of Fig. 4.8a. since L and W have been redefined by the second READ statement (line 50); their new values are printed by line 60. The results are printed in three neat columns because of the commas used in each of the three PRINT statements.

To conclude our study of the READ and DATA statements, we discuss the situation in which there are not enough numbers in the DATA statement to assign to the variables in the READ statement and the converse: the situation in which there are more numbers in the DATA statement than are needed for the variables in the READ. We first discuss the former.

In Fig. 4.9a, we see a program written to average the sum of four numbers. However, although there are four variables in the READ statement

$$20 \quad \text{READ A,B,C,D}$$

there are, by mistake, only three numbers in the DATA statement

$$10 \quad \text{DATA 85,16,-3}$$

The question is: What happens during the execution of the program? The answer is that the numbers 85, 16, and -3 in the DATA statement are matched with A, B, and C, respectively, the first three variables in the READ statement. The computer then looks for a number to assign to D. It cannot find it in this DATA statement and it cannot find any other DATA statement in the program. We represent this situation by placing the comment "Cannot find a number" for the entry corresponding to line 30 and the variable D in the table for Fig. 4.9a:

Line no.	A	B	C	D
20	85	16	-3	Cannot find a number

This situation causes an error. The computer stops executing the program at this point and produces the error message:

$$\text{OUT OF DATA   IN LINE 20}$$

as shown in Fig. 4.9b, when we run the program. The program then prints the message READY and is ready to receive another program or another statement. If we choose to, we can at this point correct the program by typing, for instance,

$$10 \quad \text{DATA 85,16,-3,14.2}$$

thereby giving the DATA statement sufficient numbers. If we then ran the program, we would get error-free results. In the type of error message just discussed, the line number—in this case line 20—refers to the READ statement that was being executed when the error occurred.

NOT ENOUGH NUMBERS IN THE DATA STATEMENT TO SATISFY THE READ STATEMENT

```
10   DATA 85,16,-3___
20   READ A,B,C,D
30   PRINT "AVERAGE=";(A+B+C+D)/4
40   END
RUN
```

Figure 4.9a. A program that calculates the average of four numbers. There are not enough numbers in the DATA statement to assign to the variables in the READ statement, i.e., there is no number in the DATA statement to assign to D.

Line no.	A	B	C	D
10		Not executed		
20	85	16	−3	Cannot find a number

Table 4.9a. How the numbers in the DATA statement are assigned to the variables in the READ statement. Note: There is no remaining number in the DATA statement to assign to the variable D.

```
RUN
OUT OF DATA  IN LINE 20
READY
```

Figure 4.9b. When the program of Fig. 4.9a is run, the READ statement cannot be successfully executed. The compiler stops the program when it realizes it cannot assign a number to D, and it prints the error message. It then prints READY and is ready to receive another program or statement. The line number in the error message refers to the line number of the READ statement.

We finally discuss what happens when there are more numbers in the DATA statement than are needed. In Fig. 4.10a, we see a program written to average the sum of three numbers. As we would expect, there are three variables in the READ statement

20   READ A,B,C

However, there are four numbers in the DATA statement

10   DATA 85,16,-3,14.2

What happens during the execution of the program? The answer is that after 85, 16, and −3 have been assigned to A, B, C, respectively, in the READ statement, as shown in line 30 of the table for Fig. 4.10a

Line no.	A	B	C
20	85	16	−3

the computer goes on to execute the remaining statements in the program. Since there are no more READ statements in the program, the computer does not have to assign 14.2, the remaining number in the DATA statement, to any variable. This does not create any difficulty for the computer so it continues its execution of the program. To check that no error is produced, we run the program. The results are as we expect; they are shown in Fig. 4.10b:

AVERAGE= 32.6667

MORE THAN ENOUGH NUMBERS IN THE DATA STATEMENT TO SATISFY THE READ STATEMENT

```
10    DATA 85,16,-3,14.2
20    READ A,B,C
30    PRINT "AVERAGE=";(A+B+C)/3
40    END
```

Figure 4.10a. A program that calculates the average of three numbers. In this program, there are more numbers in the DATA statement than variables in the READ statement: the number 14.2 is not assigned to any variable.

Line no.	A	B	C
20	85	16	−3

Table for Fig. 4.10a. How the numbers in the DATA statement are assigned to the variables in the READ statement.

```
RUN
AVERAGE= 32.6667
READY
```

Figure 4.10b. Running the program of Fig. 4.10a. The fact that the 14.2 in the DATA statement is not assigned to any variable does not cause an error.

We have now finished discussing all the facets of the operation of the DATA and READ statements. We now show how we can use these statements to greatly simplify the writing of programs. In Fig. 4.11a we show a program that calculates the salary of two workers, after having been given their hourly wage, W; the numbers of hours they worked, H; and their deductions, D. The variable N, is the worker's identification number and thus indicates the worker for whom we have calculated the salary, and S is his salary. In order to inform the person reading the program what these variables represent, we use two REM statements

```
10      REM N=WORKER NO. ,H=HOURS
20      REM W=HOURLY WAGE, D=DEDUCTIONS, S=SALARY
```

The fact that these two statements begin with the letters REM allows us to write anything we wish to in these statements. They will have no connection whatsoever with the execution of the program, but simply allow us to make comments about the program. It is another example (besides the DATA statement) of a nonexecutable statement.

REM

> The form of the REM statement is: line no.; followed by REM; followed by anything the programmer wants to type. Example:
>
> 10   REM PROGRAM CALCULATES SALARY

A worker's salary is computed by multiplying his hourly wage by the numbers of hours he works and then subtracting his deductions. This is done in line 70 for the first worker:

```
70      LET S=W*H-D
```

and in line 130 for the second worker.

```
130     LET S=W*H-D
```

When we run the program we obtain the salaries * of the two workers as shown in Fig. 4.11b.

```
SALARY FOR WORKER 110   IS $ 65.5
SALARY FOR WORKER 201   IS $ 68.7
```

* It would be nice if the computer printed the salaries as $65.50 and $68.70 instead of $65.5 and $68.7; however, the computer does not print trailing zeros. A trailing zero is defined as one which occurs to the right of the decimal point and also at the end of the number.

USING ASSIGNMENT STATEMENTS TO CALCULATE THE SALARY OF TWO WORKERS

```
10        REM  N=WORKER NO. ,H=HOURS
20        REM  W=HOURLY WAGE, D=DEDUCTIONS, S=SALARY
30        LET  N=110
40        LET  W=2
50        LET  H=35
60        LET  D=4.5
70        LET  S=W*H-D
80        PRINT "SALARY FOR WORKER";N;"IS $";S
90        LET  N=201
100       LET  W=3
110       LET  H=24
120       LET  D=3.3
130       LET  S=W*H-D
140       PRINT "SALARY FOR WORKER";N;"IS $";S
150       END
```

Figure 4.11a. A program that calculates the salary for two workers. The REM statement allows you to write anything you wish to in that statement. It has no connection whatsoever with the execution of the program. It is just used as an aid to the reader.

```
RUN
SALARY FOR WORKER 110   IS $ 65.5
SALARY FOR WORKER 201   IS $ 68.7
READY.
```

Figure 4.11b. Running the program of Fig. 4.11a.

We now use the DATA statement to simplify the program. In Fig. 4.12a

```
30    DATA 110,2,35,4.5
50    READ N,W,H,D
```

replaces

```
30        LET N=110
40        LET W=2
50        LET H=35
60        LET D=4.5
```

of the last program (Fig. 4.11a). Similarly

```
40    DATA 201,3,24,3.3
80    READ N,W,H,D
```

replaces the second set of assignment statements in Fig. 4.11a (lines 90 through 120). Since there are as many numbers in each DATA statement as there are in each READ statement, during the execution of the program the numbers in the first DATA statement

```
30    DATA 110,2,35,4.5
```

for the first worker (number 110) are assigned to the corresponding variables in the first READ statement

```
50    READ N,W,H,D
```

This is shown in line 50 of the table for Fig. 4.12a.

Line no.	N	W	H	D	S
50	110	2	35	4.5	Undef

In line 60, the salary, S, of the first worker, is calculated and in line 70, it is printed. The next READ statement is in line 80

```
80    READ N,W,H,D
```

Since the computer has already assigned all the numbers in the first DATA statement, it goes to the second DATA statement and assigns the numbers in it to the variables in this READ statement. Since the same variables—N, W, H, and D—appear in this READ statement as in the last one (line 50) these variables are redefined at this point in the program. This is seen by contrasting lines 80 and 50 of the table for Fig. 4.12a:

Line no.	N	W	H	D	S
50	110	2	35	4.5	Undef
80	201	3	24	3.3	65.5

Note that since we have not redefined S at line 80 in the program, the value of S shown in line 80 (65.5) is the one calculated for the first worker.

Next, in line 90, the computer calculates the salary for the second worker (number 201) and then in line 100 prints the results. When we run the program, we obtain the results

```
SALARY FOR WORKER 110  IS $ 65.5
SALARY FOR WORKER 201  IS $ 68.7
```

USING READ AND DATA STATEMENTS TO CALCULATE THE SALARY OF TWO WORKERS

```
10    REM N=WORKER NO.,H=HOURS
20    REM W=HOURLY WAGE,D=DEDUCTIONS, S=SALARY
30    DATA 110,2,35,4.5
40    DATA 201,3,24,3.3
50    READ N,W,H,D
60    LET S=W*H-D
70    PRINT "SALARY FOR WORKER";N;"IS $";S
80    READ N,W,H,D
90    LET S=W*H-D
100   PRINT "SALARY FOR WORKER";N;"IS $";S
110   END
```

Figure 4.12a. We simplify the program of Fig. 4.11a by using DATA statements to replace the assignment statements. Note: Although this program is briefer than the previous one, it will produce the same results.

Line no.	N	W	H	D	S
50	110	2	35	4.5	Undef
60	110	2	35	4.5	65.5
70	110	2	35	4.5	65.5
80	201	3	24	3.3	65.5
90	201	3	24	3.3	68.7
100	201	3	24	3.3	68.7

Table for Fig. 4.12a. This table shows how the numbers in the DATA statement are assigned to the variables in the READ statement. Note in line 80 of the program that all variables in the READ statement are redefined. However, S is not redefined until line 90. Thus if line 90 were accidentally omitted from the program, the salary printed for worker 201 would be the same as for worker 110.

```
RUN
SALARY FOR WORKER 110   IS $ 65.5
SALARY FOR WORKER 201   IS $ 68.7
READY
```

Figure 4.12b. Running the program of Fig. 4.12a. Note: The results are the same as those produced in the program of Fig. 4.11a.

as shown in Fig. 4.12b, which are the same as we obtained for the previous program.

When one studies the program of Fig. 4.12a, one sees that there are two sets of identical statements. The statements

```
50   READ N,W,H,D
60   LET S=W*H-D
70   PRINT "SALARY FOR WORKER";N;"IS $";S
```

are identical to statements

```
80   READ N,W,H,D
90   LET S=W*H-D
100  PRINT "SALARY FOR WORKER";N;"IS $";S
```

that follow. If a company had two thousand workers on its payroll, we would need two thousand sets of identical statements like these. In the next section we discuss a way of avoiding this.

4.2. The GO TO Statement

In every program we have written until now, the order in which the statements in the program were executed was dictated by the numerical order of their line numbers: the lowest-numbered statement was executed first, and the highest-numbered statement was executed last. It is possible—and often convenient—as we will presently show, to change the order in which the statements are executed. The GO TO statement is an example of a statement that allows us to do this. In Fig. 4.13a we give an example of the use of this statement

```
40   GOTO 10
```

This statement instructs the computer that the next line in the program it will execute is line 10. Another way of saying this is that control is transferred to line 10. Let us now see how the program in Fig. 4.13a works.

In the first statement of the program

```
10   READ N,W,H,D
```

the numbers in the lowest-numbered DATA statement

```
50   DATA 110,2,35,4.5
```

are assigned to the variables in line 10. Then in line 20, the salary, S, is calculated. All of this is shown in the first line of the table for Fig. 4.13a. We have constructed this table slightly differently from the previous tables in that we now show the assignment of variables for only one line but for each of the two times it is executed (the line we have chosen to show for this program is line 20). The line in the table describing the situation in line 20 the first time it is executed, has the entry 1st in the column labeled "Time executed"

Line no.	Time executed	N	W	H	D	S
20	1st	110	2	35	4.5	65.5

USING THE GO TO STATEMENT

```
5    REM N=WORKER NO.,H=HOURS
7    REM W=HOURLY WAGE,D=DEDUCTIONS, S=SALARY
10   READ N,W,H,D
20   LET S=W*H-D
30   PRINT "SALARY FOR WORKER";N;"IS $";S
40   GOTO 10
50   DATA 110,2,35,4.5
60   DATA 201,3,24,3.3
70   END
```

Figure 4.13a. We simplify our program even further by using the GO TO statement. This statement instructs the computer to execute line 10 after line 40 and thus changes the normal order in which the statements were executed. Statements 10 to 40 form what is called a loop. The second time line 10 is executed it reads the numbers in the second DATA statement (line 60).

Line no.	Time executed	N	W	H	D	S
20	1st	110	2	35	4.5	65.5
20	2nd	201	3	24	3.3	68.7

Table for Fig. 4.13a. This table shows the values of the variables at line 20 of the program each time line 20 is executed.

Here we see the numbers from the first DATA statement which were assigned to the variables in the READ statement, and the subsequent calculated salary, S. The results are then printed by the PRINT statement in line 30. The next line executed is line 40

$$40 \quad GOTO \ 10$$

This instructs the computer to execute line 10 next. The computer therefore goes to line 10

$$10 \quad READ \ N, W, H, D$$

where it redefines the variables in this READ statement. It does this by assigning to them the numbers from the second DATA statement. The computer then calculates the salary, using this set of numbers. We see the effect of all of this in the second line of the table for Fig. 4.13a.

Line no.	Time executed	N	W	H	D	S
20	2nd	201	3	24	3.3	68.7

The results are then printed by the PRINT statement in line 30 of the program. The next statement sends the computer back to line 10 for the third time. This time, however, the computer cannot find any more available numbers in the DATA statement. It thus prints an error message:

$$OUT \ OF \ DATA \quad IN \ LINE \ 10$$

The results of running the program are shown in Fig. 4.13b. With the exception of the error message, the results are the same as for the two previous programs.

Statements 10 to 40 form what is called a loop because during the execution of the program, the computer returns from statement 40 to statement 10 and proceeds once again along its original path. We can pictorially depict a loop by using a flow chart. A flow chart describes the order in which instructions are executed in a program. The beginning of a flow chart is represented by an oval with the word START in it. The operations that are performed in a program in assignment, READ, and PRINT statements are written inside rectangles in a flow chart. The order in which these operations are performed is described by arrows leading from one geometric figure—at this point in the discussion, either an oval or a rectangle—to another. In Fig. 4.13c we present a flow chart for the program of Fig. 4.13a. We see that the order in which the operations are performed is: Start, Read Data, Calculate Salary, and Print Salary. The arrow from the Print Salary rectangle, leads to the Read Data rectangle, thus indicating that the reading, calculating, and printing should be repeated. According to the flow chart the procedure we just described is repeated over and over again. However, as we have remarked, the program stops because it runs out of data.

GO TO

> We now describe the form of the GO TO statement. It is: line number, followed by GO TO; followed by the line number of the next statement to be executed. Example: 10 GO TO 50.

Because you can always omit spaces between the characters in a BASIC statement when you type it, you can type GO TO as GOTO.

```
RUN
SALARY FOR WORKER 110  IS $ 65.5
SALARY FOR WORKER 201  IS $ 68.7
OUT OF DATA  IN LINE 10
READY
```

Figure 4.13b. Running the program of Fig. 4.13a. Although this program is briefer than the two preceding ones, it produces the same results. The third time the program executes line 10, there are no more numbers left in the DATA statements to assign to the variables in line 10. This produces an error message. The computer then prints READY and is ready to receive another program.

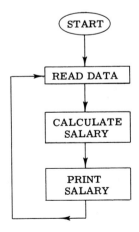

Figure 4.13c. A flow chart for the program in Fig. 4.13a.

We now discuss another application of the GO TO statement. In Fig. 4.1a we show a program that determines how many numbers there are in the DATA statement in line 60

$$60 \quad \text{DATA } 13,16,14,11,6$$

One can think of these numbers as representing the identification numbers of people in a certain company. What this program would do is to count the number of people working in the company. N will be the variable in which we will store this number. In the beginning of the program

$$10 \quad \text{LET } N=0$$

we assign 0 to N. We then assign 13, the first number in the DATA statement to X in

$$20 \quad \text{READ} \cdot X$$

The computer should now record the fact that it has encountered the first number (or person). It is instructed to do this, as we will presently explain, in

$$30 \quad \text{LET } N=N+1$$

This expression would not make sense algebraically. In BASIC, however, it does. It is interpreted as follows: The value of N on the right-hand side of the equals sign represents the last value of N, which at this point is zero (because of line 10). The number 1 is added to this and the result, which in this case is also 1, is assigned to N.

This value of N and 13, the value of X it corresponds to, are shown in the table for Fig. 4.14a:

Line no.	Time executed	X	N after line is executed
30	1st	13	1

The entry 1st notes that this is the first time line 30 was executed.

Next, the print statement in line 30 prints this value of N. Then

$$50 \quad \text{GOTO } 20$$

instructs the computer to execute line 20 next. The computer thus executes 20   READ X for the second time. It therefore assigns 16, the second number in the DATA statement, to X. The computer must now record the fact that it has encountered the second number. Consequently, in line 30 it is again instructed to add 1 to the last value of N (which is also 1) and assign the sum, which is 2, to N. Thus, each time a number is assigned to X in line 20, the value of N is increased by 1 in line 30, as is clearly shown in the table for Fig. 4.14a. The program thus counts how many numbers there are in the DATA statement. Therefore, when a variable like N has its value increased in this way, it is called a "counter."

The program prints the current count each time line 40 is executed. We see this when the program is run, as shown in Fig. 4.14b. Thus the fourth time line 40 is executed, the value

COUNTING HOW MANY NUMBERS THERE ARE IN A DATA STATEMENT

```
10    LET N=0
20    READ X
30    LET N=N+1
40    PRINT "THE NUMBER SO FAR IS";N
50    GOTO 20
60    DATA 13,16,14,11,6
70    END
```

Figure 4.14a. A program that counts the number of pieces of data in the DATA statement. In line 30, the number which was assigned to N is increased by 1 and the result is again assigned to N. When a variable like N has its value increased in this way, it is called a counter. Lines 20 to 50 form a loop.

Line no.	Time executed	X	N after line 30 is executed
30	1st	13	1
30	2nd	16	2
30	3rd	14	3
30	4th	11	4
30	5th	6	5

Table for Fig. 4.14a. This shows the value of X and N at line 30, each time the program is executed.

```
RUN
THE NUMBER SO FAR IS 1
THE NUMBER SO FAR IS 2
THE NUMBER SO FAR IS 3
THE NUMBER SO FAR IS 4
THE NUMBER SO FAR IS 5
OUT OF DATA   IN LINE 20
READY
```

Figure 4.14b. Running the program of Fig. 4.14a. Each time line 40 is executed the number currently stored in N is printed. When the READ statement (line 20) is executed the 6th time, no remaining number in the DATA statement can be found to assign to X. The computer then prints the error message OUT OF DATA IN LINE 20.

of N is 4 and the following is printed

THE NUMBER SO FAR IS 4

When the READ statement (line 20) is executed the sixth time, no remaining number can be found in the DATA statement to assign to X. The computer, as we would expect, prints

OUT OF DATA   IN LINE 20

and then READY, signifying that it is ready to receive another instruction. Since the program printed the results each time the value of N was increased by 1, we learned how many numbers were in the DATA statement. Thus the OUT OF DATA error was not a fatal one here. The flow chart for this program is shown in Fig. 4.14c.

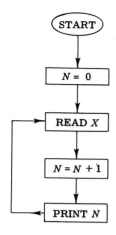

Figure 4.14c. A flow chart for the program in Fig. 4.14a.

The reader in his study of the preceding program may have wondered why, when line 50 was executed, we instructed the computer to execute line 20 and not line 10, the first statement in the program. In Fig. 4.15a we investigate what would happen if we did this, i.e., if we wrote line 50 as

```
50   GOTO 10
```

The flow chart describing this change is shown in Fig. 4.15c. Let us now follow the execution of this program. In essence, the program now consists of a loop in which the lowest-numbered statement is

```
10   LET N=0
```

and the highest-numbered statement is

```
50   GOTO 10
```

The first time the statements in the loop are executed, the values of X and N at line 30 are as is shown in the first line of the table for Fig. 4.15a:

Line no.	Time executed	X	N after line is executed
30	1st	13	1

The values are the same as they were for the same point in the execution of the last program. However, the second time the statements in the loop are executed, the value of N is again zero because of the assignment in line 10. This means that when line 30

```
30   LET N=N+1
```

is executed a second time, the value assigned to N because of this statement is not 2 as was the case in the preceding program, but still 1. This is shown in the second line of the table for Fig. 4.15a:

Line no.	Time executed	X	N after line is executed
30	2nd	16	1

Thus the second time line 40 is executed, the computer prints the same thing it did the first time

```
THE NUMBER SO FAR IS 1
```

Since line 10 is always the first statement executed in the loop, the same thing is printed each time line 40, the PRINT statement is executed. We see this when the program is run, as shown in Fig. 4.15b.

The sixth time the READ statement (line 20) is executed, no more available numbers remain in the DATA statement. The computer thus prints

```
OUT OF DATA   IN LINE 20
```

The message READY is printed, signifying that the computer is ready to receive another instruction.

INCORRECT WAY OF COUNTING HOW MANY NUMBERS THERE ARE IN A DATA STATEMENT

```
10   LET N=0
20   READ X
30   LET N=N+1
40   PRINT "THE NUMBER SO FAR IS";N
50   GOTO 10
60   DATA 13,16,14,11,6
70   END
```

Figure 4.15a. An incorrect version of the program in Fig. 4.14a. If written correctly, it would count the numbers in the DATA statement. The loop (statements 10 to 50) begins at the wrong point. Thus the value of N is always 0 at the beginning of the loop each time the statements in the loop are executed. The loop should begin at line 20.

Line no.	Time executed	X	N after line 30 is executed
30	1st	13	1
30	2nd	16	1
30	3rd	14	1

Table for Fig. 4.15a. The values of X and N the first three times line 30 is executed. Note that the value of N is always 1.

```
RUN
THE NUMBER SO FAR IS 1
THE NUMBER SO FAR IS 1
THE NUMBER SO FAR IS 1
THE NUMBER SO FAR IS 1
THE NUMBER SO FAR IS 1
OUT OF DATA   IN LINE 20
READY
```

Figure 4.15b. Running the program of Fig. 4.15a. Each time line 40 is executed, the computer prints the same thing. The sixth time the READ statement is executed, no more available numbers remain in the DATA statement. The computer thus prints OUT OF DATA IN LINE 20.

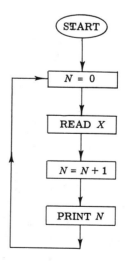

Figure 4.15c. Flow chart for the program of Fig. 4.15a. Each time the loop is executed, the value of N is incorrectly set equal to zero.

The printed results of the correct version of the program shown in Fig. 4.14b were not aesthetically pleasing. We would prefer the results to consist of one line that says TOTAL NUMBER IS 5. In order to obtain this, it is typical for novices to write a program such as that shown in Fig. 4.16a, in which the print statement

```
60    PRINT "TOTAL NUMBER IS";N
```

falls outside of the loop formed by lines 20 to 40. The hope is that, after the last piece of data is read, the computer will automatically execute line 60 and print the final results. This does not happen, however, as the flow chart in Fig. 4.16c indicates. We see that the rectangle containing PRINT N is never reached. We now explain why the program does not perform the task we want it to.

When the program is run, each time a new value of X is read, the value of N is increased by 1, as is shown in the table for Fig. 4.16a. Nothing, however, is printed by the computer. When line 20 is executed for the sixth time, there are no more data left in line 50 to assign to X. The computer then prints the error message

```
OUT OF DATA   IN LINE 20
```

as is shown in Fig. 4.16b, and the program is finished. Line 60 was never executed. The next thing printed is

```
READY
```

and the computer is ready to receive another instruction. In a short time, we will see how to write a program that will produce the results we desired here, i.e., one line of results informing us of how many numbers are in the DATA statement.

ANOTHER INCORRECT WAY OF COUNTING THE NUMBERS IN A DATA STATEMENT

```
10    LET N=0
20    READ X
30    LET N=N+1
40    GOTO 20
50    DATA 13,16,14,11,6
60    PRINT "TOTAL NUMBER IS";N
70    END
```

O.K

Figure 4.16a. A second incorrect version of the program in Fig. 4.14a. Written correctly, it would print one line of results at the end of the program, telling how many numbers there are in the DATA statement. Since the PRINT statement is outside the loop (statements 20 to 40), it is never reached by the program. After line 40, the computer continues to return to line 20 until it has run out of data.

```
RUN
OUT OF DATA   IN LINE 20
READY
```

Figure 4.16b. Running the program of Fig. 4.16a. When line 20 is executed the 6th time there are no more data left in line 50 to assign to X. We thus get an error message which informs us of this.

Line no.	Time executed	X	N after line 30 is executed
30	1st	13	1
30	2nd	16	2
30	3rd	14	3
30	4th	11	4
30	5th	6	5

Table for Fig. 4.16a. The values of X and N each time line 30 is executed.

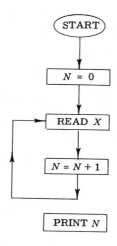

Figure 4.16c. A flow chart for the program of Fig. 4.16a. The PRINT statement is never reached.

We now investigate another application of the GO TO statement in which we use not only a counter, but an accumulator as well. The program shown in Fig. 4.17a calculates T, the sum of the deposits, X, in a bank, and N, the number of deposits made. We will use the variable N as the counter

$$70 \quad LET \ N=N+1$$

and the variable T, as the accumulator

$$60 \quad LET \ T=T+X$$

As you will recall, we discussed the use of an accumulator in Fig. 2.21a of Chapter 2. When using an accumulator, we add some quantity, in this case the deposit, X, to the previous value of the accumulator, T, and then assign the resulting sum again to the accumulator. Let us now study the program.

The program starts by assigning zeros to N and T:

$$30 \quad LET \ N=0$$
$$40 \quad LET \ T=0$$

In the READ statement in line 50, the first number in the DATA statement (and thus the first deposit), 12.6, is assigned to X. Then in line 60

$$60 \quad LET \ T=T+X$$

this value of X is added to the previous value of the accumulator T—which at this point is zero—and the resulting sum, 12.6, is assigned to T (this represents the total amount deposited so far). In line 70, the computer records the fact that this was the first deposit

$$70 \quad LET \ N=N+1$$

Thus the value of N is increased by 1, thereby making it 1. Then in line 80 the results are printed. The values of the variables at this point in the program are shown in the first line of the table for Fig. 4.17a:

Line no.	Time executed	X	T	N
80	1st	12.6	12.6	1

In line 100, the computer is instructed to again execute the READ statement at line 50. This time at line 50, the second number in the DATA statement (and thus the second deposit), 13.2, is assigned to X. In line 60, this value of X is added to the previous value of T, which is 12.6, and the resulting sum, 25.8, is assigned to T (this represents $25.80, the total amount deposited so far). In line 70, the value of N is again increased by 1, so now its value is 2. The computer has thus recorded that it encountered the second deposit. Finally, in lines 80 and 90 the results are printed. This is now the second time line 80 was executed. The second line in the table for Fig. 4.17a displays the values of the variables at this point in the program

Line no.	Time executed	X	T	N
80	2nd	13.2	25.8	2

Each time the loop (lines 50 to 100) is executed, the value of N is increased by 1 and the new sum of the deposits is assigned to T. This is shown in the remaining part of the table for Fig. 4.17a.

USING AN ACCUMULATOR

```
10    REM  T=ACCUMULATED DEPOSITS
20    REM  X=DEPOSITS;N=NUMBER OF DEPOSITS
30    LET N=0
40    LET T=0
50    READ X
60    LET T=T+X
70    LET N=N+1
80    PRINT "TOTAL AMOUNT DEPOSITED SO FAR IS $";T;
90    PRINT "NUMBER OF DEPOSITS IS ";N
100     GOTO 50
110     DATA 12.6,13.2,14.8,16.7
120     END
```

Figure 4.17a. Program in which an accumulator, T, is used to sum the deposits, X, in a bank. In line 60, the value of X just read is added to the previous value of T, and thus becomes the current value of T.

Line no.	Time executed	X	T	N
80	1st	12.6	12.6	1
80	2nd	13.2	25.8	2
80	3rd	14.8	40.6	3
80	4th	16.7	57.3	4

Table for Fig. 4.17a. This table shows how the accumulator T is increased by the value of X for each execution of the loop. The value of T for a line is obtained by adding the value of X for that line to the value of T for the preceding line. This is the result of: 60 LET T = T + X.

Figure 4.17b shows the results when the program is run. Each time lines 80 and 90 are executed, the values of T and N are printed. For instance on the fourth time, the computer prints

```
TOTAL AMOUNT DEPOSITED SO FAR IS $ 57.3    NUMBER OF DEPOSITS IS  4
```

The fifth time the READ statement in line 50 is executed, there are no longer any data to be read; we thus see the message

```
                    OUT OF DATA   IN LINE 50
```

printed on the teletypewriter followed by

```
                    READY
```

which indicates that the computer is ready to receive another instruction.

```
RUN
TOTAL AMOUNT DEPOSITED SO FAR IS $ 12.6       NUMBER OF DEPOSITS IS  1
TOTAL AMOUNT DEPOSITED SO FAR IS $ 25.8       NUMBER OF DEPOSITS IS  2
TOTAL AMOUNT DEPOSITED SO FAR IS $ 40.6       NUMBER OF DEPOSITS IS  3
TOTAL AMOUNT DEPOSITED SO FAR IS $ 57.3       NUMBER OF DEPOSITS IS  4
OUT OF DATA   IN LINE 50
READY
```

Figure 4.17b. Running the program of Fig. 4.17a. The program stops when it has executed the READ statement for the fifth time and finds that there are no more data in the DATA statement. The dollar signs in the results are obtained from the strings in the PRINT statements.

We now write a program that sums the numbers 1, 2, 3, 4 . . . . to a number that we will determine during the running of the program. The program shown in Fig. 4.18a uses an accumulator, T, to add the numbers being produced by the counter, N. This is done in lines 50 and 60 of the program

```
50    LET N=N+1
60    LET T=T+N
```

as we shall presently explain. The loop in the program consists of statements 50 to 80. The flow chart for the program is shown in Fig. 4.18c.

At the beginning of the program

```
30    LET N=0
40    LET T=0
```

zeros are assigned to N and T. Then in line 50, the value of the counter, N, is increased by 1, so that it is now 1; and in line 60, this value of N is added to the previous value of T, which is 0, and the result, 1, is assigned to T. This is now the new value of T, and it is the sum of the numbers generated so far, i.e., from 1 to 1. The computer prints the results of this calculation in line 70. In the first line of the table for Fig. 4.18a we show the values that the variables have at this point in the program

Line no.	Time executed	N	T
70	1st	1	1

After the computer has printed the results, it is instructed in line 80 to execute line 50 again. Here the value of N is again increased by 1, so that it is now 2. In line 60, this is added to the previous value of T, which is 1, and the result, 3, is assigned to T. The computer has at this point added the numbers from 1 to 2 obtaining the result, 3. In line 70, the results are printed. This is the second time that line 70 has been executed. All of this is shown in the second line of the table for Fig. 4.18a

Line no.	Time executed	N	T
70	2nd	2	3

Each time line 70 is executed, the value of N is increased by 1. Thus the next number is produced. This number is then added to the previous value of T (which represents the previous sum), producing the present value of T (which represents the present sum). This is shown in the table for Fig. 4.18a.

Figure 4.18b shows the printed results when the program is run. Every time line 70 is executed, the present values of N and T are printed; for example, on the third time, the computer prints

```
SUM OF #'S FROM 1 TO 3    IS 6
```

SUMMING THE WHOLE NUMBERS FROM 1 ON UP

```
10    REM T=ACCUMULATOR;N=COUNTER
20    REM THIS PROGRAM SUMS THE NOS. FROM 1 UP
30    LET N=0
40    LET T=0
50    LET N=N+1
60    LET T=T+N
70    PRINT "SUM OF #'S FROM 1 TO";N;"IS";T
80    GOTO 50
90    END
```

Figure 4.18a. Program sums the numbers from 1 to the point where you stop the program. The accumulator, T, sums the numbers that the counter, N, produces. Note there are no data in this program. Statements 50 to 80 comprise the loop.

Line no.	Time executed	N	T
70	1st	1	1
70	2nd	2	3
70	3rd	3	6
70	4th	4	10

Table for Fig. 4.18a. The values of N and T each time line 70 is executed. Each value of N is added to the previous value of T, producing the current value of T, which is the sum of the numbers from 1 to the present value of N.

```
RUN
SUM OF #'S FROM 1 TO 1     IS 1
SUM OF #'S FROM 1 TO 2     IS 3
SUM OF #'S FROM 1 TO 3     IS 6
SUM OF #'S
USER ABORT
READY
```

Figure 4.18b. Running the program of Fig. 4.18a. If we permit it, the program will run indefinitely. In order to stop the program we have to hit the "BREAK" key or the "CTRL" key and another key simultaneously, depending on the system we use. This produces a message on the teletype which indicates that we have stopped the program.

If we do not interfere with the program, it will run until the computer is shut off. In order to stop the program, depending on the computer we use, we either depress the BREAK key or simultaneously depress the CTRL key and another key.* The computer then either prints a message indicating that we stopped the program, e.g., STOP or, as here:

USER ABORT

or types nothing at all, depending on the system we are using. The computer then types READY, indicating that it is ready to receive more instructions.

---

* If you do not know which key to press, ask someone who works for the computer center to tell you. Be sure you understand the correct procedure for doing this before you write and run a program such as that described in Fig. 4.18a.

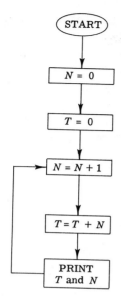

Figure 4.18c. A flow chart for the program shown in Fig. 4.18a. If this program were not stopped, it would run indefinitely.

4.3.   The IF **Statement; Relational Operators; Trailer; Multiplicative Accumulators**

Up to now, the execution of the statements in a loop stopped either because the program was out of data, as in Fig. 4.17b, or because we hit the BREAK key, as in Fig. 4.18b. In either case, when the computer stopped executing the statements in the loop, it printed **READY** and the program was finished. Using the program in Fig. 4.19a, which sums the numbers from 1 to 4, we discuss a method of instructing the computer to go from a statement in the loop:

        80   IF N=4 THEN 100

to one outside the loop:

        100   PRINT "SUM OF #'S FROM 1 TO";N;"IS";T

without ending the program. The programming device that enables us to do this is called an IF statement, an example of which is given in line 80 of the program. This particular IF statement instructs the computer to go to statement 100—and thus print the sum of the numbers—if the value of N equals 4. However, if the value of N does not equal 4, the computer automatically executes the next statement in the program, which is

        90   GOTO 60

and thus continues to sum the numbers.

In this program, the lowest-numbered statement in the loop is

        60   LET N=N+1

and the highest-numbered statement is

        90   GOTO 60

The only way to get out of the loop is for the value of N to be 4. The first time line 80 is executed in the program, the values of N (the counter) and T (the accumulator) are both 1, as shown in the first line of the table for Fig. 4.19a:

Line no.	Time executed	N	T	Next statement
80	1st	1	1	90

Since the value of N is 1, the condition N=4 is false. Therefore, the computer proceeds to line 90. (This is shown in the table by the fact that the number 90 appears in the first line as the entry under the heading Next statement.) It then proceeds to line 60, the lowest-numbered statement in the loop. There it increases the value of N by 1. Now the value of N equals 2; the condition in line 80 N=4 is still false. Consequently, the second time line 80 is executed, the computer again proceeds to line 90. It then executes the statements in the loop

USING THE IF STATEMENT TO SUM THE NUMBERS FROM 1 TO 4

```
10    REM T=ACCUMULATOR
20    REM N=COUNTER
30    REM PROGRAM SUMS THE NOS. FROM 1 TO 4
40    LET N=0
50    LET T=0
60    LET N=N+1
70    LET T=T+N
80    IF N=4 THEN 100
90    GOTO 60
100   PRINT "SUM OF #'S FROM 1 TO";N;"IS";T
110   END
```

Imp
O.K
If

Figure 4.19a. A program that sums the numbers from 1 to 4. An IF statement is used to instruct the computer to leave the loop, formed by lines 60 to 90. When the condition N=4 in this statement is false, the computer proceeds to line 90 and then executes the loop again. However, when the condition N=4 is true, the computer follows the instruction THEN 100 in the second part of the IF statement and executes line 100.

Line no.	Time executed	N	T	Next statement
80	1st	1	1	90
80	2nd	2	3	90
80	3rd	3	6	90
80	4th	4	10	100

Table for Fig. 4.19a. This table shows how the statement 80 IF N=4 THEN 100 works and the values of T and N each time line 80 is executed. When N does not equal 4, the condition N=4 is false, so the next statement executed is line 90 (the next statement in the program). However, when N equals 4 the condition N=4 is true, the next statement executed is 100, as is stated in the THEN 100 part of the IF statement.

```
RUN
SUM OF #'S FROM 1 TO 4      IS 10
READY
```

Figure 4.19b. Running the program of Fig. 4.19a.

for a third time. This time the value of N equals 3 and the condition in line 80 N = 4 is still false. The computer then executes the statements in the loop the fourth time. The value of N now is 4 as is shown in the fourth line of the table for Fig. 4.19a:

Line no.	Time executed	N	T	Next statement
80	4th	4	10	100

Thus the condition in line 80, N = 4, is true and the computer proceeds to line 100, as is shown in this line of the table. There it prints the results. Each time the statements in the loop are executed, the value of N for that execution is added to the value of the accumulator, T, as we see in the table for Fig. 4.19a. In order to see how the printed results appear, we run the program. The results are shown in Fig. 4.19b.

IF

> The form of the IF statement is: line number, followed by the word IF; followed by a condition that can be either true or false; followed by the word THEN; followed by the line number the computer is to go if the condition is true. If it is false, the computer executes the next statement in the program. Example:
>
> 20   IF A+2=B+3 THEN 200
>
> A condition consists of a relational operator sandwiched between two expressions. In the present example, the condition is A + 2 = B + 3, the relational operator is the equals sign, and the two expressions are A + 2 and B + 3.

We will give more examples of relational operators and their use in conditions below. The IF statement represents a point in the program where the computer in effect makes a decision as to which statement to execute next; in our case, the value of N determines which statement the computer will execute next. Points like this in the program are called branch points. A branch point is represented in a flow chart by a diamond. Inside the diamond, we write the condition that determines the next statement executed. Leaving the diamond are two arrows—one labeled YES and the other NO. The YES arrow is followed if the condition in the diamond is true. The NO arrow is followed if the condition in the diamond is false. In Fig. 4.19c, we present a flow chart for this program.

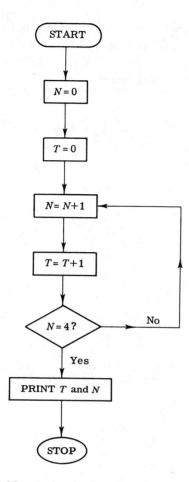

Figure 4.19c. A flow chart for the program of
Fig. 4.19a. The diamond represents the branch
at **IF N = 4 THEN 100.**

We now discuss the different relational operators and their use in conditions by giving several examples. This is shown in Table 4.1. In order to make these examples easier to follow, we have assigned the following numerical values to the variables used in the conditions: A=1, B=2, C=2, and D=1. We have also included an assignment statement

$$60 \quad \text{LET A}=10$$

as the statement that follows the IF statement. It is thus the statement that is executed if the condition in the IF statement is false. The examples given below are just segments of programs—their only use is to illustrate the use of the IF statement.

Example 1:

```
50   IF  A+B = D  THEN  80
60   LET A= 10
```

During the execution, the computer will interpret line 50 as: 50 IF 1+2=1 THEN 80. Since the condition $1+2=1$ is false, the next statement executed is line 60.

Example 2:

```
50   IF  C*D<>A+B  THEN  80
60   LET A= 10
```

Here we have used $< >$, the operator for "not equal." It consists of two characters: $<$ followed by $>$. During execution, the computer will interpret line 50 as 50 IF 3*1 $< >$ 1+2 THEN 80. Since 3 obviously equals 3, the condition "3*1 $< >$ 1+2" is false. Thus the next statement executed is line 60.

Example 3:

```
50   IF  A↑2>B  THEN  80
60   LET A= 10
```

Here we have used $>$, the operator for "greater than." During execution, the computer will interpret line 50 as 50 IF 1 ↑ 2 > 2 THEN 80. Since 1 ↑ 2, which is 1, is not greater than 2, the condition 1 ↑ 2 > 2 is false. Thus the next statement executed is line 60.

Example 4:

```
50   IF  A<4.2  THEN  80
60   LET A= 10
```

Here we have used $<$, the operator for "less than." During execution, the computer will interpret line 50 as 50 IF 1 < 4.2 THEN 80. Since 1 is indeed less than 4.2, the condition 1 < 4.2 is true. This time the next statement executed is line 80.

Example 5:

```
50   IFC>=1+2  THEN  80
60   LET A= 10
```

Here we have used $> =$, the operator for "greater than or equal to." It consists of two characters: $>$ followed by $=$. In the condition, only one of the relations "greater than" or "equal to" need be true in order for the condition to be true (if both relations are true, the condition is certainly true; if both are false, the condition is false). Thus, in 50 IF 3 >= 1+2 THEN 80, 3 is equal to 3; consequently, the condition "3 >= 1+2" is true. Thus the

THE RELATIONAL OPERATORS

Imp. O.K

				Evaluation of conditions for A = 1, B = 2, C = 3, and D = 1		
Example	Relational operator	Meaning		Example of use in a condition	Numerical equivalent of the condition when the IF statement which contains the condition is executed	True or False value of the condition
1	=	Equal		A + B = D	1 + 2 = 1	False
2	< >	Not equal		C*D < > A + B	3*1 < > 1 + 2	False
3	>	Greater than		A ↑ 2 > B	1 ↑ 2 > 2	False
4	<	Less than		A < 4.2	1 < 4.2	True
5	> =	Greater than or equal to		C > = 1 + 2	3 > = 3	True
6	< =	Less than or equal to		C < = A*B	3 < = 1*2	False

Table 4.1. The use of the relational operators in different conditions. An example of the use of each operator in a condition is given, as well as the numerical value of the condition for A = 1, B = 2, C = 3, and D = 1. The True or False value of the condition is given in the last column. When using the operators > = and < =, on most systems one cannot write the operator with the characters reversed, e.g., = > or = <.

next statement executed is 80. Note: On most systems you *cannot* write this operator with the characters reversed: $=>$.

Example 6:

$$50 \quad IF \quad C<=A+B \quad THEN \quad 80$$
$$60 \quad LET \quad A=10$$

Here we have used $<=$, the operator for "less than or equal to." It consists of two characters: the $<$ followed by the $=$. In the condition, only one of the relations "greater than" or "equal to" need be true in order for the condition to be true (if both relations are true, the condition is certainly true; if both are false, the condition is false). During execution, the computer will interpret line 50 as 50   IF 3 $< = 1*2$ THEN 80. Since 3 is not less than 2 nor is 3 equal to 2, the condition 3 $< = 1*2$ is false. Thus, the next statement executed is line 60. Again, note that on most systems you cannot write this operator with the characters reversed: $= <$.

Implicit in our evaluation of these conditions has been the fact that the relational operators have a lower priority than the arithmetic operations, as shown in Table 4.2. Thus, in evaluating the expression

$$A + B > C - D$$

the addition and subtraction have the highest priority. Since the addition is to the left of the subtraction, the addition in $A+B$ is done first and then the subtraction in $C-D$ is performed. Finally, the computer determines whether $A+B$ is greater than $C-D$, thus determining the "true" or "false" value for the condition, as shown in Table 4.3.

THE PRIORITY OF THE DIFFERENT OPERATIONS

Operator	Priority
↑	1st
*	2nd
/	2nd
+	3rd
−	3rd
=	4th
< >	4th
>	4th
<	4th
> =	4th
= <	4th

Table 4.2. The priority of the arithmetic operators in comparison to the relational operators.

STEPS IN EVALUATING CONDITIONS IN IF STATEMENTS

Step	Part of the condition evaluated	How the computer interprets the part of the condition	True or false value
1	A+B	1+2	Not applicable
2	C−D	3−1	Not applicable
3	A+B>C−D	3>2	True

Table 4.3 Steps in evaluating $A+B>C-D$ where $A=1, B=2, C=3,$ and $D=1$.

Armed with this new supply of relational operators, we now rewrite the program of Fig. 4.19a (it summed the numbers from 1 to 4) so that we can eliminate the GO TO statement in line 80. We do this by writing the IF statement as

```
80   IF N <> 4 THEN 60
```

as shown in Fig. 4.20a. Statements 60 to 80 comprise the loop. The first three times that line 80 is executed, the value of N is not equal to 4. The expression in the IF statement is thus true, and the computer is next instructed to execute line 60, the lowest-numbered statement in the loop. This is shown in the table for Fig. 4.20a; for example, the third line reads:

Line no.	Time executed	N	T	Next statement
80	3rd	3	6	60

The fourth time line 80 is executed, N equals 4. Thus the condition in the IF statement is false; consequently, the computer is instructed to leave the loop, and it executes line 90 next. This is clearly shown in the table:

Line no.	Time executed	N	T	Next statement
80	4th	4	10	90

At line 90 the computer prints the results, and then the program is finished.

In order to see how the printed results look, we run the program. The results are shown in Fig. 4.20b:

```
SUM OF #'S FROM 1 TO 4    IS 10
```

As we expect, this is the identical result we obtained from the program shown in Fig. 4.19b. Thus changing the IF statement and eliminating the GO TO statement did not change the results of the program. However, it did make the program shorter by one statement.

WRITING THE PREVIOUS PROGRAM IN ONE LESS STEP USING THE INEQUALITY OPERATOR

```
10    REM  T=ACCUMULATOR
20    REM  N=COUNTER
30    REM  PROGRAM SUMS THE NOS. FROM 1 TO 4
40    LET  N=0
50    LET  T=0
60    LET  N=N+1
70    LET  T=T+N
80    IF N <> 4 THEN 60
90    PRINT "SUM OF #'S FROM 1 TO";N;"IS";T
100   END
```

Figure 4.20a. A program that does the same thing as the previous program (Fig. 4.19a), i.e., sums the numbers from 1 to 4, but in one less step. The IF statement has been rewritten so that when N does not equal 4, the computer goes back to line 60. This eliminates the GO TO statement in line 90 of the previous program. Indeed, the results are the same as those shown in Fig. 4.19b. Statements 60 to 80 comprise the loop.

Line no.	Time executed	N	T	Next statement
80	1st	1	1	60
80	2nd	2	3	60
80	3rd	3	6	60
80	4th	4	10	90

Table for Fig. 4.20a. This table shows how the statement 80 IF N $<>$ 4 THEN 60 works and the values of T and N each time line 80 is executed. When N does not equal 4, the condition N$<>$4 is true; so the next statement executed is line 60 (as is stated in the THEN 60 part of the IF statement). However, when N equals 4, the condition N$<>$4 is false; so the next statement executed is line 90, (the next statement in the program).

```
RUN
SUM OF #'S FROM 1 TO 4      IS 10
READY
```

Figure 4.20b. The results of running the program of Fig. 4.20a.

We next discuss a method of leaving a loop in a program that has a DATA statement containing an undetermined amount of numbers. The program we will study, shown in Fig. 4.21a, determines the sum of all the deposits, T, in a bank, together with the total number of deposits, N. This program is similar to the one we studied in Fig. 4.17a, but because we use an IF statement, the results of the present program will consist of only one line. The deposits appear in the DATA statement

$$140 \quad DATA \; 12.6,13.2,14.8,16.7,999$$

The last number, 999, does not represent a deposit, but is placed in the DATA statement to signal the program that there are no more deposits. Since it appears as the last number in the DATA statement, it is called a trailer. The trailer, as we shall soon see, is not included in either the sum of deposits or the number of deposits. Let us now follow what happens when the program is executed.

In lines 50 and 60, the counter, N, and the accumulator, T, are assigned the value zero. Then in line 70

$$70 \quad READ \; X$$

the first deposit, 12.6, is read from the DATA statement and assigned to X. Then in line 80, the computer tests whether this value of X is the trailer

$$80 \quad IF \; X=999 \; THEN \; 120$$

If it is not, as is the case for the first piece of the data, the value of X is added to the accumulator, T

$$90 \quad LET \; T=T+X$$

and the counter is increased by 1

$$100 \quad LET \; N=N+1$$

The computer is then instructed to next execute line 70, the beginning of the loop. Each time a new number is read and it is not equal to 999, the computer processes the number in the same way, adding it to the previous value of the accumulator. Thus, for the third deposit, 14.8, we see from the third line of the table for Fig. 4.21a:

Line no.	Time executed	X	T	N
110	3rd	14.8	40.6	3

that T, the accumulator for deposits, has had its value increased to 40.6.

When the trailer is read from the DATA statement, the value assigned to X is 999. Thus in the IF statement of line 80, the condition $X=999$ is true and the computer is instructed to leave the loop and to execute line 120 next. There it prints the results. In order to see how the results look, we run the program. The results are as shown in Fig. 4.21b

$$TOTAL \; OF \; DEPOSITS \; IS \; \$ \; 57.3 \qquad \# \; OF \; DEPOSITS \; IS \; 4$$

This program produced one line of results but accomplished the same thing as the program of Fig. 4.17a, which produced 4 lines of results as shown in Fig. 4.17b.

USING A TRAILER TO INDICATE THE END OF A DATA STATEMENT

```
10    REM  T=ACCUMULATOR
20    REM  N=COUNTER;X=DEPOSIT
30    REM  PROGRAM CALCULATES TOTAL
40    REM  AND NUMBER OF DEPOSITS
50    LET N=0
60    LET T=0
70    READ X
80    IF X=999 THEN 120
90    LET T=T+X
100   LET N=N+1
110   GOTO 70
120   PRINT "TOTAL OF DEPOSITS IS $";T;
130   PRINT "# OF DEPOSITS IS";N
140   DATA 12.6,13.2,14.8,16.7,999
150   END
```

Figure 4.21a. A program that calculates the sum of the deposits and the total number of deposits made in a bank. The last number—here 999—in the DATA statement is called a trailer. It is not considered a deposit. Its function is to signal the computer in 80 IF X = 999 THEN 120 to print the results. For all other values of X, the computer performs the calculations in lines 90 and 100.

Line no.	Time executed	X	T	N
110	1st	14.6	12.6	1
110	2nd	13.2	25.8	2
110	3rd	14.8	40.6	3
110	4th	16.7	57.3	4

Table for Fig. 4.21a. The values assigned to X, T, and N each time line 110 is executed. We see that the trailer is not included in the results.

```
RUN
TOTAL OF DEPOSITS IS $ 57.3          # OF DEPOSITS IS 4
READY
```

Figure 4.21b. Running the program of Fig. 4.21a. Note: In comparison to Fig. 4.17b, only one line of results is printed.

We now discuss a common mistake made in writing programs such as the one we have just discussed. The mistake is to place the IF statement (which instructs the computer to leave the loop) at the wrong place in the program. As an example, we have placed the IF statement

100   IF X=999 THEN 120

in the program shown in Fig. 4.22a after

90   LET N=N+1

instead of at the correct point in the program—directly after the READ statement as shown in the previous program. The point in the program where this mistake has an effect is when the trailer, 999 is read and assigned to X. Up to that point the program operates in the same was as did the previous one. When the trailer is read, it is first added to the accumulator, in line 80, and then the value of N is increase by 1. The result of this is shown in the last line of the table for Fig. 4.22a:

Line no.	Time executed	X	T	N	Next statement
100	5th	999	1056.3	5	120

The value of T is 1056.3, or 999 more than it should be. The value of N is 5, or 1 more than it should be (there were only 4 deposits). After line 100 has been executed, the next statement executed is line 120, where the results are printed.

In order to see how the results are printed, we run the program, as shown in Fig. 4.22b. The results

TOTAL DEPOSITS = $ 1056.3   # OF DEPOSITS IS 5

because they include the contribution of the trailer, are incorrect.

INCORRECT USE OF TRAILER

```
10    REM T=ACCUMULATOR
20    REM N=COUNTER;X=DEPOSIT
30    REM CALCULATES THE TOTAL AND
40    REM THE NUMBER OF DEPOSITS
50    LET N=0
60    LET T=0
70    READ X
80    LET T=T+X
90    LET N=N+1
100   IF X=999 THEN 120
110   GOTO 70
120   PRINT "TOTAL DEPOSITS = $";T;
130   PRINT "# OF DEPOSITS IS";N
140   DATA 12.6,13.2,14.8,16.7,999
150   END
```

Figure 4.22a. Incorrect version of the program that calculates the sum of the deposits and the number of deposits made in a bank. In this program, the statement that causes the computer to exit from the loop is placed in the wrong point in the program (it should be directly after the READ statement, as in Fig. 4.21a). The result is that the trailer is included as a deposit.

Line no.	Time exe-cuted	X	T	N	Next statement
100	1st	12.6	12.6	1	110
100	2nd	13.2	25.8	2	110
100	3rd	14.8	40.6	3	110
100	4th	16.7	57.3	4	110
100	5th	999	1056.3	5	120

Table for Fig. 4.22a. The values assigned to the variables X, T, and N at line 100 each time that line is executed. Because of the incorrect location of line 100 in the program, the trailer, 999, has been included in the sum T, making its value 1056.30, or 999.00 larger than it should be. It has also made the total number of deposits equal 5 instead of 4.

```
RUN
TOTAL DEPOSITS = $ 1056.3
READY
```

Figure 4.22b. Running the program of Fig. 4.22a. Since the trailer is included as a deposit, both the total deposits and the number of deposits are to large.

```
# OF DEPOSITS IS 5
```

Using some of the techniques we have learned so far, we now write a program—shown in Fig. 4.23a—that calculates the product of the numbers from 1 to 4. Instead of using the type of accumulator we have used until now, which has been an additive one, we now use a multiplicative accumulator, which we represent by the variable P. Later we will slightly alter the program so that it will calculate the product of the numbers from 1 to any number, R. In mathematics, this product is called R factorial and is written as R! It is used in many probability calculations. Let us now investigate the program.

In the beginning of the program, the computer assigns zero to the counter, N, and 1 to the accumulator, P, in lines 50 and 60, respectively. It then adds 1 to the value of N, making it 1.

$$70 \quad \text{LET} \quad N = N + 1$$

Next it takes the previous value of P (which is 1), multiplies it by the value of N (which is also 1), and assigns the result (which is 1) to P as shown in

$$80 \quad \text{LET} \quad P = P * N$$

At line 90, since N is not 4, the computer is instructed to go to line 70, the beginning of the loop. There, the value of N is increased to 2. Then at line 80, the previous value of P is multiplied by 2 and the result (which is 2) is assigned to P. We have thus multiplied the first two numbers, 1×2 and assigned the product to P. The results are shown in the second line of the table for Fig. 4.23a:

Line no.	Time executed	N	P	Next statement
90	2nd	2	2	70

Since N does not equal 4, the next line executed is 70, the beginning of the loop. In this, the third execution of the statements in the loop, N is increased to 3. Then the previous value of P (which is 1×2) is multiplied by 3, and the result (which is 6) is assigned to P. We have thus multiplied the first three numbers $1 \times 2 \times 3$ and assigned the product to P. This process is repeated each time the loop is executed, as can be seen from the table for Fig. 4.23a. Thus if we study any two consecutive lines of the table, e.g.,

Line no.	Time executed	N	P	Next statement
90	2nd	2	2	70
90	3rd	3	6	70

we see that the value of P for the second line is obtained by multiplying the value of N for that line by the value of P for the preceding line. This is precisely the meaning of

$$80 \quad \text{LET} \quad P = P * N$$

On the fourth execution of the loop, N equals 4, so the product 4×6 (which is 24) is assigned to P. At line 90, since N now equals 4, the condition $N <> 4$ is false. Consequently, the computer is instructed to execute line 100 next. It thus leaves the loop and prints the results. We observe this result

$$\text{THE PRODUCT OF THE \#S FROM 1 TO 4} \quad \text{IS 24}$$

when the program is run, as shown in Fig. 4.23b. If we had initially assigned P the value zero instead of 1, the value of P would have been zero for the rest of the program.

USING THE MULTIPLICATIVE ACCUMULATOR

```
10    REM P=MULTIPLICATIVE ACCUMULATOR
20    REM N= COUNTER
30    REM PROGRAM FINDS THE PRODUCT OF
40    REM THE NUMBERS FROM 1 TO 4
50    LET N=0
60    LET P=1
70    LET N=N+1
80    LET P=P*N
90    IF N <> 4 THEN 70
100   PRINT "THE PRODUCT OF THE #S FROM 1 TO";
110   PRINT N;"IS";P
120   END
```

Figure 4.23a. This program finds the product of the numbers from 1 to 4. P is the multiplicative accumulator. Each time line 80 it executed, the value of the counter N is multiplied by the previous value of P and the result is assigned to P. Thus the number assigned to P on the third execution of line 80 is 2×3, or 6. Hence, on the fourth time it will be 6×4.

Line no.	Time executed	N	P	Next statement
90	1st	1	1	70
90	2nd	2	2	70
90	3rd	3	6	70
90	4th	4	24	100

Table for Fig. 4.23a. This table shows the values of the variables in the program at line 90, the IF statement, each time that line is executed. Also shown is the next statement to be executed. Note: For a given line, the value of P is obtained from the product of N for that line and P for the preceding line. This corresponds to: 80 LET P=P*N.

```
RUN
THE PRODUCT OF THE #S FROM 1 TO 4    IS 24
READY
```

Figure 4.23b. Running the program of Fig. 4.23a.

We now generalize our program so that it will calculate the product of the numbers from 1 to any number we choose. The program which does this is shown in Fig. 4.24a.

The main difference between this program and that of Fig. 4.23a is that 4, used in the IF statement of the previous program

$$90 \quad \text{IF N} <> 4 \text{ THEN } 70$$

which determined the product the program calculated, is now replaced by the variable R as shown in the IF statement of the present program:

$$100 \quad \text{IF N} <> R \text{ THEN } 80$$

The value of R is determined by the number from the DATA statement

$$130 \quad \text{DATA } 5$$

which is assigned to R when line 70

$$70 \quad \text{READ R}$$

is executed. Just by changing the number in the DATA statement, we can change the product which the program calculates.

When the IF statement in line 100 is executed, the value of R is already determined. Thus, in the case of the present program, the computer uses the value of 5 assigned to R and interprets line 100 as

$$100 \quad \text{IF N} <> 5 \text{ THEN } 80$$

When the computer executes this statement, the only time it is not instructed to go to line 80, the beginning of the loop, is when the value of N equals 5. This clearly shown in the fifth line of the table for Fig. 4.24a:

Line no.	Time executed	N	R	P	Next statement
100	5th	5	5	120	110

Thus the computer proceeds to line 110. Note that when the computer executes this line and the next line

```
110   PRINT "THE PRODUCT OF THE #S FROM 1 TO";
120   PRINT R;"IS";P
```

the number it will print after the word TO will be the value of R used to calculate the product. This is exactly what we want. In order to see how these results appear we run the program as shown in Fig. 4.24b and obtain

```
THE PRODUCT OF THE #S FROM 1 TO 5    IS 120
```

CALCULATING THE PRODUCT OF THE NUMBERS FROM 1 TO R

```
10    REM P=MULTIPLICATIVE ACCUM.
20    REM N=COUNTER
30    REM PROGRAM FINDS THE PRODUCT OF
40    REM THE NUMBERS FROM 1 TO R
45    REM WHERE R IS ANY NUMBER
50    LET N=0
60    LET P=1
70    READ R
80    LET N=N+1
90    LET P=P*N
100   IF N <> R THEN 80
110   PRINT "THE PRODUCT OF THE #S FROM 1 TO";
120   PRINT R;"IS";P
130   DATA 5
140   END
```

O.K

Figure 4.24a. This program is the same as the preceding one, but it finds the product of the numbers from 1 to R, where R is defined by the READ and DATA statements. After R is assigned the value 5 in line 70, the computer interprets line 100 as: IF N<>5 THEN 70. This, in effect, instructs the computer to calculate the product of the numbers from 1 to 5.

Line no.	Time executed	N	R	P	Next statement
100	1st	1	5	1	80
100	2nd	2	5	2	80
100	3rd	3	5	6	80
100	4th	4	5	24	80
100	5th	5	5	120	110

Table for Fig. 4.24a. This table shows the values of the variables in the program at line 100. Note that the value of R is always 5. Also, when the value of N does not equal R, the next statement executed is 80. However, when the value of N and R are the same, the next statement executed is 110, where the results are printed.

```
RUN
THE PRODUCT OF THE #S FROM 1 TO 5     IS 120
READY
```

Figure 4.24b. Running the program of Fig. 4.24a. We can change 5, the value of R, to any number we wish simply by changing the number in the DATA statement.

Using the program of Fig. 4.25a, we now study how we can calculate the products of the numbers from 1 to R, for many values of R. The important difference between the present program and the previous one is that now the statements (line 60 to 140) which essentially formed the previous program are executed many times, once for each number in the DATA statement

160   DATA 6,5,8,999

except for the trailer, 999. Let us now investigate the operations of the program.

In line 60, the first number in the DATA statement, 6, is assigned to R. The program then tests whether this value of R is the trailer

70   IF R=999 THEN 180

since it is not, the next set of statements is executed, and the product of the numbers from 1 to 6 is calculated. The computer is then instructed to go to line 60, the READ statement, where now the number 5 is assigned to R. Thus lines 60 to 150 constitute a loop, which we will call the outer loop. If you look closely at this loop, you can see that a group of the statements in the loop—lines 100 to 120—themselves form a loop. We will call this the inner loop. Each time a given number is assigned to R in the READ statement, the inner loop is executed that number of times, e.g., since the first value of R is 6, the statements in the inner loop are executed 6 times. Note that each time after a new number is assigned to R, N is set equal to zero and P is set equal to 1. If this were not done, the product for the new number would include the contributions from the product of the old numbers and would thus be incorrect.

In order to see what the output looks like, we run the program. The results are shown in Fig. 4.25b.

PLACING A LOOP WITHIN A LOOP

```
10    REM P=MULTIPLICATIVE ACCUM
20    REM N=COUNTER
30    REM PROGRAM FINDS THE PRODUCT OF
40    REM THE NUMBERS FROM 1 TO R
50    REM FOR MANY VALUES OF R
60    READ R
70    IF R=999 THEN 180
80    LET N=0
90    LET P=1
100   LET N=N+1
110   LET P=P*N
120   IF N <> R THEN 100
130   PRINT "THE PRODUCT OF THE #S FROM 1 TO";
140   PRINT R;"IS";P
150   GOTO 60
160   DATA 6,5,8,999
180   END
```

O.K

Figure 4.25a. A program that calculates the product of the numbers from 1 to R, where R is each of the numbers, 6, 5, and 8 in the DATA statement. There are two loops in the program. Lines 60 to 150 form the outer loop. Each time this loop is executed, the inner loop (lines 100 to 120) is executed a number of times equal to the value of R read in the outer loop. It thus calculates the product of the numners from 1 to R.

```
RUN
THE PRODUCT OF THE #S FROM 1 TO 6    IS 720
THE PRODUCT OF THE #S FROM 1 TO 5    IS 120
THE PRODUCT OF THE #S FROM 1 TO 8    IS 40320.
READY
```

Figure 4.25b. Running the program of Fig. 4.25a. Each time a new number is assigned to R in line 60, the program calculates the appropriate product.

4.4. The INPUT Statement

We have discussed, so far, two ways of assigning numbers to variables. The first is the assignment statement, and the second is the combination of the READ and DATA statements. When the programmer uses either of these two methods, he must make assignments while he is writing the program. There is still another way of assigning numbers to variables, as shown in Fig. 4.26a, that is, to use the INPUT statement

40   INPUT M, G

As opposed to the two previous methods, when the programmer uses the INPUT statement, he makes the assignments while the program is running. Thus the INPUT statement *is not* used to read numbers from a DATA statement.

INPUT

> The form of the INPUT statement is: line number, followed by the word INPUT, followed by one or more variables. If there is more than one variable, the variables are separated by commas. They cannot be separated by semicolons. Examples:
>
> 10   INPUT   A1, A2, C
15   INPUT   B

We now demonstrate the use of the INPUT statement. The program in Fig. 4.26a calculates the miles per gallon for a given number of miles and a given number of gallons. When the program is run, line 30, the first statement executed, causes the message

TYPE IN MILES, A COMMA AND THEN GALLONS

to be typed on the teletype as shown in Fig. 4.26b. This instructs the programmer in what order to type the required numbers. The next statement executed is the INPUT statement; this causes a question mark to be typed by the computer on the teletypewriter. Whenever an INPUT statement is executed, the question mark is typed. It is the signal to the programmer to type numbers on the teletypewriter as input to the program. It is always a good idea when using an INPUT statement to precede it with a PRINT statement that will produce a message that will instruct the programmer what information the program requires and how to type this information on the teletype.

The general procedure that a programmer must follow in order to satisfy an INPUT statement is: type one or more numbers and then a carriage return. If one types more than one number, one must separate them by commas, e.g.,

? 205, 18

as shown in figure 4.26b. Note: The programmer must type the numbers on the same line on which the question mark appears. We now return to the execution of the program.

After the numbers for the miles and gallons, 205 and 18 respectively, have been typed in, they are assigned to the variables M and G as shown in the first line of the table for Fig. 4.26a:

USING THE INPUT STATEMENT

```
10      REM CALCULATES MILES PER GALLON
20      REM M=MILES;G=GALLONS
30      PRINT "TYPE IN MILES,A COMMA AND THEN GALLONS"
40      INPUT M,G
50      PRINT "FOR";M;"MILES AND";G;"GALLONS,THE";
60      PRINT " MILES PER GALLONS=";M/G
70      GO TO 30
80      END
```

Figure 4.26a. A program which uses an INPUT statement and then calculates the miles per gallon for the two numbers typed in. The variables in the INPUT statement are assigned values by you after you have typed RUN. As in a READ statement, these variables must be separated by a comma. The INPUT statement cannot be used with a DATA statement. Lines 30 to 70 form a loop.

Line no.	M	G	Time executed
40	205	18	1st
40	125	10	2nd
40	150	12	3rd

Table for Fig. 4.26a. The values assigned to M and G each time line 40 is executed. These numbers are typed in by the programmer when line 40 is executed.

```
TYPE IN MILES,A COMMA AND THEN GALLONS
? 205,18
FOR 205   MILES AND 18    GALLONS,THE MILES PER GALLONS= 11.3889
```

Figure 4.26b. Running the program of Fig. 4.26a. When the execution of the INPUT statement begins, the computer types a question mark. The programmer types in the required numbers, separating them by a comma, and then hits the RETURN key. The computer then prints the results.

Line no.	M	G	Time executed
40	205	18	1st

These numbers are then used to calculate the miles per gallon in the PRINT statements

```
50      PRINT "FOR";M;"MILES AND";G;"GALLONS,THE ";
60      PRINT "MILES PER GALLON=";M/G
```

Once the results are printed the computer is instructed to go back to line 30, and the entire process begins again. In Fig. 4.26c, we show that the second time the program asks for the miles and gallons to be typed in, the programmer carelessly only types in the miles

```
? 125
```

and then hits the carriage return. This does not satisfy the requirements of the INPUT statement. Depending on the system you use, the computer will type either two question marks or some appropriate message like

```
NOT ENOUGH DATA, TYPE IN MORE
```

as we have also shown in Fig. 4.26c. The programmer then types in the second number

```
10
```

and then hits the carriage return key. He does not type in a comma. The program then assigns these numbers to M and G as shown in the second line of the table for Fig. 4.26a:

Line no.	M	G	Time executed
40	125	10	2nd

TYPING TOO FEW NUMBERS IN RESPONSE TO AN INPUT STATEMENT

```
TYPE IN MILES,A COMMA AND THEN GALLONS
? 125
NOT ENOUGH DATA, TYPE IN MORE
10
FOR 125  MILES AND 10   GALLONS,THE MILES PER GALLONS= 12.5
```

Figure 4.26c. If the programmer forgets to type the second number, the computer prints NOT ENOUGH DATA, TYPE IN MORE and waits for the second number before continuing to execute the program. We type 10. Then the computer prints the results for 125 miles and 10 gallons.

You may remember that, if you do not provide enough numbers in a DATA statement to satisfy a READ statement, the execution is terminated. As we have just seen, this is not the case when the programmer forgets to type all the numbers required by the INPUT statement. He is given a second chance. We now investigate what happens when the programmer types in too many numbers after the question mark is printed, as shown in Fig. 4.26d:

```
?  150,12,2
```

The computer responds to this by typing a warning message

```
TOO MUCH DATA,RETYPE INPUT     AT   40
```

The 40 refers to the INPUT statement at line 40. We retype the data as shown, and the computer then assigns 150 to M and 125 to G as shown in the third line of the table for Fig. 4.26a:

Line no.	M	G	Time executed
40	150	12	3rd

The computer then uses these numbers to calculate the miles per gallon and prints

```
FOR 150   MILES AND 12    GALLONS,THE MILES PER GALLONS= 12.5
```

The computer would then go back to line 30 and this entire process would go on indefinitely. We use the same method employed previously to stop a program—we hit the BREAK key. On some systems, a special procedure must be followed to end a program in which an INPUT statement is being executed: For example, on the Hewlett-Packard 2000C, the programmer must simultaneously hit the CTRL and C keys to end a program at this point; on some other systems, the programmer must type STOP.

TYPING TOO MANY NUMBERS IN RESPONSE TO AN INPUT **STATEMENT**

```
TYPE IN MILES,A COMMA AND THEN GALLONS
? 150,12,2
TOO MUCH DATA,RETYPE INPUT    AT   40
? 150,12
FOR 150   MILES AND 12     GALLONS,THE MILES PER GALLONS= 12.5
TYPE IN MILES,A COMMA AND THEN GALLONS
?

READY.
```

Figure 4.26d. If the programmer types too many numbers, the computer informs him of this by typing TOO MUCH DATA, RETYPE INPUT AT 40. The 40 is the line number of the INPUT statement in question. The programmer retypes the first two numbers and then hits the RETURN key. In order to stop the program, the programmer must hit the BREAK key or simultaneously hit the CTRL key and some other key or type STOP. The procedure depends on the system used on your computer.

In Fig. 4.27a, for the sake of comparison we present the same program as the one we have just studied with one change. Now the INPUT statement has been replaced with a READ statement

        20   READ M, G

and a therefore a DATA statement

        60   DATA 205, 18, 125, 10

has been included in the program. It contains the first two sets of numbers we used in the previous program. The table for Fig. 4.27a shows the variable assignment at line 20. Once the programmer types RUN, the program does all the calculations and then runs out of data as shown in Fig. 4.27b. If the programmer wants to find out the miles per gallon for the last set of data used in the previous program, 150 and 12, he must now type

        60 DATA 150, 12
        RUN

as shown in Fig. 4.27c; i.e., he must change the DATA statement and rerun the program. This is a more tedious operation to perform than simply typing two numbers, as we did when we wrote the program with an INPUT statement.

USING A READ AND DATA STATEMENT TO CALCULATE MILES PER GALLON

```
10      REM CALCULATES MILES PER GALLON
20      READ M,G
30      PRINT "FOR";M;"MILES AND";G;"GALLONS, THE ";
40      PRINT "MILES PER GALLON=";M/G
50      GO TO 20
60      DATA 205,18,125,10
70      END
```

Figure 4.27a. Second version of the program that calculates miles per gallon. This program, however, uses a DATA statement. In order to give the program more data, the programmer must change the DATA statement. Thus it is now more difficult for the programmer to interact with the computer.

Line no.	M	G	Time executed
20	205	18	1st
20	125	10	2nd

Table for Fig. 4.27a. The values assigned to M and G each time line 20 is executed. The assignments are the same as in the previous program.

```
RUN
FOR 205  MILES AND 18    GALLONS, THE MILES PER GALLON= 11.3889
FOR 125  MILES AND 10    GALLONS, THE MILES PER GALLON= 12.5
END OF DATA    AT   20
READY.
```

Figure 4.27b. Running the program of Fig. 4.27a.

```
60 DATA 150,12
RUN
FOR 150  MILES AND 12    GALLONS, THE MILES PER GALLON= 12.5
END OF DATA    AT   20
READY.
```

Figure 4.27c. If the programmer now wants to calculate the miles per gallon for more data, e.g., for 150 miles and 12 gallons, he has to change line 60 and then type RUN, and rerun the program.

We now alter the program of Fig. 4.26a so that the program ends without our having to hit the BREAK key. We do this in Fig. 4.28a by including in the program another pair of PRINT and INPUT statements and an IF statement

```
70        PRINT "TO CONTINUE TYPE 1;ELSE,0";
80        INPUT T
90        IF T=1 THEN 30
```

The loop in the program consists of lines 30 to 90. After the miles per gallon have been calculated and printed, statement 70 is executed; the computer asks whether you want to continue by printing:

TO CONTINUE TYPE 1;ELSE,0 ?1

If you type 1, the loop (lines 30 to 90) is executed again. On the other hand, if you type 0, the next statement executed is

```
100       END
```

and the program is finished. Note, since line 70 ends in a semicolon, the question mark typed when the INPUT statement is executed, is typed on the same line as the message produced by line 70. We must therefore type our response on this line, as is shown in Fig. 4.28b.

OPTIONAL ENDING OF A PROGRAM WITH AN INPUT STATEMENT

```
10        REM CALCULATES MILES PER GALLON
20        REM M=MILES;G=GALLONS
30        PRINT "TYPE IN MILES, A COMMA AND THEN GALLONS"
40        INPUT M,G
50        PRINT "FOR";M;"MILES AND";G;"GALLONS,THE ";
60        PRINT "MILES PER GALLON=";M/G
70        PRINT "TO CONTINUE TYPE 1;ELSE,0";
80        INPUT T
90        IF T=1 THEN 30
100       END
```

Figure 4.28a. Same as program in Fig. 4.26a except that the programmer is given the option of ending the program by typing 0. The semicolon at the end of line 70 causes the question mark to be printed on the same line immediately after ELSE 0, as we see in Fig. 4.28b.

```
RUN
TYPE IN MILES, A COMMA AND THEN GALLONS
?205,18
FOR 205   MILES AND 18    GALLONS,THE MILES PER GALLON= 11.3889
TO CONTINUE TYPE 1;ELSE,0 ?1
TYPE IN MILES, A COMMA AND THEN GALLONS
? 125,10
FOR 125   MILES AND 10    GALLONS,THE MILES PER GALLON= 12.5
TO CONTINUE TYPE 1;ELSE,0 ?0
READY.
```

Figure 4.28b. Running the program of Fig. 4.28a.

PROBLEMS

1. What is wrong with the following statements?
   a. 10   READ A,B,C,D
   b. 10   READ A,B;C,D
   c. 10   READ,A,B,C,D,

2. What is wrong with the following statements?
   a. 10   DATA 10.2,20.6;30.7,6
   b. 10   DATA, 10.2,20.6,7,6

3. What are the results of the following program?
   ```
   10    READ A,B,C,D,E
   20    PRINT "SUM=";A+B+C+D+E
   30    DATA 1,2,3
   40    DATA 4,5
   50    END
   ```

4. What are the results of the following program?
   ```
   10    READ A
   20    READ B,C
   30    READ D
   40    PRINT "PRODUCT=";A*B*C*D
   50    DATA 1,2,3
   60    DATA 4,5
   70    END
   ```

5. Write a program that contains the following DATA statement and averages the the numbers in it: DATA 16.2, 17.4, 3.96, 17.1.

6. Given a DATA statement in which the first piece of data indicates how many other pieces of data follow it, write a program that contains this DATA statement and averages the numbers following the first piece of data.

7. Given the following table, write a program that calculates each worker's salary and then prints the salary and all the items in the table relating to that worker

Worker number	Hourly wage	Hours	Tax rate
110	$4.00	40	12%
111	$6.40	40	15%
112	$5.00	40	13%

Note: A worker's salary = HOURS × HOURLY WAGE − TAX RATE × HOURS × HOURLY WAGE.

8. Given the following table, write a program that for each sale calculates the number of square feet of plywood sold and the amount of the sale in dollars. The price per square foot of plywood is $.06.

Sale number	Length	Width
1001	8 ft.	4 ft.
1006	12 ft.	4 ft.
1012	5 ft.	3 ft.

9. Given the table in problem 8, write a program that not only calculates the dollar amount of each sale, but also determines, for each purchase, how many sales including the present sale have been made (use a counter for this) and the total dollar amount of sales (use an accumulator for this).

10. The formula to convert from Fahrenheit to Centigrade is $C = 5/9 \ (F - 32)$. Given the following Fahrenheit temperature readings 0°, 32°, 80°, 150°, 212°, write a program that converts them to Centigrade and prints both temperatures and reading number.

11. What is wrong with each of the following lines?

```
a. 10   IF N=4 GO TO 30
b. 10   IF N EQUALS 4 THEN 30
c. 10   IF N=>4 THEN 40
d. 10   IF N=<4 THEN 30
```

12. What are the results of the following program?

```
10   DATA 30,61,3,92,4
20   READ X
30   IF X=3 THEN 60
40   PRINT X;
50   GO TO 20
60   END
```

13. Given A=1, B=3, C=3, D=1. What statement is executed after the IF statement in each of the following sets of lines?

```
a. 20   IF A+B>C THEN 80
   30   PRINT A
```

```
b. 20   IF A*B<>C*D THEN 80
   30   PRINT A
```

c. 20   IF A↑2+B↑2>B↑2+C↑2 THEN 80
   30   PRINT A

d. 20   IF A<=(B+C)/(A+B) THEN 80
   30   PRINT A

e. 20   IF A*B<C+D THEN 80
   30   PRINT A

f. 20   IF A*B*C>=9 THEN 80
   30   PRINT A

14. Write a program that, given the numbers in the DATA statement 10   DATA 13,12,6,7,999 calculates the square and cube of each number except the last and then prints the original number and the results. The printed results should appear in columns labeled NUMBER, SQUARE, and CUBE, respectively. The number 999 is a trailer and should not be used in the calculations but should signal the computer to print I AM FINISHED.

15. Write a program that calculates the product of the odd numbers from 1 to 15.

16. Write a program that calculates the product of the odd numbers from 1 to 7, from 1 to 11, and from 1 to 13.

17. Write a program that, given the numbers in the DATA statement 10   DATA 13, 12, 6, 7, calculates the square and cube of each number and then prints the original number plus these results. The printed results should appear in columns labeled NUMBER, SQUARE, and CUBE. After the calculations are done for the last number, 7, the computer should print: I CAN'T THINK, THEREFORE I AM NOT.

18. Write a program that calculates
$$Y = \sum_{N=0}^{N=4} X^N, \qquad \text{i.e., } Y = 1 + X + X^2 + X^3 + X^4$$
where the value of X is 3 and is read from a DATA statement. Hint: use LET $Y = Y + X \uparrow N$, where N is the counter.

19. Write a program that calculates
$$Y = \sum_{N=0}^{M} X^N, \qquad \text{i.e., } Y = 1 + X + X^2 + X^3 + \ldots + X^M$$
The values of M and X should be read from a DATA statement.

20. Repeat problem 19, but this time the values of M and X should be typed in response to an INPUT statement.

 21. Do problem 10 using an INPUT statement instead of a READ and DATA statement.

22. Is the following line, because of the word REMARK, a misuse of the REM statement?

```
10    REMARK  PROGRAM
```

23. What is printed by the following program?

```
10    READ A, A
20    PRINT A
30    GO TO 10
40    DATA 1, 2, 3, 4
50    END
```

5

The FOR-NEXT Loop

5.1. Numbers

We begin by defining a number. A number consists of a group of digits that may or may not include a decimal point. A digit is any of the following: 0, 1, 2, 3, 4, 5, 6, 7, 8, 9.

Now that we have defined a number, let us see how numbers are used in BASIC. When the computer prints a number, it will print it in one of three different ways, depending on the number itself.

1. If the number includes a fractional part, e.g., 4¾, the number will be printed with a decimal point: 4.75

2. If the number is a whole number—and it is not too large, as defined in the next paragraph—it will be printed without a decimal point: 236

3. There is a limit to the maximum number of digits a computer can accommodate. This limit is fixed for each make of computer. Depending on the computer you use, this limit varies between 6 and 16 digits. If a number used in a program has more than the maximum number of digits allowed, it will be printed in what is called exponential form (sometimes called power of ten or scientific notation). As an example of this, in Fig. 5.1a we show a program in which a 9-digit number

```
10 PRINT 123456789
```

is used. The program was run on a computer that can accommodate a maximum of 6 digits. The computer handles this 9-digit number in the same way it would handle a 9-digit number resulting from a calculation. For pedagogic reasons, we can think of the computer as first converting the number to exponential form

$$1.23456789 \times 10^8$$

and then rounding the 1.23456789 part to 6 digits

$$1.23457$$

Thus the result printed when the program is run, is

$$1.23457E+08$$

as shown in Fig. 5.1b. The $+08$ means that 1.23457 is multiplied by 10^8; i.e., it indicates

154

HOW NUMBERS ARE PRINTED

```
10 PRINT 123456789
20 END
```

Figure 5.1a. A program in which a number appears having more digits than a given computer can accommodate. The number has 9 digits, but the computer on which we ran the program could accommodate only 6.

```
RUN
1.23457E+08
READY
```

Figure 5.1b. Running the program of Fig. 5.1a. The number is converted to exponential form and then rounded to 6 digits.

that the exponent of 10 multiplying 1.23457 is $+08$ or simply 8. If the computer prints

$$1.11111E+02$$

for the results of a program, the value of the number is 1.11111×10^2. Similarly a printed result of

$$2.67131E-03$$

corresponds to the value 2.67131×10^{-3}.

You may write numbers in a BASIC program using these three methods: with a decimal point, without a decimal point, or in exponential form. Numbers that have a fractional part must be written with a decimal point. Numbers that have more digits than your computer can accommodate, whether they are very large or very small numbers, should be written in exponential form. If you do not write them in exponential form, the computer, depending on which version of BASIC you are using, will either convert the number to exponential form, as we showed in Fig. 5.1b, or tell you that the number has too many digits.

When you write numbers in exponential form, you may omit the plus sign in the exponential part. Thus $1.231E+3$ may be written as $1.231E3$. However when you write a number that has a negative exponent you cannot omit the minus sign. Thus, if you write 1.23×10^{-3} as $1.23E3$, the computer will interpret it as 1.23×10^3.

You cannot use commas in writing numbers. Thus

```
10   LET X=27,321
```

would cause a grammatical error. Finally, if you want to use a negative number in a program you must place a minus sign before the number; for example,

```
10   LET X=-273
```

Fig. 5.1c includes examples of various types of numbers used in writing programs. The results are shown in Fig. 5.1d.

We summarize much of what we have said in this section by considering a program in which we have written the whole number 90 in the three possible ways:

```
10 PRINT 90,90.0,9.0E1
```

as shown in the program of Fig. 5.1e. Since this number is a whole number, the computer will always print it as 90, no matter how we write it in the program, as is shown in Fig. 5.1f.

```
10  LETX=-237
20  LET Y=13.6712
30  LET R=.631E+12
40  LET Z=1.231E+03
50  LET Z1=1.231E03
60  LET Z2=1.231E3
70  LET A=1.23E-03
80  LET A1=1.23E-3
90  PRINT "X=";X;"Y=";Y;"R=";R;"Z=";Z
100 PRINT "Z1=";Z1;"Z2=";Z2;"A=";A;"A1=";A1
110 END
```

Figure 5.1c. Examples of the three types of numbers that can be used in a BASIC program: whole numbers, numbers that have a fractional part, and exponential numbers. A number that has a positive exponent may be written without the plus sign in the exponential part. Numbers that have negative exponents must always be written with the minus sign in the exponential part.

```
RUN
X=-237   Y= 13.6712     R= 6.31000E+11    Z= 1231
Z1= 1231      Z2= 1231      A= .00123      A1= .00123
READY
```

Figure 5.1d. Running the program of Fig. 5.1c. Numbers that have fewer than 6 digits are not printed as exponential numbers even though they were written as exponential numbers in the program.

```
10 PRINT 90,90.0,9.0E1
20 END
```

Figure 5.1e. Program in which the number 90 is written in all three of the possible forms: without a decimal point, 90; with a decimal point, 90.0; in exponential form 9.0E1.

```
RUN
90               90              90
READY
```

Figure 5.1f. Running the program of Fig. 5.1e. We see that no matter how the whole number 90 is written in Fig. 5.1e, the computer prints it as the whole number 90.

5.2. The FOR-NEXT Loop

We now introduce a method that will enable us to form loops with fewer statements and with greater facility then we did previously. As an example of the previous method we show in Fig. 5.2a, a program that reads and prints each of the pieces of data in:

```
60   DATA 16,14,11,31
```

We instruct the computer to do this four times by using a counter, N, which we first set equal to zero in

```
10   LET N=0
```

then adding 1 to this value in

```
40   LET N=N+1
```

each time we read and print a piece of data; and then finally testing whether the value of N is 4

```
50   IF N <> 4 THEN 20
```

If it is not, we read and print the next piece of data. Each time 20 READ X is executed, the next number in the DATA statement is assigned to X. In the table for Fig. 5.2a, we show the values of the variables used in the program each time line 50 is executed. In Fig. 5.2b we show the results of running the program. The results are as expected. The numbers are all printed on one line because of the semicolon at the end of line 30:

```
30   PRINT X;
```

MOTIVATING THE FOR–NEXT LOOP

```
10    LET N=0
20    READ X
30    PRINT X;
40    LET N=N+1
50    IF N <> 4 THEN 20
60    DATA 16,14,11,31
70    END
```

O.K

Figure 5.2a. Program reads and prints each of 4 pieces of data in line 60.

Line no.	Time executed	N	X	Next statement
50	1st	1	16	20
50	2nd	2	14	20
50	3rd	3	11	20
50	4th	4	31	70

Table for Fig. 5.2a. The values of N and X each time line 50 is executed. The next statement executed is also shown.

```
RUN
 16     14      11      31
READY
```

Figure 5.2b. Running the program of Fig. 5.2a.

An easier way of writing this program is to use a FOR–NEXT loop, as shown in the program of Fig. 5.3a. We do this by sandwiching the statements in the loop of the preceding program that do not contain the counter N

```
30    READ X
40    PRINT X;
```

between a statement that begins with FOR and one that begins with the word NEXT.

The FOR statement

```
20    FOR N=1 TO 4
```

instructs the computer to execute the statements (lines 30 and 40) included between this and the NEXT statement

```
50    NEXT N
```

for N=1, N=2, N=3, and finally N=4.

In using the FOR–NEXT loop in this program, the programmer does not have to write statements which set N=0 or increase N by 1 or test the value of N as we did in Fig 5.2a. This is now all done "behind the scenes" in the computer—when the FOR and NEXT statements are translated. To be sure, because of the FOR statement in this program, the NEXT statement

```
50    NEXT N
```

can be thought of as increasing N by 1 and testing whether N equals 4. If N does not equal 4, then the statements in the loop starting with line 30 are executed again.

Let us now follow the execution of the program. In line 20, the value of N is initially set equal to 1. Then 16, the first number in the DATA statement, is assigned to X in the READ statement and is immediately printed in the PRINT statement. In line 50, NEXT N increased the value of N to 2. The program then proceeds to line 30, the READ statement. There 14, the second number in the DATA statement, is assigned to X. The value of the variables there is shown in the second line of the table for Fig. 5.3a.

Line no.	Time executed	N	X
30	2nd	2	14

In line 50, N is again increased by 1 so that it now equals 3. The program executes the loop for the third time, and then finally executes it for the fourth time. The computer has now executed the loop for N=1 to 4. The instruction in

```
20    FOR N=1 TO 4
```

is now satisfied. Hence, the computer now leaves the loop and goes to the next executable statement after the loop

```
70    END
```

and the program is finished. The DATA statement in line 60 was skipped because it is a non-executable statement. The results of running the program are shown in Fig. 5.3b.

USING THE FOR–NEXT LOOP

```
10    REM INTRODUCT TO FOR-NEXT
20    FOR N=1 TO 4
30    READ X
40    PRINT X;
50    NEXT N
60    DATA 16,14,11,31
70    END
```

Figure 5.3a. A second version of the program which reads and prints each of four pieces of data. It uses a FOR–NEXT loop to do this. The FOR–NEXT loop operates as follows: because of FOR N=1 TO 4, the statements (lines 30 and 40) which lie between the FOR and NEXT statements are executed for N=1, N=2, N=3, N=4. *Note:* The variable that follows the word NEXT (in this case N) must be the same as the one that follows the word FOR; it is called the index of the loop.

Line no.	Time executed	N	X
30	1st	1	16
30	2nd	2	14
30	3rd	3	11
30	4th	4	31

Table for Fig. 5.3a. The values of N and X each time line 30 is executed.

prob.
REM
O.K

```
RUN
16      14      11      31
READY
```

Figure 5.3b. Running the program of Fig. 5.3a. The results are the same as for Fig. 5.2a.

The variable (in this case N), called the index of the loop, which appears after the word FOR must be the same one that appears after the word NEXT. Thus if the loop ends with the statement

    40   NEXT P

as shown in Fig. 5.3c, an error occurs. When the program is run, the compiler cannot find the FOR P = ... statement which should begin the loop ending with NEXT P. It thus prints the message

    NEXT WITHOUT MATCHING FOR   IN LINE 40

as shown in Fig. 5.3d. The exact wording in this error message depends on the make of computer you use.

We now apply the FOR-NEXT loop to the program we studied in Fig. 4.11 and 4.13, in which we calculated S (the salary) from R (the hourly wage), H (the number of hours), and D (the union dues) of workers in a given organization. The variable N is used to identify the workers. The program is shown in Fig. 5.4a. In it, we calculate the salary of four workers. The statement

    50   READ N,R,H,D

reads the information required for a given worker. The statement

    60   LET S=R*H-D

calculates his salary, and the statement

    70   PRINT "SALARY FOR WORKER";N;"IS $";S

prints the results. These statements are sandwiched between

    40   FOR Z=1 TO 4

which begins the loop and determines that these statements will be executed 4 times, and

    80   NEXT Z

which marks the end of the loop.

When the loop has been executed for the fourth time, the next statement executed after line 80 is

    130   END

Figure 5.4b shows the results when the program is run. Each time line 70 is executed, it prints the appropriate line of results for each of the four workers. Thus the first line printed

    SALARY FOR WORKER 3   IS $ 65.5

shows that the value of the variable S is 65.5 for the worker whose identification number, N, is 3.

AN INCORRECT FOR-NEXT LOOP

```
10    FOR N=1 TO 4
20    READ X
30    PRINT X;
40    NEXT P
50    DATA 16,14,11,31
60    END
```

Figure 5.3c. Program in which a mistake is made in writing the **NEXT** statement: the wrong variable follows the word NEXT. Line 40 should read 40 NEXT N.

```
RUN
NEXT WITHOUT MATCHING FOR  IN LINE 40
READY
```

Figure 5.3d. Running the program of Fig. 5.3c. We obtain an error message.

USING A FOR-NEXT LOOP TO CALCULATE A WORKER'S SALARY

```
10    REM N=I.D.#;R=HOURLY WAGE
20    REM H=HOURS; D=DUES; S=SALARY
30    REM PROGRAM CALCULATES WORKERS7 SALARY
40    FOR Z=1 TO 4
50    READ N,R,H,D
60    LET S=R*H-D
70    PRINT "SALARY FOR WORKER";N;"IS $";S
80    NEXT Z
90    DATA 3,2,35,4.5
100   DATA 7,3,24,3.3
110   DATA 8,5.6,38,22.2
120   DATA 9,6.2,40,73
130   END
```

Figure 5.4a. A program which uses the FOR-NEXT loop to calculate the salaries of four workers. We now use Z as the index in the FOR-NEXT loop.

```
RUN
SALARY FOR WORKER 3    IS $ 65.5
SALARY FOR WORKER 7    IS $ 68.7
SALARY FOR WORKER 8    IS $ 190.6
SALARY FOR WORKER 9    IS $ 175
READY
```

Figure 5.4b. Running the program of Fig. 5.4a.

Our next application of the FOR–NEXT loop is to a very pertinent problem: determining the number of columns on the teletypewriter you are using. The number of columns per line on the teletypewriter is usually 70, 72, or 75. We determine this number in the program shown in Fig. 5.5a.

The program is very simple; it consists of a FOR–NEXT loop in which, because of 10 FOR I=1 TO 10, the line

```
20    PRINT "123456789-";
```

is executed 10 times. We again exploit the fact that when a PRINT statement ends with a semicolon its results will be printed on the same line as the results of the last PRINT statement executed. Thus, the second time line 20 is executed, the string 123456789—will be printed on the same line that it was printed on the first time line 20 was executed. This process is repeated each time line 20 is executed until there is no more room on the line. The computer then follows the procedure it follows whenever it finds that it cannot print all the required information on one line: it prints the remaining information on the next line. It thus prints the remaining strings on the next line. If, however, only part of the repeated string fits on the last part of the first line, the computer prints the rest of the string as well as the remaining strings on the next line.

When we run the program we see, as shown in Fig. 5.5b, that seven complete strings were printed on one line. Since there are 10 characters in the string, our teletypewriter has 70 columns per line. If in addition to the seven times the string was printed on the line, one string was partially printed on the first line and partially on the second line, we would add the number of characters printed on the first line to 70 and thus obtain the total number of columns on the line.*

---

* On some systems, if part of a string does not fit on a line, the computer prints the entire string on the next line. Thus the results of this program when run on those systems may be misleading since there may be more columns on a line than the results indicate. To avoid this, one should add

    32 FOR I = 1 TO 100
    34 PRINT "X";
    36 NEXT I

to the program of Fig. 5.5a. This will print a row of Xs on the same line as the last 123456789– was printed on (the second line of results) until there is no more room on the line. Since the string X consists of only one character, every available column on the second line will be occupied. Thus by comparing the first two lines of results, we can determine how many columns are available on a teletypewriter line.

DETERMINING HOW MANY COLUMNS YOUR TELETYPEWRITER PAGE HAS

```
10   FOR I=1 TO 10
20   PRINT "123456789-";
30   NEXT I
40   END
```

Figure 5.5a. A program that determines how many columns there are on a teletypewriter line. The PRINT statement is executed 10 times. Since this statement ends with a semicolon, each time it is executed the computer continues to print the quoted strings on the same line. It does this until there is no more room on the line. If only part of a repeated string fits on the line, the computer prints the rest of the string, as well as the remaining strings on the next line.

```
RUN
123456789-123456789-123456789-123456789-123456789-123456789-123456789-
123456789-123456789-123456789-
READY
```

Figure 5.5b. Running the program of Fig. 5.5a. In order to determine the number of columns in a line, we multiply the number of times the string is completely printed on the first line by 10, the number of characters in the string. We then add to this the number of characters printed in the string which is only partially printed on the rest of the line. In our case, no string was partially printed on the first line. Hence, the number of columns on a line of our teletypewriter is 7*10, or 70.

We now investigate a program in which the index—in this case D—is used in a statement in the loop. This is shown in line 20 of the program of Fig. 5.6a.

20   PRINT "D=";D:

This statement is executed for D=1 to 6, i.e., six times. Each time it is executed, the value of D is printed. Since this line ends with a semicolon, all the results are printed on one line. We see this when we run the program, as shown in Fig. 5.6b.

USING THE INDEX OF THE LOOP IN A STATEMENT WITHIN THE LOOP

```
10    FOR D=1 TO 6
20    PRINT "D=";D;
30    NEXT D
40    END
```

Figure 5.6a. A program in which the variable D, used as the index for the loop, is also used in a statement within the loop.

```
RUN
D= 1      D= 2      D= 3      D= 4      D= 5      D= 6
READY
```

Figure 5.6b. Running the program of Fig. 59a. Each time line 20 is executed the value of the index, D, is printed. Again, because line 20 ends with a semicolon, all the results are printed on one line.

We now study the application of the FOR–NEXT loop to two programs, in which the index of the loop is itself used in a calculation with the loop, for example, in the program of Fig. 5.7a

```
20    PRINT 10↑R
```

is in a FOR–NEXT loop where R is the loop index. The purpose of these programs is to demonstrate again something we learned at the beginning of this chapter: the size of a number calculated by the computer determines the form in which the number is printed. Thus, very large numbers and very small fractions are printed in exponential form whereas all other numbers are printed with a decimal point if they have a fractional part, or without a decimal point if they are whole numbers. The programs were run on a machine that could accommodate a maximum of 6 digits.

The first program, shown in Fig. 5.7a, produces the numbers 1, 10, 100, 1000, 10000, etc., using a FOR–NEXT loop containing

```
20    PRINT 10↑R
```

where R is the variable used as the index of the loop. Thus in successive executions of the loop, as the value of R goes from 1 to 7, the computer interprets line 20 as   20 PRINT 10 ↑ 1, 20 PRINT 10 ↑ 2, 20 PRINT 10 ↑ 3 ⋯   20 PRINT 10 ↑ 7. In order to determine how these numbers are printed, we run the program, as shown in Fig. 5.7b. We see that as long as the number calculated in the PRINT statement contains fewer than 6 digits, the number *will not* be printed in exponential form. Thus on the fourth execution of the loop, the number appearing in the PRINT statement (10 ↑ 4) is printed as

```
10000
```

Since it is a whole number, it does not contain a decimal point.

However, once a number contains more than 6 digits, it is printed in exponential form. For example, on the seventh execution of the loop, the number appearing in the PRINT statement (10 ↑ 7) if it *were not* printed in exponential form, would contain 8 digits. It thus is printed in exponential form as

```
1.00000E+07
```

In the problems, you are asked to write a similar program that will determine the maximum number of digits your computer can accommodate.

The second program, shown in Fig. 5.8a, produces the numbers 1/10, 1/1000, etc., using a FOR–NEXT loop that contains

```
20    PRINT 1/(10↑R)
```

In successive executions of the loop, as the value of R goes from 1 to 8, the computer interprets line 20 as: 20 PRINT 1/(10 ↑ 1),   20 PRINT 1/(10 ↑ 2),   20 PRINT 1/(10 ↑ 3) ⋯,   20 PRINT 1/(10 ↑ 8). In order to determine how these numbers are printed, we run the program as shown in Fig. 5.8b. We see that as long as the number calculated in the PRINT statement, contains fewer than 6 digits, the number *will not* be printed in exponential form. Thus on the fourth execution of the loop, the number appearing in the PRINT statement [1/(10 ↑ 4)] is printed as

```
.0001
```

Once a number contains more than 6 digits, it is printed in exponential form. For example, on the seventh execution of the loop, the number appearing in the PRINT statement [1/(10 ↑ 7)], if it *were not* printed in exponential form, would contain more than 6 digits. It is thus printed in exponential form as

```
1.00000E-07
```

HOW THE VALUE OF A NUMBER DETERMINES THE FORM IN WHICH THE NUMBER IS PRINTED

```
10    FOR R=1 TO 7
20    PRINT 10↑R
30    NEXT R
40    END
```

Figure 5.7a. This program shows that large numbers will be printed in exponential form. The loop index, R, is used in a calculation within the loop.

```
RUN
 10
 100
 1000
 10000
 100000
 1.00000E+06
 1.00000E+07
READY
```

Figure 5.7b. Running the program of Fig. 5.7a on a machine that can accommodate a maximum of 6 digits. If a number contains more than 6 digits, it is printed in exponential form.

```
10    FOR R=1 TO 8
20    PRINT 1/(10↑R)
30    NEXT R
40    END
```

Figure 5.8a. This program shows that very small fractions will be printed in exponential form.

```
RUN
 .1
 .01
 .001
 .0001
 .00001
 .000001
 1.00000E-07
 1.00000E-08
READY
```

Figure 5.8b. Running the program of Fig. 5.8a on a machine that can accommodate a maximum of 6 digits. If a number contains more than 6 digits, it is printed in exponential form.

Another program in which the index—this time N—is used within a loop is shown in Fig. 5.9a. This program does the same thing as the one in Fig. 4.24, i.e., it calculates the product of the numbers from 1 to R, where R is a number read in the program. The variable N, besides being the index of the loop is also used within the loop for calculating the product

70   LET P=P*N

This is reflected in the table for Fig. 5.9a since, for every line, the value of N used in the calculation equals the time the loop was executed; for example, for the fourth line of the table

Line no.	Time executed	R	N used in calculation	P on left of =
70	4th	9	4	24

the value of N used in the calculation is 4 for the fourth time line 70 is executed.

Another feature of this program which is new is that in the FOR statement the upper limits of the index N is not a number but a variable R, as shown in line 60:

60   FOR N=1 TO R

This value of R is read from the DATA statement when the program is executed—the value of R is 9. The computer therefore translates this statement as

60   FOR N=1 TO 9

We see from the table for Fig. 5.9 that the last time line 70 is executed is when both R and N equal 9.

Line no.	Time executed	R	N used in calculation	P on left of =
70	9th	9	9	362880

The results when the program is run are shown in Fig. 5.9b:

THE PRODUCT OF THE #'S FROM 1 TO 9   IS 362880.

We note that not only is the product 362880 printed, but the value of R, which is 9, is printed as well. This is because R appears in the PRINT statement in line 100

100   PRINT "1 TO";R;"IS";P

CALCULATING R !

```
10    REM PROGRAM CALCULATES THE PRODUCT
20    REM OF THE NUMBERS FROM 1 TO R
30    REM P=THE MULTIPLICATIVE ACCUMULATOR
40    LET P=1
50    READ R
60    FOR N=1 TO R
70    LET P=P*N
80    NEXT N
90    PRINT "THE PRODUCT OF THE #'S FROM";
100   PRINT "1 TO";R;"IS";P
110   DATA 9
120   END
```

Figure 5.9a. A progam in which a FOR-NEXT loop is used to calculate the product of the numbers from 1 to R, a number which is read in. The index, N, is itself used in the loop in the calculation to determine the product, P.

Line no.	Time executed	R	N used in calculation	P on left of =
70	1st	9	1	1
70	2nd	9	2	2
70	3rd	9	3	6
70	4th	9	4	24
70	5th	9	5	120
70	6th	9	6	720
70	7th	9	7	5040
70	8th	9	8	40320
70	9th	9	9	362880

Table for Fig. 5.9a. The values of R and N; and the value of P on the left-hand side of the equals sign in line 70. The value of N corresponds to the time the loop is being executed. This is as we expect, since not only is N used in the calculation of the product, but it is also the index for the loop. Also note that the value of R is the upper limit for the number of times the loop is executed.

```
RUN
THE PRODUCT OF THE #'S FROM1 TO 9      IS 362880.
READY
```

Figure 5.9b. Running the program of Fig. 5.9a. Note: Not only is the product 362880 printed, but the value of R, which is 9, is printed as well.

We next consider a program, shown in Fig. 5.10a, that calculates the product of the numbers from 1 to R for many values of R. This program does the same thing as the one we studied in Fig. 4.25.

The program consists of two loops. The inner loop (which we will call the N loop since N is the loop index) consists of the statements

```
70    FOR N=1 TO R
80    LET P=P*N
90    NEXT N
```

It calculates, as we see, the products of the numbers from 1 to R. Before this loop is executed, we must read in R. We must also assign the value 1 to P, otherwise the product will always be zero. Thus we write

```
50    READ R
60    LET P=.1
```

After the inner loop is executed the required number of times—the value of R—the computer is instructed in lines 100 and 110 to print the results.

This entire process must be done three times, once for each number in the DATA statement. We thus form an outer loop (the T loop) by sandwiching lines 50 through 110 between

```
40    FOR T=1 TO 3
```

and

```
120   NEXT T
```

What we have done is called nesting loops. In order to enable you to better understand this procedure, we compare what we have done with the loops—placing the inner loop entirely within the outer loop—with the practice used by shippers of items such as wastepaper baskets. To conserve space they stack—or "nest"—the baskets, one within the other. Just as we can nest many baskets within each other, we may nest many loops within each other. However, we must take care to use a different index for each loop. For example, if we had used the same index, T, for both loops in this program, the value of T would simultaneously have been 1 for the first execution of the outer loop and 6 for the sixth execution of the inner loop. This is an impossibility because a variable can assume only one value at a time. If by mistake one uses the same index for nested loops, one will get an error message when the program is run.

The concept of nesting means that an inner loop (in this case the N loop) must be totally contained within an outer loop (T loop). In other words, since   40 FOR T=1 TO 3 precedes   70 FOR N=1 TO R, the reverse order must be followed in the placement of the NEXT statements. Thus NEXT N must precede NEXT T. Figure 5.10b shows the printed results when the program is run.

On some systems there is a limit to the number of loops that one can nest within each other; for instance on the CDC 6600 one can nest loops only 10 deep. On other systems this limit is affected only by the size of the computer's memory.

NESTING FOR-NEXT LOOPS

```
10    REM PROGRAM CALCULATES THE PRODUCT
20    REM OF THE NUMBERS FROM 1 TO R
30    REM FOR MANY VALUES OF R
40    FOR T=1 TO 3
50    READ R
60    LET P=.1
70    FOR N=1 TO R
80    LET P=P*N
90    NEXT N
100   PRINT "THE PRODUCT OF THE #'S ";
110   PRINT "FROM 1 TO":R;"IS";P
120   NEXT T
130   DATA 6,17,23
140   END
```

Figure 5.10a. A program that calculates the product of the <u>numbers from 1 to R, for many values of R</u>. The T loop is executed for each number in the DATA statement. Each time the T loop is executed, the N loop is executed for N=1 to the value of R just read in. Note that the index for each loop must have different variable names. The loops, as we have used them here, are said to be nested. Also, since FOR T=1 TO 3 precedes FOR N=1 TO R, then NEXT N must precede NEXT T in order for the loops to be properly nested.

```
RUN
THE PRODUCT OF THE #'S FROM 1 TO 6     IS 720
THE PRODUCT OF THE #'S FROM 1 TO 17    IS 3.55687E+14
THE PRODUCT OF THE #'S FROM 1 TO 23    IS 2.58520E+22
READY
```

Figure 5.10b. Running the program of Figure 5.10a.

We now discuss another program that uses nested loops. This program, shown in Fig. 5.11a, calculates the area of rectangles, whose length, L, and width, W, are the indices of the two loops. Each time the statements in the W loop (outer loop) are executed once, the statements in the L loop (inner loop)

```
40   FOR L=1 TO 4
50   PRINT "L=";L;"W=";W;"A=";L*W
60   NEXT L
```

are executed four times. The table for Fig. 5.11a demonstrates this; for example, the first four lines

Line no.	W	L	A
50	1	1	1
50	1	2	2
50	1	3	3
50	1	4	4

show that at line 50 while the value of W is 1, the value of L goes from 1 to 4 and therefore the area A also goes from 1 to 4. In Fig. 5.11b are shown the results when the program is run.

CALCULATING THE AREA OF RECTANGLES

```
10    REM CALCULATES RECTANGLES'S AREA
20    REM LOOPS PROPERLY NESTED
30    FOR W=1 TO 4
40    FOR L=1 TO 4
50    PRINT "L=";L;"W=";W;"A=";L*W
60    NEXT L
70    NEXT W
80    END
```

Figure 5.11a. A program that uses nested FOR–NEXT loops to calculate the area of various-sized rectangles. Each time the statements in the W loop are executed, the statements in the L loop are executed four times.

Line	W	L	A
50	1	1	1
50	1	2	2
50	1	3	3
50	1	4	4
50	2	1	2
50	2	2	4
50	2	3	6
50	2	4	8
.	.	.	.
.	.	.	.
.	.	.	.
50	4	1	4
50	4	2	8
50	4	3	12
50	4	4	16

Table for Fig. 5.11a. Values of W, L, and A at line 50. For each value of W, L assumes 4 values.

```
RUN
L= 1      W= 1      A= 1
L= 2      W= 1      A= 2
L= 3      W= 1      A= 3
L= 4      W= 1      A= 4
L= 1      W= 2      A= 2
L= 2      W= 2      A= 4
L= 3      W= 2      A= 6
L= 4      W= 2      A= 8
L= 1      W= 3      A= 3
L= 2      W= 3      A= 6
L= 3      W= 3      A= 9
L= 4      W= 3      A= 12
L= 1      W= 4      A= 4
L= 2      W= 4      A= 8
L= 3      W= 4      A= 12
L= 4      W= 4      A= 16
READY
```

Figure 5.11b. Running the program of Figure 5.11a.

In Fig. 5.12a we show the same program as in Fig. 5.11a, but this time the loops are not nested properly. If the loops had been properly nested, since the FOR W... precedes the FOR L..., the NEXT L should precede the NEXT W. As we see, this is not the case in Fig. 5.12a; there the NEXT W precedes the NEXT L. When we run the program, as shown in Fig. 5.12b, the computer produces the following error message

NEXT WITHOUT MATCHING FOR   IN LINE 60

One can nest more than one inner loop in an outer loop. Thus in Fig. 5.13 we see that the A3 loop and the A2 loop are nested in the A1 loop.

IMPROPERLY NESTED FOR—NEXT LOOPS

```
10    REM CALCULATES RECTANGLES' AREA
20    REM LOOPS IMPROPERLY NESTED
30    FOR W=1 TO 4
40    FOR L=1 TO 4
50    PRINT "L=";L;"W=";W;"A=";L*W
60    NEXT W
70    NEXT L
80    END
```

Figure 5.12a. Same program as in Figure 5.11a, but this time the loops are improperly nested. The NEXT L should precede the NEXT W.

```
RUN
NEXT WITHOUT MATCHING FOR   IN LINE 60
READY
```

Figure 5.12b. When we run the program of Figure 5.12a we obtain an error message.

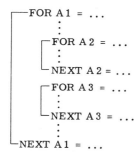

Figure 5.13. Diagram showing that more than one inner loop (the A2 loop and the A3 loop) can be nested in an outer loop (the A1 loop).

We next rewrite the program of Fig. 5.11a so that the areas of the rectangles will be printed in tabular form: the lengths of the rectangles will label the top of the table, and the widths will label the left-hand side of the table. In order to label the top of the table, we start the program, which is shown in Fig. 5.14a, with

```
30   PRINT "LENGTH=",
```

and the loop

```
40   FOR T=1 TO 4
50   PRINT T,
60   NEXT T
```

This produces the first line of results shown in Fig. 5.14b

```
LENGTH=       1          2          3          4
```

Everything here was printed on one line because the PRINT statements in lines 30 and 50 both end with a comma. The next statement

```
70   PRINT
```

since it does not end with a comma and since it does not print any characters, has the effect of removing the comma from line 50 the last time line 50 is executed. This enables the computer to print the next group of results on a new line.

The W loop and the nested L loop produce the rest of the table. Each time the W loop is executed, it prints another line of the table. The first statement after the beginning of the W loop

```
90   PRINT "WIDTH=";W,
```

prints WIDTH= and then the appropriate value of W for each line of the table. Because this statement ends with a comma, the L loop

```
100   FOR L=1 TO 4
110   PRINT L*W,
120   NEXT L
```

prints on the same line as WIDTH=, the four areas calculated for the appropriate value of W and each of the four values of L. For instance when W=2, we obtain the third line of results shown in Fig. 5.14b

```
WIDTH= 2       2          4          6          8
```

The values of the areas are in the proper columns because there are the same number of commas in lines 30 and 50 when they are executed as there are in lines 90 and 110 when they are executed. If we upset this equality by changing the semicolon in line 90 to a comma, thus writing it as

```
90   PRINT "WIDTH=",W,
```

the values of the areas would not have been in the proper column.

Imp ↓

AREAS OF RECTANGLES PRODUCED IN TABULAR FORM

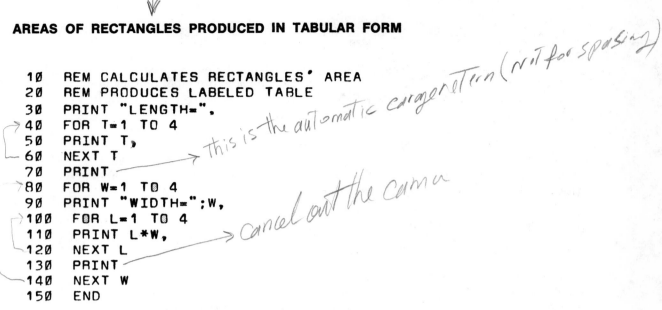

```
 10    REM CALCULATES RECTANGLES' AREA
 20    REM PRODUCES LABELED TABLE
 30    PRINT "LENGTH=",
 40    FOR T=1 TO 4
 50    PRINT T,
 60    NEXT T
 70    PRINT
 80    FOR W=1 TO 4
 90    PRINT "WIDTH=";W,
100    FOR L=1 TO 4
110    PRINT L*W,
120    NEXT L
130    PRINT
140    NEXT W
150    END
```

this is the automatic carriage return (not for spacing)

Cancel out the comma

Figure 5.14a. The program of Figure 5.11a rewritten so that a table is produced. The T loop produces the numbers on the first line of results. The W loop produces each subsequent line of the table; the nested L loop produces the areas for each line of the table.

```
RUN
LENGTH=            1          2          3          4
WIDTH= 1           1          2          3          4
WIDTH= 2           2          4          6          8
WIDTH= 3           3          6          9         12
WIDTH= 4           4          8         12         16
READY
```

Figure 5.14b. Running the program of Figure 5.14a.

So far, we have limited our study of the FOR–NEXT loop to programs in which the index was always increased by 1 for each execution of the loop. This need not be the case. The index can be increased by any fixed amount each time the loop is executed, as we shall see in the program of Fig. 5.15a. This program calculates the principal that accumulates when a given balance is kept in the bank at 5% interest for a number of years. The statement

60   FOR N=1 TO 5 STEP 2

in the program is a more generalized version of the FOR statement we have been using. By including the STEP 2 in line 60 we have instructed the computer to increase the index, N, by 2 each time the loop is executed. Thus the second time the statements in the loop are executed, N equals 3. This is shown in the second line of the table for Fig. 5.15a:

Line no.	Time executed	N	B	P
80	2nd	3	200	231.525

The next time the loop is executed, N is equal to 5. Since this is the maximum allowed value of the index (as dictated by the TO 5 in line 60), this is the last time the statements in the loop are executed. The results of the program are shown in Fig. 5.15b.

USE OF THE STEP IN FOR-NEXT LOOP

```
10   REM CALCULATES PRINCIPAL ON
20   REM A BALANCE AT 5% INTEREST
30   REM B=ORIGINAL BALANCE, P=PRINCIPAL
40   READ B
50   PRINT "PRINCIPAL","BALANCE","YEARS"
60   FOR N=1 TO 5 STEP 2
70   LET P=B*1.05↑N
80   PRINT P,B,N
90   NEXT N
100  DATA 200
110  END
```

Figure 5.15a. The program produces a table of principal that accrues at 5% interest for a minimum of 1 year to a maximum of 5 years for increments of 2 years. These values of the year are dictated by 60 FOR N=1 TO 5 STEP 2. The STEP 2 in line 60 means that each time the N loop is executed, the value of N is increased by 2.

Line no.	Time executed	N	B	P
70	1st	1	200	210
70	2nd	3	200	231.525
70	3rd	5	200	255.256

Table for Fig. 5.15a. The values of N, B, and P each time line 70 is executed. Note: The change in N is 2. This corresponds to the STEP 2 in line 60 of the program.

```
RUN
PRINCIPAL        BALANCE        YEARS
 210               200            1
 231.525           200            3
 255.256           200            5
READY
```

Figure 5.15b. Running the program of Figure 5.15a. The results are in tabular form, as was explained in Chapter 2, because of the commas used in both PRINT statements.

If the programmer so desires, he can write line 60 as

$$60 \quad \text{FOR } N=5 \text{ TO } 1 \text{ STEP } -2$$

as shown in Fig. 5.16a. This means that each time the loop is executed the value of N is decreased by 2 as dictated by the STEP -2 at the end of line 60. Also, the first time line 70 is executed, the value of N is 5 as shown in the first line of the table for Fig. 5.16a:

Line no.	Time executed	N	B	P
70	1st	5	200	255.256

However, the second time the loop statements are executed, the value of N is decreased by 2 as dictated by the STEP -2, and consequently the value of N this time is 3. The third and last time the loop statements are executed, the value of N is 1. All of this is shown in the table for Fig. 5.16a.

Because no changes were made in this program except for reversing the order of the years for which the balance is calculated, the results of this program should be identical to that of the program shown in Fig. 5.15a except for the order in which the results are printed. To check this, we run the program. The results are as we expected; they are shown in Fig. 5.16b.

USING A STEP THAT HAS A NEGATIVE VALUE

```
10   REM CALCULATES PRINCIPAL ON
20   REM A BALANCE AT 5% INTEREST
30   REM B=ORIGINAL BALANCE, P=PRINCIPAL
40   READ B
50   PRINT "PRINCIPAL","BALANCE","YEARS"
60   FOR N=5 TO 1 STEP -2
70   LET P=B*1.05↑N
80   PRINT P,B,N
90   NEXT N
100  DATA 200
110  END
```

Figure 5.16a. Second version of the program (shown in Figure 5.15a); this version calculates the principal that accrues at 5% interest. As we see in 60   FOR N=5 TO 1 STEP -2, the initial value of the index is its maximum (5) and its final value, is its minimum (1). The STEP -2 means that each time the loop is executed, the index N is decreased by 2.

Line no.	Time executed	N	B	P
70	1st	5	200	255.256
70	2nd	3	200	231.525
70	3rd	1	200	210

Table for Fig. 5.16a. The values of N, B, and P each time line 70 is evaluated. Note: The change in N is -2. This corresponds to the STEP -2 in line 60 of the program.

```
RUN
PRINCIPAL        BALANCE        YEARS
   255.256         200            5
   231.525         200            3
   210             200            1
READY
```

Figure 5.16b. Running the program of Figure 5.16a. Since as compared with the previous program no change has been made in the program except for the order in which the index is evaluated, the results shown in this figure and Figure 5.15b are identical, except for the order in which the results are printed.

Had we wished to do so, we could have written the FOR statement in line 50 of the program of Fig. 5.15a so that all the numbers in the statement would have been replaced by variables, as we show now in line 80 of Fig. 5.17a

```
80    FOR N=N1 TO N2 STEP S2
```

The values of the variables N1, N2, and S2 are read in line 60

```
60    READ B,N1,N2,S2
```

and they are 1, 5, and 2, respectively. These along with 200, the value of B, are obtained from the DATA statement

```
120    DATA 200,1,5,2
```

When line 80 is executed, the computer interprets it as

```
80    FOR N=1 TO 5 STEP 2
```

In order to see what the printed results look like, we run the program. As we expect, the results, as shown in Fig. 5.17b, are the same as in Fig. 5.15b.

FOR

> The form of the FOR statement is: line number followed by FOR followed by the variable that is the index of the loop; followed by a number, a variable, or an expression involving a mathematical operation; followed by TO; followed by a number, a variable, or an expression involving a mathematical operation; followed by STEP, followed by a number, a variable, or an expression involving a mathematical operation. If the index is increased by 1 each time the loop is executed, STEP 1, as we have seen, can be omitted. Examples are:
>
> ```
> 40    FOR A1=2 TO 4
> 30    FOR N=-2 TO R STEP 0.2
> ```

Another example of a valid FOR statement is

```
60    FOR N=A*B TO S↑2+3 STEP C+D-3
```

It is not as complicated as it seems. For instance, if the variables in the statement were previously defined in the program as: A = 1, B = 2, S = 3, C = 2, and D = 3, this statement would be evaluated by the computer as

```
60    FOR N=2 TO 12 STEP 2
```

A FOR–NEXT LOOP IN WHICH THE LIMITS OF THE INDEX AND THE VALUE OF THE STEP ARE ALL VARIABLES

```
10    REM CALCULATES PRINCIPAL ON
20    REM A BALANCE AT 5% INTEREST
30    REM B=ORIGINAL BALANCE, P=PRINCIPAL
40    REM N1=MINIMUM VALUE FOR YEARS
50    REM N2=MAXIMUM VALUE FOR YEARS,S2=CHANGE IN YEARS
60    READ B,N1,N2,S2
70    PRINT "PRINCIPAL","BALANCE","YEARS"
80    FOR N=N1 TO N2 STEP S2
90    LET P=B*1.05↑N
100   PRINT P,B,N
110   NEXT N
120   DATA 200,1,5,2
130   END
```

Figure 5.17a. Third version of the program shown in Figure 5.15a; this version calculates the principal that accrues at 5% interest. The numbers that appeared in the FOR statement of Figure 5.15a have been replaced by variables.

```
RUN
PRINCIPAL          BALANCE              YEARS
 210               200                  1
 231.525           200                  3
 255.256           200                  5
READY
```

Figure 5.17b. Running the program of Figure 5.17a. The results are the same as for the program of Figure 5.15a.

We next discuss a program in which the index in the FOR-NEXT loop is increased by a fraction of a whole number each time the loop is executed. For example, in line 80 of Fig. 5.18a

```
80   FOR Z=M1 TO M2 STEP D
```

the value of D is a fraction of a whole number. The program shown in Fig. 5.18a calculates the value, *H,* of the normal curve

$$H = \frac{e^{\frac{-Z^2}{2}}}{\sqrt{2\pi}}$$

for a given *Z,* the variable which is normally distributed. This curve is indeed one of those most commonly used in statistics. It certainly looks menacing. We, however, do not have to understand its derivation; all we have to do is write this expression in BASIC. The value of *e* is 2.71828 and the value of π is 3.14159, both to 6-figure accuracy. Hopefully, we remember that the square root of a variable, *X,* can be written as $X^{1/2}$ algebraically. Thus it can be written as $X \uparrow .5$ in BASIC, since 1/2 equals 0.5. Remembering the rules for forming expressions in BASIC, we write this formula using the following steps:

1. $\sqrt{2\pi}$ is equal to $(2\pi)^{1/2}$ and is written in BASIC as $(2*3.14159)\uparrow.5$

2. $\frac{-Z^2}{2}$ is written in BASIC as $(-Z\uparrow 2/2)$

3.   So $e^{\frac{-Z^2}{2}}$ is written in BASIC as $2.71828 \uparrow (-Z\uparrow 2/2)$. Thus the entire expression is written as is shown in the program:

```
90   LET H=2.71828↑(-Z↑2/2)/(2*3.14159)↑.5
```

We have chosen to write the FOR statement so that the index's original value is M1, its greatest value is M2, and the amount by which it is increased for each execution of the loop is D. Therefore we write

```
80   FOR Z=M1 TO M2 STEP D
```

These values are read in

```
70   READ M1,M2,D
```

using

```
120   DATA -3,3,.5
```

Consequently, the value of D (the value of the STEP) is 0.5, so the computer interprets line 80 as

```
80   FOR Z=-3 TO 3 STEP .5
```

Thus the first value of the index Z is −3, and the program calculates the value of H for it. The second value of Z is −2.5, and the program calculates the value of H for this Z. This process continues as is shown in Fig. 5.18b, until the loop statements have been executed 13 times.

A STEP THAT HAS NONINTEGRAL VALUES

```
10   REM PRODUCES A TABLE FOR
20   REM THE NORMAL CURVE
30   REM M1=MINIMUM VALUE OF Z
40   REM M2=MAXIMUM VALUE OF Z
50   REM D= CHANGE IN Z
60   PRINT "HEIGHT","Z"
70   READ M1,M2,D
80   FOR Z=M1 TO M2 STEP D
90   LET H=2.71828↑(-Z↑2/2)/(2*3.14159)↑.5
100   PRINT H,Z
110   NEXT Z
120   DATA -3,3,.5
130   END
```

Figure 5.18a. Program that produces the normal curve. Each time the statements of the Z loop are executed, the value of Z is increased by 0.5 (the value of D).

```
RUN
HEIGHT           Z
  4.43186E-03    -3
  1.75283E-02    -2.5
  .053991        -2
  .129518        -1.5
  .241971        -1
  .352066        -.5
  .398942         0
  .352066         .5
  .241971        1
  .129518        1.5
  .053991        2
  1.75283E-02    2.5
  4.43186E-03    3
READY
```

Figure 5.18b. Running the program of Figure 5.18a.

We now present a program, shown in Fig. 5.19a, that finds the largest number in a group of numbers. This group of numbers consists of the last five numbers in the DATA statement

$$140 \quad \text{DATA } 5,1,8,3,9,2$$

i.e., 1,8,3,9,2. The first number, 5, is used in the program to indicate that five numbers will follow in the DATA statement; it is assigned to N at the beginning of the program when

$$50 \quad \text{READ N,X}$$

is executed. Then 1, the first of the numbers in the group, is assigned to X. The program will always assign the largest number it has encountered so far to the variable L. Since 1 is the only number of the group that the program has encountered so far and since it has been assigned to X, X is in turn assigned to L.

$$60 \quad \text{LET L=X}$$

This is shown in the first line of the table for Fig. 5.19a:

Line no.	Time executed	X	L	Next statement
60	1st	1	1	70

Since N equals 5, the FOR–NEXT loop which begins with

$$70 \quad \text{FOR C=1 TO N-1}$$

will be executed four times, once for each of the remaining four numbers in the group. The first time the statements of the loop are executed, the number 8 is assigned to X in

$$80 \quad \text{READ X}$$

Then the following statement in the program tests whether this new value of X is larger than the number that was just assigned to L

$$90 \quad \text{IF X>L THEN } 110$$

Since it is, its value (which is 8) is assigned to L, in

$$110 \quad \text{LET L=X}$$

thus replacing the old value of L. The loop statements are then executed again. This time the value of X is 3. It is obviously not larger than the value stored in L, so after

$$90 \quad \text{IF X>L THEN } 110$$

is executed, line 110 is skipped and thus the value of L is not changed. In the next execution of the loop, the number 9 is assigned to X. Since this is the largest number the computer has encountered so far, it assigns this number to L. The loop is then executed for the fourth and last time. The value of X is now 2. The situation that exists when the IF statement (line 90) is executed this time is shown in the last line of the table for Fig. 5.19a:

Line no.	Time executed	X	L	Next statement
90	4th	2	9	100

Since the condition $X > L$ in the IF statement is not true, line 100 is executed next, as shown

Read on from here carfully

FINDING THE LARGEST NUMBER IN A GROUP

```
10    REM PROGRAM FINDS THE LARGEST
20    REM NUMBER IN THE DATA STATEMENT
30    REM N=# OF NUMBERS IN DATA STATEMENT
40    REM L=LARGEST #,X= ANY # IN DATA
50    READ N,X
60    LET L=X
70    FOR C=1 TO N-1
80    READ X
90    IF X>L THEN 110
100    GOTO 120
110    LET L=X
120    NEXT C
130    PRINT "LARGEST # IS";L
140    DATA 5,1,8,3,9,2
150    END
```

Figure 5.19a. A program that finds the largest number in the group consisting of 1, 8, 3, 9, and 2. The first number in the DATA statement indicates to the computer how many numbers are in the group. It is assigned to N. The largest number encountered as the program is executed is assigned to L. The value of X is the number just read from the group. If the value of X is larger than the current value of L, it is assigned to L in line 110. If it is not larger, the value of L remains unchanged. Thus at the end of the program, L contains the largest number in the group.

Line no.	Time executed	X	L	Next statement
60	1st	1	1	70
90	1st	8	1	110
90	2nd	3	8	100
90	3rd	9	8	110
90	4th	2	9	100

Table for Fig. 5.19a. The value of X and L at two points (lines 60 and 90) in the program. If the value of X is larger than the value of L in a given line of the table, it replaces the value of L for the next line. Thus the value of L in the last line of the table is the largest number in the group.

```
RUN
LARGEST # IS 9
READY
```

Figure 5.19b. Running the program of Figure 5.19a. The last number assigned to L is the largest of the group.

in the table. Thus line 110 is skipped and the value of L remains unchanged. At this point the loop is finished. The next statement executed is

130   PRINT "LARGEST # IS";L

Since the last number assigned to L is the largest number in the group of numbers, this statement prints the largest number, as shown in Fig. 5.19b, when the program is run

LARGEST # IS 9

We conclude this section by discussing three aspects of the writing of FOR—NEXT loops.

1. You can transfer out of a FOR—NEXT loop before the loop is finished. Thus in the program of Fig. 5.20a, when the value of N is 5, the statement

30   IF N>4 THEN 60

transfers execution out of the loop to line 60. Thus the complete loop is executed only 4 times. The value of N when the computer leaves the loop is 5, as is shown in Fig. 5.20b.

2. You can increase the value of the loop index in the statements sandwiched between the FOR and the NEXT. Thus in Fig. 5.21a, each time the loop is executed, the value of the index, N, is increased by 2 in

30   LET N=N+2

besides being increased by 1—as usual—in line 50. We see from Fig. 5.21b that the loop was executed only 4 times.

3. You can transfer into a loop from outside a loop. This is in general not advisable because you are defeating the purpose of the FOR—NEXT loop. The results of doing this are unexpected. In line 30 of Fig. 5.22a we transfer into the loop, setting the value of N equal to 4. The result on the system on which this program was run is that the PRINT statement in the loop is executed only once, as we see in Fig. 5.22b. On other systems, the result of transferring into a loop would produce other unexpected results.

OTHER FEATURES OF THE FOR-NEXT **LOOP**

```
10    REM TRANSFERRING OUT OF LOOP
20    FOR N=1 TO 10
30    IF N>4 THEN 60
40    PRINT N
50    NEXT N
60    PRINT "THE HIGHEST VALUE OF N IS";N
70    END
```

Figure 5.20a. The computer can leave a loop before the loop is finished.

```
RUN
 1
 2
 3
 4
THE HIGHEST VALUE OF N IS 5
READY
```

Figure 5.20b. Running the program of Figure 5.20a. Although the maximum value of N in the FOR statement is 10, the computer leaves the loop when the value of N is 5.

```
10    REM INCREASING VALUE OF INDEX IN LOOP
20    FOR N=1 TO 10
30    LET N=N+2
40    PRINT N
50    NEXT N
70    END
```

```
RUN
 3
 6
 9
 12
READY
```

Figure 5.21a. In line 30 we increase the value of the index, N, by 2. The value of N, as usual, is also increased by 1 in NEXT N.

Figure 5.21b. Running the program of Figure 5.21a. The results show the effect of 30 LET N=N+2.

```
10    REM TRANSFERRING INTO LOOP
20    LET N=4
30    GOTO 50
40    FOR N=1 TO 10
50    PRINT N
60    NEXT N
70    END
```

```
RUN
 4
READY
```

Figure 5.22a. We enter the loop without first executing the FOR statement. This is allowed, but it leads to unexpected results.

Figure 5.22b. On the computer that Fig. 5.22a was run on, the N loop was executed only once.

5.3   The RESTORE Statement

In Fig. 5.23a we present a program that attempts to execute the loop

```
20    READ A,B,C
30    PRINT "A=";A;"B=";B;"C=";C
```

indefinitely. Because there are only three numbers in the DATA statements

```
50    DATA 11,12
60    DATA 13
```

the program stops the second time line 20 is executed and prints

```
OUT OF DATA    IN LINE 20
```

as shown in Fig. 5.23b. We have presented this program in order to introduce a statement that will enable the computer to read the values in DATA statements more than once. The statement is called the RESTORE statement. When it is executed, the effect on the program is the same as though none of the numbers in any DATA statement in the program had been read. Thus when the next READ statement is executed, the next number read is the first one in the lowest-numbered DATA statement. We demonstrate the use of the RESTORE statement in Fig. 5.24a. This program is the same as the previous one except for the inclusion of the RESTORE statement. The loop, which can be executed indefinitely if we wish, is

```
20    READ A,B,C
30    PRINT "A=";A;"B=";B;"C=";C
35    RESTORE
40    GOTO 20
```

The first time the READ statement is executed, the variables A, B, and C are assigned the numbers 11, 12, and 13, respectively. These are the numbers in the DATA statements:

```
50    DATA 11,12
60    DATA 13
```

The second time the READ statement is executed, because of the RESTORE statement the situation in the DATA statement is restored to the point where it was at the beginning of the program. Thus the READ statement can be executed again, and therefore the numbers 11, 12, and 13 are again assigned to A, B, and C, respectively. This process continues—as we see from the printed results in Fig. 5.24b—until we wish to stop it; we do this by pressing the BREAK key.

USING THE RESTORE STATEMENT

```
10   REM PROGRAM WITHOUT RESTORE
20   READ A,B,C
30   PRINT "A=";A;"B=";B;"C=";C
40   GOTO 20
50   DATA 11,12
60   DATA 13
70   END
```

```
RUN
A= 11    B= 12    C= 13
OUT OF DATA   IN LINE 20
READY
```

Figure 5.23a. The second time line 20 is executed, there are no more numbers to assign to A, B, and C. The program thus stops.

Figure 5.23b. Running the program of Figure 5.23a. The second time line 20 is executed the computer prints the error message

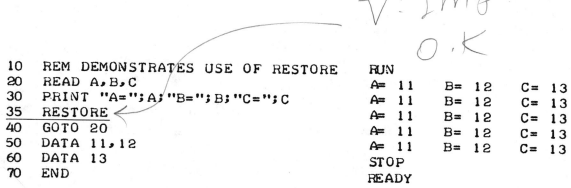

```
10   REM DEMONSTRATES USE OF RESTORE
20   READ A,B,C
30   PRINT "A=";A;"B=";B;"C=";C
35   RESTORE
40   GOTO 20
50   DATA 11,12
60   DATA 13
70   END
```

```
RUN
A= 11    B= 12    C= 13
A= 11    B= 12    C= 13
A= 11    B= 12    C= 13
A= 11    B= 12    C= 13
A= 11    B= 12    C= 13
STOP
READY
```

V: IMP
O.K

Figure 5.24a. Same program as Figure 5.23a except for the inclusion of the RESTORE statement. After a RESTORE is executed, the next number read is the first one in the lowest-numbered DATA statement. Thus each time line 20 is executed, A is assigned the value 11.

Figure 5.24b. Running the program of Figure 5.24a. Because of the RESTORE statement, the program can run indefinitely. We stop it by hitting the BREAK key.

We now apply the RESTORE statement to a program, shown in Fig. 5.25a, that determines whether certain numbers—these numbers could represent student identification numbers—are in the DATA statement. Executing line 30, the computer instructs us to type the number we are looking for. When we do this, the number is assigned to the variable A in 40 INPUT A.

In the loop

```
50    FOR J=1 TO 5
60    READ B
70    IF B=A THEN 110
80    NEXT J
```

a number is read from the DATA statement and assigned to B. If the value of B does not equal the value of A, then the desired number has not been found. The statements in the loop are therefore executed again. If, however, the value of B equals the value of A, then the desired number has been found. The computer is then instructed to leave the J loop and execute: 110 PRINT B; "WAS FOUND". The next statement executed, 120 RESTORE, restores the situation in the DATA statement to what it was before the first READ was executed. This enables the computer to read the numbers in the DATA statement, again starting with the number 1022.

Thus when, executing line 30, the computer instructs us to type the next number we are looking for, the entire process can begin again.

If the first number we type in is not in the DATA statement, the computer executes the loop the required 5 times and then executes: 90 PRINT "CAN'T FIND ID #" ; A. Then 120 RESTORE is executed and—as we mentioned before—the entire process starts again. If the RESTORE statement were not present, the computer could search for only one number.

Figure 5.25b shows what happens when the program is run. In response to

TYPE ID#, THEN HIT RETURN

We type in 1116. The table for Fig. 5.25a shows how 70 IF B＝A THEN 110 works. In the first line of the table

Line no.	Time executed	A	B	Next statement
70	1st	1116	1022	80

we see that, since 1022 (the first number assigned to B in the READ statement) does not equal 1116 (the number we typed in), the next statement executed is   80 NEXT J. The loop thus is executed again. We see from the third line of the table

Line no.	Time executed	A	B	Next statement
70	3rd	1116	1116	110

that the value of B read from the DATA statement this time, is the same as the one we typed in, and which was therefore assigned to A. The computer therefore leaves the loop and executes line 110, printing

1116   WAS FOUND

SEARCHING THE DATA STATEMENT FOR A GIVEN NUMBER

```
10    REM SEARCHES THE DATA
20    REM STATEMENT FOR CERTAIN ID#S
30    PRINT "TYPE ID#, THEN HIT RETURN"
40    INPUT A
50    FOR J=1 TO 5
60    READ B
70    IF B=A THEN 110
80    NEXT J
90    PRINT "CAN'T FIND ID #";A
100    GOTO 120
110    PRINT B;"WAS FOUND"
120    RESTORE
130    GOTO 30
140    DATA 1022,1023,1116,1004,1192
150    END
```

Figure 5.25a. Program searches the DATA statement for a given number, which we assign to A in the INPUT statement when we run the program. The RESTORE statement (line 120) enables the program to search the DATA statement starting from the first number in it each time one wishes to search for a number.

Line no.	Time executed	A	B	Next statement
70	1st	1116	1022	80
70	2nd	1116	1023	80
70	3rd	1116	1116	110

Table for Fig. 5.25a. How 70 IF B=A THEN 110 works. This statement tests whether the given number is in the DATA statement. If the value of A equals the value of B, the computer leaves the J loop.

```
RUN
TYPE ID#, THEN HIT RETURN
?1116
 1116     WAS FOUND
TYPE ID#, THEN HIT RETURN
?1110
CAN'T FIND ID # 1110
TYPE ID#, THEN HIT RETURN
?
READY
```

Figure 5.25b. Running the program of Fig. 5.25a. We stopped the program by hitting the BREAK key.

The program then requests another number. We type the number 1110. The computer then searches the DATA statement for this number. Since this number is not in the DATA statement, the computer executes the statements in the J loop five times. It then executes

```
90  PRINT "CAN'T FIND ID #";A
```

and therefore prints CAN'T FIND ID # 1110. The program then requests another number. Since we want to stop the program at this point, we hit the BREAK key.

PROBLEMS

1. Write the following numbers in BASIC in exponential form:
   a. 1.2378×10^{11}
   b. 1.2387×10^{-11}
   c. 62.34×10^{4}
   d. 62.34×10^{-4}

2. Translate the following BASIC exponential numbers into exponential form:
   a. 6.238E+08
   b. 3.781E4
   c. 4.932E+9
   d. 8.94E−04
   e. 6.731E−8

3. Given the following table, write a program using a FOR—NEXT loop that calculates each worker's salary and then prints the salary and all the items in the table for that worker.

Worker number	Hourly wage	Hours	Tax Rate
110	$4.00	40	12%
111	$6.40	40	15%
112	$5.00	40	13%

Hours x Hourly wage − Tax Rat xTows x Hourly wage

14   **4.** The formula to convert from Fahrenheit to Centigrade is C = 5/9 (F−32). Write a program using a **FOR–NEXT** loop that converts the Fahrenheit temperatures from 1° to 100° (in steps of 1°) to their equivalent Centigrade values. Label the columns.

5. a. Write a program similar to the one shown in Fig. 5.7a that will determine the maximum number of digits your computer can accommodate in a number.

b. Change line 10 in Fig. 5.7a to read

```
10   FOR R=1 TO 1000
```

and run the altered program. This will enable you to determine approximately what is the largest number your computer can accommodate. When the computer encounters a number larger than this, it prints OVERFLOW.

c. Change line 10 in Fig. 5.8a to read

```
10   FOR R=1 TO 1000
```

and run the altered program. This will enable you to determine approximately what is the smallest number your computer can accommodate. When the computer encounters a number smaller than this, it prints UNDERFLOW.

6. What is wrong with the following program which should calculate the product of the numbers from 1 to 4.

```
10   LET X=0
20   FOR I=1,4
30   LET X=X*J
40   PRINT THE PRODUCT OF THE NUMBERS FROM;
50   PRINT 1 TO 4 IS; X
```

15   **7.** Given the following table, which describes the dimensions of plywood sold in a given sale

Sale number	Length	Width
1001	8 ft.	4 ft.
1006	12 ft.	4 ft.
1012	5 ft.	3 ft.

write a program that calculates the dollar amount of each purchase and determines for each purchase how many purchases, including the present purchase, have been made (use the loop index for this) and the total dollar amount of sales (use an accumulator for this). The price of plywood is $.06 per square foot.

8. Write a program that produces a multiplication table for the numbers from 1 to 8.

9. Write a program that calculates $Y = \sum_{N=0}^{M} X^N$ where M and X are read from a DATA statement.

10. What are the results for the following program?

```
10    FOR I=1 TO 7 STEP 2
20    PRINT I;
30    NEXT I
40    END
```

11. Write a program that calculates the product of the odd numbers from 1 to 11.

12. Write a program that determines the smallest number in a group.

13. What is printed by the following programs?

```
10    FOR R=1 TO 10 STEP 3
20    IF N=3 THEN 50
30    PRINT R;
40    NEXT R
50    END
```

```
10    FOR R=1 TO 10 STEP 3
20    LET R=R+2
30    PRINT R
40    NEXT R
50    END
```

14. Type and run the following program to determine what is the value of the loop index (in this case I) on your computer after the loop has been executed

```
10    FOR I=1 TO 5
20    NEXT I
30    PRINT I
40    END
```

15. What are the results of running the following program?

```
10    FOR K=1 TO 3
20    READ A,B
30    PRINT A,B
40    RESTORE
50    NEXT K
70    DATA 4,3,2,1,8
80    END
```

16. Write a program that produces a vertical line of asterisks.

17. Write a program that produces a horizontal line of asterisks.

18. Write a program that produces the following repeating pattern.

```
XXX - - XXX - - XXX - - XXX - -
- - - XX - - - XX - - - XX - - - XX
XXX - -  XXX - - XXX - - XXX - -
- - - XX - - - XX - - - XX - - - XX
```

6

Strings and Library Functions

6.1. Strings

Thus far we have discussed how one can assign numbers to variables by using the assignment, READ, DATA, and INPUT statements. We now demonstrate how one can assign strings to variables as well using these statements. We note that when strings are assigned to variables the form of the above-mentioned statements remains the same.

In Fig. 6.1a we show a program in which strings are assigned to the variables in assignment statements. The variables to which strings are assigned are called string variables. We note the form of the variable name that must be used for string variables: it must consist of a letter followed by a dollar sign as shown in 20 LET A\$ = "CAT". We also note that in an assignment statement the string (here CAT) assigned to the string variable must be in quotation marks. Although A1 is a legal nonstring variable, A1\$ would be an illegal string variable. In Table 6.1 we show both legal and illegal variables.

When we want to print the strings assigned to the string variables, we place the string variables in a PRINT statement

40 PRINT A\$,B\$

in the same way as we did for nonstring variables, henceforth called simple variables.

When the program is executed, first the string CAT is assigned to the string variable, A\$, as shown in the first line of the table for Fig. 6.1a.

Line no.	A\$	B\$
20	CAT	Undef

Since in the 20 B\$ has not yet been defined, the entry "Undef" appears for this variable. By the time line 30 is executed, both variables have been defined. Thus when line 40 is executed, the computer will have no difficulty in printing the two strings, as shown in the first line of results in Fig. 6.1b

CAT   DOG

200

STRING VARIABLES

Legal string variables	Illegal string variables
R$, S$, A$	A2$, AB$, 2$

Table 6.1. The name of a string variable must consist of a letter of the alphabet followed by a dollar sign.

USING STRINGS IN THE ASSIGNMENT STATEMENT

```
10 REM USE OF STRINGS IN ASSIGNMENT STATEMENT
20 LET A$="CAT"
30 LET B$="DOG"
40 PRINT A$,B$
50 PRINT "CAT","DOG"
60 END
```

Figure 6.1a. Program shows the assignment of strings to string variables in a program. The form of the PRINT and assignment statements is the same as before. The string must always appear in quotes in the assignment statement.

Line no.	A$	B$
20	CAT	Undef
30	CAT	DOG
40	CAT	DOG
50	CAT	DOG

Table for Fig. 6.1a. This table shows the assignment of string variables on a line-by-line basis. We see that by line 30, CAT has been assigned to A$ and DOG to B$.

```
RUN
CAT          DOG  ←── Printed by line 40
CAT          DOG  ←── Printed by line 50
READY
```

Figure 6.1b. Running the program of Fig. 6.1a. The results of lines 40 and 50 are the same. Thus comas used in a PRINT statement have the same effect on string variables as they do on strings, i.e., the strings will be printed starting in either column 16, 31, 45, or 61, etc.

In order to show that the comma in a PRINT statement has the same effect on string variables as it has on strings, we have included line 50 in the program

50 PRINT "CAT","DOG"

When it is executed it produces the same results as line 40

CAT   DOG

as shown in the second line of results in Fig. 6.1b. Thus when a string variable is preceded by a comma, it will be printed starting in the 16th, 31st, 46st, 61st, etc., column. The string is printed in the lowest-numbered of these columns which has not already been printed in.

If one attempts to print an undefined string variable in a PRINT statement, for example, by inserting in the program of Fig. 6.1a

25   PRINT A$,B$

where B$ is at that point undefined, the results will depend on the system one is using. Some systems* will produce an error message. Other systems will print a blank for the value of the undefined string variable.

In Fig. 6.2a, we show how to assign strings to string variables using the READ and DATA statements

20   READ A$,B$
50   DATA "CAT","DOG"

Although on most systems strings do not always have to be placed in quotes in a DATA statement, as we will discuss below, it is always simpler to place them in quotes.

When the program is executed, the first string in the DATA statement is assigned to the first string variable in the READ statement, the second string in the DATA statement is assigned to the second string variable in the READ statement, as we expect. This is shown in line 20 of the table for Fig. 6.2a:

Line no.	A$	B$
20	CAT	DOG

Since a semicolon appears between the two string variables in the PRINT statement

30   PRINT A$;B$

when the program is run, the strings assigned to these string variables will be printed without any intervening spaces. This is shown in the first line of results in Fig. 6.2b.

CATDOG

In order to remind you that this is the same effect semicolons have on strings, we have included line 40 in the program

40   PRINT "CAT";"DOG"

When it is executed, it produces the same results as line 30. This is shown in the second line of Fig. 6.2b

---

* For instance, this is the case on the HP 2000C. Also, if the programs described in this section are run on this system, the string variables must be dimensioned in a DIM statement (see Section 8.3).

USING STRINGS IN THE READ AND DATA STATEMENTS

```
10      REM USE OF STRINGS IN READ STATEMENT
20      READ A$,B$
30      PRINT A$;B$
40      PRINT "CAT";"DOG"
50      DATA "CAT","DOG"
60      END
```

Figure 6.2a. This program shows the use of string variables in the READ statement and use of strings in the DATA statement. You may place the strings in quotes in the DATA statement. However, when the string consists only of letters, on most systems you can eliminate the quotes.

Line no.	A$	B$
20	CAT	DOG
30	CAT	DOG
40	CAT	DOG

Table for Fig. 6.2a. The assignment of the strings to the string variables in Fig. 6.2a.

```
RUN
CATDOG  ←—— Printed by line 30
CATDOG  ←—— Printed by line 40
READY
```

Figure 6.2b. Running the program of Fig. 6.2a. The results of lines 40 and 50 are the same. Thus semicolons used in PRINT statements have the same effect on string variables as they do on strings, i.e., they are printed without any intervening spaces.

As you might expect, string variables and simple variables can appear together in the same READ and PRINT statement, as we see in Fig. 6.3a:

```
20        READ A$,R2,B$
30        PRINT A$,R2,B$
```

Also strings and numbers may appear together in the same DATA statement, as we see in

```
40        DATA "CAT",32.2,"DOG"
```

The assignment of the strings and the number to the proper variables are shown in the table for Fig. 6.3a. The results of running the program

```
CAT                32.2              DOG
```

are shown in Fig. 6.3b. Note that we must position the strings and numbers in a DATA statement so that strings will be assigned to string variables and numbers will be assigned to simple variables *; otherwise an error will result. Thus the string DOG could not be assigned to the simple variable R2.

---

* The number 32.2 on some systems is considered to be a string if it is assigned to a string variable, and a number if it is assigned to a simple variable.

USING STRING VARIABLES AND SIMPLE VARIABLES TOGETHER

```
10      REM STRING AND SIMPLE VARIABLES TOGETHER
20      READ A$,R2,B$
30      PRINT A$,R2,B$
40      DATA "CAT",32.2,"DOG"
50      END
```

Figure 6.3a. String variables (A$ and B$) and simple variables (R2) can be used together in a READ statement. Strings (CAT and DOG) and numbers (32.2) can be used together in a DATA statement.

Line no.	A$	B$	R2
20	CAT	DOG	32.2
30	CAT	DOG	32.2

Table for Fig. 6.3a. The assignment of the strings and the number in Fig. 6.3a to the proper variables.

```
RUN
CAT            32.2          DOG
READY
```

Figure 6.3b. Running the program of 6.3a.

In Fig. 6.4a we show how to assign strings to string variables using the INPUT statement

30   INPUT A$,B$,A

Please note that we can, as is shown here, include a simple variable, A, together with the string variables A$ and B$ in an INPUT statement. When the program is run, line 20 causes the message

TYPE STRING, COMMA, STRING,COMMA,NUMBER

to be printed on the teletypewriter. We follow these instructions and type

? "CAT","DOG",32.1

as shown in Fig. 6.4b. (Although here we do not always have to type strings in quotes, as we will discuss below, it is simpler to type them in quotes.) The two strings are assigned to the string variables, and the number is assigned to the simple variable, as shown in line 30 of Table 6.3a.

Line no.	A$	B$	A
30	CAT	DOG	32.1

We note again that we can only assign strings to string variables and numbers to simple variables. Thus had we typed in

32.1, "DOG","CAT"

in response to 30   INPUT A$,B$,A the computer could not assign CAT to A, and depending on the system you are using, the computer might not be able to assign 32.1 to A$. The computer would inform us of this by typing an error message.

Since a comma precedes B$ in

40   PRINT A$,B$;A

the strings will be printed with spaces between them; i.e., the value of B$ would be printed starting in column 16. Since a semicolon precedes A and follows B$ in this statement, the number assigned to A will be printed after the value of B$, with one intervening space left between them for the sign of the number. This is shown in Fig. 6.4b when the program is run

CAT   DOG 32.1

In order to show that this is the same result we would obtain if we had used strings in the PRINT statement instead of string variables, we include line 50 in the program

50   PRINT "CAT","DOG";A

As we expect, this statement produces

CAT   DOG 32.1

the same results as those produced by line 40.

USING STRINGS IN THE INPUT STATEMENT

```
10      REM STRINGS IN INPUT STATEMENTS
20      PRINT "TYPE STRING, COMMA, STRING,COMMA,NUMBER"
30      INPUT A$,B$,A
40      PRINT A$,B$;A
50      PRINT "CAT","DOG";A
60      END
```

Figure 6.4a. Program shows the use of string variables in an INPUT statement. String variables and simple variables can be used together in an INPUT statement.

Line no.	A$	B$	A
20	Undef	Undef	Undef
30	CAT	DOG	32.1
40	CAT	DOG	32.1
50	CAT	DOG	32.1

Table for Fig. 6.4a. The assignment of the strings and the number in Fig. 6.4a to the proper variables.

```
RUN
TYPE STRING, COMMA, STRING,COMMA,NUMBER
? "CAT","DOG",32.1
CAT             DOG 32.1
CAT             DOG 32.1
READY
```

Figure 6.4b. Running the program of Fig. 6.4a. After the computer types the instructions for entering the data, we respond by typing CAT, DOG, 32.1.

The rules that dictate when you must place quotation marks around the strings in DATA statements and around the string typed in response to an INPUT statement, vary from one system to another. As a general rule, if the string contains a comma as in

JULY 4, 1974

or begins with a nonalphabetic character as in

12TH OF MAY

or begins with blanks—(we use the symbol b to represent a blank) as in

bbTHE

or ends with blanks as in *

THEbb

we must then place the string in quotes: otherwise, we can write the string without quotes. In Table 6.2 we show these four examples in tabular form.

As we remarked previously, it is always permissible to place quotes around strings when they are used in a DATA statement or in response to an INPUT statement; however, one must always place quotes around strings used in assignment statements.

---

* Conversely, on some systems like the CDC 6600 the computer may append blanks to the last string in a DATA statement, if that string is not in quotes.

QUOTATION MARKS AROUND STRINGS IN READ AND INPUT STATEMENTS

Case	Example	Reason
1	JULY 4, 1974	Contains a comma
2	12 OF MAY	Begins with a nonalphabetic character
3	bbTHE	Begins with blanks (b)
4	THEbb	Ends with blanks (b)

Table 6.2. Rules for when you must place quotes around strings used with READ or INPUT statements. These rules—especially rule 2—vary from one system to another. For example, on some systems you can assign a string that consists of a number like 12 to a string variable in an INPUT or READ statement without placing the string in quotes.

In Fig. 6.5a, we demonstrate how string variables can be redefined in a program. When line 20

20   READ A$

is executed, the string CAT is assigned to A$, as we see in the table for Fig. 6.5a.

Line no.	A$
20	CAT

In line 40, the string HORSE is assigned to A$, thus redefining it. This is reflected in line 40 of the table for Fig. 6.5a.

Line no.	A$
40	HORSE

where we see that the value of A$ is no longer CAT but is now HORSE. When the computer executes line 50 of the program it will now print HORSE as the value of A$. The results of the program are as we expect and are shown in Fig. 6.5b. Line 30 produces

CA T

and line 50 produces

HORSE

We can summarize all of this by saying that we can place only one string at a time in a memory location, and the string that remains, is the string placed there last.

6.2. Comparing Strings

Just as numbers can be compared in an IF statement, so too can strings be compared there. At this point in the book the only two relation operators we will use to compare strings are the = and < >. Thus if the string COW was assigned to R$, then the condition R$ = "COW" would be true; consequently the next statement executed after, for instance

20   IF R$="COW" THEN 40

would be statement 40. We note here that the form of a condition involving strings is: a string or string variable; followed by a relational operator; followed by a string or string variable.

REDEFINING STRINGS

```
10        REM REDEFINES STRINGS
20        READ A$
30        PRINT A$
40        READ A$
50        PRINT A$
60        DATA "CAT","HORSE"
70        END
```

Figure 6.5a. A program in which a string variable, A$, is redefined in line 40.

Line no.	A$
20	CAT
30	CAT
40	HORSE
50	HORSE

Table for Fig. 6.5a. We see that the string variable A$ is redefined in line 40. We can place only one string at a time in a memory location. The string that remains, is the one placed there last.

```
RUN
CAT
HORSE
READY
```

Figure 6.5b. Running the program of Fig. 6.5a. Since A$ is redefined in line 50, the computer prints the redefined value of A$ there.

We now demonstrate the application of string comparisons to a program that, once given a person's name, searches the DATA statement in the program to determine whether the person's name is there. The program is shown in Fig. 6.6a. It is similar to the one that searched the DATA statement for a given identification number (see Fig. 5.25a). One could use this type of program to determine whether a person lived in a certain town. Let us now investigate how the program works.

We are first instructed at line 30

```
30      PRINT "TYPE NAME,THEN HIT RETURN"
```

to type the name of the person we are looking for. We type "JILL" as shown in Fig. 6.6b. This name is assigned to A$ in

```
40      INPUT A$
```

The computer then searches the DATA statement for this name by executing the statements of the FOR–NEXT loop, which extends from line 50 to 80:

```
50      FOR J=1 TO 5
60      READ B$
70      IF B$=A$ THEN 110
80      NEXT J
```

The first time

```
60      READ B$
```

is executed, the computer assigns JOHN to B$. Thus when line 70

```
70      IF B$=A$ THEN 110
```

is executed, the assignments made to the string variables are as shown in the first line of the table for Fig. 6.6a:

Line no.	Time executed	A$	B$	Next statement
70	1st	JILL	JOHN	80

Consequently, the computer interprets line 70 as

```
70   IF "JOHN"="JILL" THEN 110
```

Since JOHN does not equal JILL, the next statement executed is line 80, and so the statements in the loop are executed again. This time BOB is assigned to A$, so the computer will now interpret line 70 as

```
70   IF "BOB"="JILL" THEN 110
```

We see that the next statement executed will again be line 80.

The third time the statements in the loop are executed, JILL is assigned to A$. The computer thus interprets line 70 as

```
70   IF "JILL"="JILL" THEN 110
```

SEARCHING THE DATA STATEMENT FOR CERTAIN STRINGS

```
10      REM PROGRAM SEARCHES THE DATA STATEMENT
20      REM FOR A CERTAIN NAME
30      PRINT "TYPE NAME,THEN HIT RETURN"
40      INPUT A$
50      FOR J=1 TO 5
60      READ B$
70      IF B$=A$ THEN 110
80      NEXT J
90      PRINT "CANT FIND NAME"
100     GO TO 120
110     PRINT B$;" WAS FOUND"
120     PRINT "TO CONTINUE TYPE YES;ELSE,NO."
130     INPUT C$
140     IF C$<>"YES" THEN 180
150     DATA "JOHN","BOB","JILL","MARY","FRED"
160     RESTORE
170     GO TO 30
180     END
```

Figure 6.6a. Program searches the DATA statement for a name we type in when line 40 is executed. This search is done by the loop which extends from lines 50 to 80. When the search is finished, if the user wishes to search for another name, the RESTORE statement is executed. This means the next string read will be JOHN, the first string in the DATA statement.

Line no.	Time executed	A$	B$	Next statement
70	1st	JILL	JOHN	80
70	2nd	JILL	BOB	80
70	3rd	JILL	JILL	110

Table for Fig. 6.6a. The strings assigned to A$ and B$ each time line 70 is executed in the search for JILL. The first time it is executed, the computer interprets line 70 as: 70 IF JILL = JOHN THEN 110. The last column shows the next statement executed. In this case, it would be line 80, the next statement in the program. When the value of A$ equals that of B$, the computer leaves the loop.

Since JILL equals JILL, the next statement executed is line 110, which is out of the loop. Thus we are instructed by the computer to leave the loop before the statements in the loop are executed the number of times required in the FOR statement. This permits us to eliminate unnecessary searches of the DATA statement. Since B$ equals JILL when 100 PRINT B$; "WAS FOUND" is executed, it prints

JILL WAS FOUND

as shown in Fig. 6.6b. We are then asked whether we wish to search for more names. We type YES, so YES is assigned to C$ in line 130. The computer then interprets line 140 as

140   IF"YES"<>"YES" THEN 180

Since the condition in the IF statement is false, and since the DATA statement in line 150 is nonexecutable, the next statement executed is

160   RESTORE

Thus the next time a READ statement is executed, the string read will be the first string in the DATA statement, i.e., JOHN.

The GO TO statement in line 170 transfers control to line 30 where the computer prints

TYPE NAME,THEN HIT RETURN

This time we type TED. The computer executes the statements in the FOR—NEXT loop five times, since TED is not in the DATA statement. Then the statement

90   PRINT "CANT FIND NAME"

is executed.

We are then informed to type YES if we wish to continue, NO if we do not, as shown in Fig. 6.6b. We type NO. The computer then interprets line 140 as

140   IF"NO"<>"YES" THEN 180

Since the condition in this IF statement is now true, the computer proceeds to the END statement in line 180.

6.3. Library Functions: SQR, INT, ABS, SGN, EXP, LOG, SIN, COS, TAN, RND

We have mentioned before that if one wishes to obtain the square root of a number, e.g., 180, one can write the following statement in BASIC

20   LET Y=180↑0.5

```
RUN
TYPE NAME,THEN HIT RETURN
? "JILL"
JILL WAS FOUND
TO CONTINUE TYPE YES;ELSE,NO.
? "YES"
TYPE NAME,THEN HIT RETURN
? "TED"
CANT FIND NAME
TO CONTINUE TYPE YES;ELSE,NO.
? "NO"
READY
```

Figure 6.6b. Running the program of Fig. 6.6a.

This corresponds to the algebraic expression $Y = 180^{1/2}$, which in turn corresponds to $Y = \sqrt{180}$, the most familar way of writing a square root. There is, however, an easier way for nonmathematically oriented people to obtain a square root in BASIC. They may obtain the square root of 180 by writing

```
20    LET Y=SQR(180)
```

The appearance of SQR( ) in a program automatically activates another program, referred to as SQR, which is stored in the memory; this program calculates the square root of whatever is between the parentheses, be it written as a number, a variable, or an expression. SQR is called a library function and is but one of many that we will study. What appears between the parentheses is called the argument of the function. In our discussion below we will refer to SQR as the SQR function.

We remember from the beginning of high school that if we are given the length of the two sides of a right triangle, *A,* and *B,* we can obtain C^2, the square of the hypotenuse, by using the pythagorean theorem:

$$C^2 = A^2 + B^2$$

Using the SQR function, we now discuss a program shown in Fig. 6.7a which calculates, not the hypotenuse squared, but the hypotenuse itself. The program starts in line 30 by printing the column labels SIDE A, SIDE B, and HYPOTENUSE:

```
30    PRINT "SIDE A","SIDE B","HYPOTENUSE"
```

Lines 40 to 80 constitute a FOR–NEXT loop, in which the computer first reads the lengths of the two sides A and B

```
50    READ A,B
```

The length of the hypotenuse is calculated in

```
60    LET C=SQR(A↑2+B↑2)
```

The results are then printed. The loop is executed 3 times and produces the results shown in Fig. 6.7b. Again the results are in a neat columnar form because of the corresponding commas in both PRINT statements.

Examples of the ways in which a function can be used in a program follow:

1. Alone in an assignment statement, as we have shown here.

2. In a PRINT statement. Thus we could have eliminated line 60 in Fig. 6.7a and written line 70 as

```
70    PRINT A,B,SQR(A↑2+B↑2)
```

3. In mathematical expressions. Thus, when we wrote the program of Fig. 5.19a, we could have used the SQR function to write the algebraic expression

$$H = \frac{e^{\frac{-Z^2}{2}}}{\sqrt{2\pi}}$$

as

```
90    LET H=2.71828↑(-Z↑2/2)/SQR(2*3.14159)
```

where $e = 2.71828$ and $\pi = 3.14159$ are both expressed to 6 figures.

USING FUNCTIONS

```
10    REM CALCULATES THE HYPOTENUSE
20    REM OF A RIGHT TRIANGLE
30    PRINT "SIDE A","SIDE B","HYPOTENUSE"
40    FOR R=1 TO 3
50    READ A,B
60    LET C=SQR(A↑2+B↑2)
70    PRINT A,B,C
80    NEXT R
90    DATA 3,4,6,8,1,1
100   END
```

Figure 6.7a. A program that uses the SQR function to calculate the hypotenuse of a right triangle. The appearance of SQR in your program, signals the computer to calculate the square root of what is between the parentheses that follow SQR. In this case it would be $A \uparrow 2 + B \uparrow 2$.

```
RUN
SIDE A          SIDE B          HYPOTENUSE
  3               4               5
  6               8               10
  1               1               1.41421
READY
```

Figure 6.7b. Running the program of Fig. 6.7a.

The next library function we will discuss is the INT function. The appearance of INT(X) in a program automatically activates another program referred to as INT, which is stored in the machine. This determines the greatest integer less than or equal to X, where X can be expressed as a number, a variable, or an expression involving a mathematical operation. In mathematics we say that INT(X) truncates the value of X. Thus when X is a positive number which has a fractional part, INT(X) removes that part of X to the right of the decimal point. For example, the value of INT(3.9) is 3. When X is a whole number, INT(X) does nothing to X. For example, the value of INT(3) is just 3.

On the other hand, if X is a negative number which has a fractional part, INT(X) gives the next lowest integer; thus the value of INT(−3.9) is −4. If X is a negative integer, INT(X) gives X. Thus the value of INT(−3) is −3.

We can use the INT function to round numbers since the value of INT(X+.5) is always the rounded value of X. For example, if the value of X is 14.2 then INT(X+.5) is the same as INT(14.7). The value of INT(14.7) is 14, therefore 14.2 was correctly rounded to 14. On the other hand if the value of X is 14.6, then INT(X+.5) is the same as INT(15.1). The value of INT(15.1) is 15, therefore 14.6 was correctly rounded to 15.

In Fig. 6.8a we see a program that used the INT function to round numbers in that DATA statement. The numbers are placed in

```
80 · DATA 16.6,14.8,25.6,4.8,87.8,67.2,35,93
```

The main part of the program consists of the FOR–NEXT loop, which extends from line 30 to line 70. This loop is executed 8 times, once for each number in the DATA statement. Each number is successively assigned to X in

```
40   READ X
```

The first number assigned to X, is 16.6. The number is then rounded to 17 in

```
50   LET Y=INT(X+.5)
```

How this is done is shown in the table for Fig. 6.8a:

Line no.	X	X+.5	Y
50	16.6	17.1	17

The remaining part of the table shows how the rest of the numbers in the DATA statement are processed. The results of running the program are shown in Fig. 6.8b..

USING THE `INT` FUNCTION TO ROUND NUMBERS

```
10    REM ROUNDS NUMBERS
20    PRINT "NUMBER","ROUNDED #"
30    FOR A=1 TO 8
40    READ X
50    LET Y=INT(X+.5)
60    PRINT X,Y
70    NEXT A
80    DATA 16.6,14.8,25.6,4.8,87.8,67.2,35,93
90    END
```

Figure 6.8a. A program that in line 50 rounds the value of X. The function INT(X) removes the numbers after the decimal point from the value of X, i.e., it truncates the value of X. Thus INT(X+.5) rounds the value of X to the nearest whole number, as is shown in the table for Fig. 6.8a. The values of X are read from the DATA statement.

Line no.	X	X+.5	Y
50	16.6	17.1	17
50	14.8	15.3	15
50	25.6	26.1	26
50	4.8	5.3	5
50	87.7	88.3	88
50	67.2	67.7	67
50	35	35.5	35
50	93	93.5	93

Table for Fig. 6.8a. How the computer evaluates 50 LET Y=INT(X+.5): First the value of X is increased by 0.5. Then any digit that appears to the right of the decimal point of this new number is dropped.

```
RUN
NUMBER              ROUNDED #
  16.6                17
  14.8                15
  25.6                26
   4.8                 5
  87.8                88
  67.2                67
  35                  35
  93                  93
READY
```

Figure 6.8b. Running the program of Fig. 6.8a.

In Table 6.3 are displayed the library functions that are generally available on most systems. ABS(X) finds the absolute value of X: it gives the positive value of X, independent of whether X is itself positive or negative. Thus the value of ABS($-$11.3) is 11.3. The value of ABS(11.3) is 11.3.

The value of SGN(X) is 1 if X is positive; its value is 0, if X is zero; $-$1, if X is negative. Thus the value of SGN(16.2) is 1, SGN(0) is 0 and SGN($-$17.1) is $-$1.

EXP(X) is the value of e^x where $e = 2.71828$. Using this and the SQR function we can now write the formula for the normal curve

$$H = \frac{e^{\frac{-Z^2}{2}}}{\sqrt{2\pi}}$$

as

```
LET H=EXP(-Z↑2/2)/SQR(2*3.14159)
```

in BASIC.

LOG(X) calculates the logarithm of X to the base e. The value of X must be greater than zero.

AVAILABLE LIBRARY FUNCTIONS

Function	Description	Restrictions on X
SQR(X)	Square root	X must be positive
INT(X)	Greatest integer less than or equal to X	None
ABS(X)	Absolute value of X; i.e., always gives the positive value of X	None
SGN(X)	If X is positive SGN(X) is 1; if X is zero SGN(X) is 0; if X is negative SGN(X) is -1	None
EXP(X)	e^x	None
LOG(X)	$\log_e X$	X must be greater than zero
SIN(X)	Sin X	X in radians
COS(X)	Cos X	X in radians
TAN(X)	Tan X	X in radians
ATN(X)	Arc tan X; results in radians	None
RND(X)	Produces a random number between zero and one	None

Table 6.3. Library functions. These functions are stored in the computer's memory. What appears between the parentheses—in this case X—is called the argument of the function.

The trigonometric functions SIN(X), COS(X), and TAN(X) require that X be in radians. It is more convenient, however, to work with angles measured in degrees. We know that there are 360 degrees in a circle. It is also true that there are 2π radians in a circle. Thus to convert from degrees to radians we must multiply the angle measured in degrees by $2\pi/360$ or by $\pi/180$, which to 6 significant figures is 3.14159/180. Knowing this, we can now write a program that will produce a trigonometric table. The program is shown in Fig. 6.9a.

The main part of the program is the loop

```
40    FOR A=0 TO 90 STEP 15
50    LET R=C*A
60    PRINT A,R,SIN(R),COS(R),TAN(R)
70    NEXT A
```

The variable A serves two purposes: it is obviously the index of the loop, however it also represents the specific angle for which the SIN, COS, and TAN will be calculated. From the FOR statement, one can see that we are varying the angle from zero to 90 degrees in steps of 15 degrees. The statement

```
50    LET R=C*A
```

converts the angle A (measured in degrees) to the angle R (measured in radians). The conversion constant, C, is calculated outside of the loop

```
30    LET C=3.14159/180
```

Had we calculated this constant inside the loop, we would have performed this division needlessly for each execution of the loop except the first. Statement 60

```
60    PRINT A,R,SIN(R),COS(R),TAN(R)
```

calculates and then prints the trigonometric functions. The results,* shown in Fig. 6.9b, look like the tables you would see at the end of a trigonometry book.

The ATN(X) function calculates the angle whose tangent is X. It is called the arc tangent function. The angle † is given in radians.

---

* Because of the approximation used by the computer, some of the results differ somewhat from the true results. Thus the cosine of 90° should be zero. We get the value 1.12352E–06, which is very close to zero.

† ATN(X) gives the principal value of the angle.

USING THE TRIGONOMETRIC FUNCTIONS TO PRODUCE A TRIGONOMETRIC TABLE

```
10    REM PRODUCES TRIG TABLE
20    PRINT "ANGLE","RADIAN","SIN","COS","TAN"
30    LET C=3.14159/180
40    FOR A=0 TO 90 STEP 15
50    LET R=C*A
60    PRINT A,R,SIN(R),COS(R),TAN(R)
70    NEXT A
80    END
```

Figure 6.9a. A program uses the SIN, COS, and TAN functions to produce a trigonometric table. The A loop—lines 40 to 70—is executed for angles A varying from 0° to 90° in steps of 15°. In line 50, the computer converts from degrees to radians, R so that the computer in line 60 will calculate the right result for a given angle.

```
RUN
ANGLE         RADIAN        SIN            COS              TAN
0             0             0              1.               0
15            .261799       .258819        .965926          .267949
30            .523598       .5             .866026          .57735
45            .785398       .707106        .707107          .999999
60            1.0472        .866025        .5               1.73205
75            1.309         .965926        .25882           3.73204
90            1.5708        1.             1.12352E-06      890059.
READY
```

Figure 6.9b. Running the program of 6.9a. The results are in neat tabular form because of the corresponding commas in the PRINT statements of the lines 20 and 60.

We now discuss the function whose form varies the most from one computer to another: the RND function. The RND function produces random numbers from 0 to 1. A random number is one whose value you cannot predict. For example, the results when you roll dice are random numbers. Random numbers are useful for simulating games of chance—such as all card games—and other situations that are described by random processes—such as nuclear decay. We will give examples of the applications of random numbers in this and future chapters.

On some systems, the RND function is written simply as RND, for example

20   LET Y=RND

On most systems, however, the function must be written with an argument, e.g., 20   LET Y=RND(X). On some of these systems, the value assigned to X does not affect the random numbers produced by the computer, i.e., RND(6) and RND(−27.1) would produce the same result. On others of these systems, if the value of X is zero the computer will generate the same set of random numbers each time the program is run; and if X is negative or positive, it will generate a different set of random numbers each time the program is run. On yet others, the scheme is different. In this book, we will write this function as RND(0). We now present a program, shown in Fig. 6.10a, in which we use this function. The program simulates a game of choosing played by kids—the one that begins with the words, "once, twice, three, shoot!" The game is played by two players. One player calls, "odds" or "evens." Let us say he calls, "odds." Then both players simultaneously each put out one or two fingers. If the sum of the total numbers of extended fingers is an odd number and if the player who did the calling called "odds," he wins. However, if he called "evens," he loses.

In the program we have written, the user plays against the computer; the program does not decide who wins. The program begins with

20   LET Y=RND(0)

Here the computer generates a random number between 0 and 1. Since we cannot predict what number it will generate, let us say that the first time it generates 0.63. It assigns this to Y. The next statement executed is

30   LET X=INT(2*Y)+1

This converts the random number to either a 1 or a 2, which corresponds to the computer putting out one finger or two fingers. The first line of the table for Fig. 6.10a shows what happens in this statement when the value of Y is 0.63

Line no.	Time executed	Y	2*Y	INT(2*Y)	X
30	1st	0.63	1.26	1	2

Here the value of Y, 0.63, is multiplied by 2, giving 1.26; then INT(1.26) is calculated, giving 1; finally 1 is added to this, giving 2. This is the value assigned to X. Again, it is the number of fingers the computer will put out. The player, however, does not know this. The computer gives him the following instructions:

TYPE ODDS OR EVENS, COMMA, THEN 1 OR 2

A SIMPLE MONTE CARLO PROGRAM

```
10   REM SIMULATES GAME OF CHOOSING
20   LET Y=RND(O)
30   LET X=INT(2*Y)+1
40   PRINT "TYPE ODDS OR EVENS, COMMA, THEN 1 OR 2"
50   INPUT C$,N
60   PRINT "MINE WAS";X;"YOURS WAS";N
70   PRINT "YOU CALLED ";C$
80   GOTO 20
90   END
```

Figure 6.10a. The program uses random numbers to simulate a game of choosing. You play against the computer. The computer produces the number 1 or 2 randomly in lines 20 and 30. In response to line 40 you type either ODDS or EVENS and a 1 or 2. If you type ODDS, the sum of your number and the computer's number must be 3 in order for you to win. If you type EVENS, the sum of your number and the computer's number must be 2 or 4 in order for you to win.

Line no.	Time executed	Y	2*Y	INT(2*Y)	X
30	1st	0.63	1.26	1	2
30	2nd	0.24	0.48	0	1
30	3rd	0.48	0.96	0	1

Table for Fig. 6.10a. The table shows how the computer produces a 1 or 2 randomly.

when line 40 is executed. The ODDS or EVENS is what the player calls out, and the 1 or 2 corresponds to the number of fingers that player puts out. The person playing against the computer in this instance types

```
"ODDS",2
```

as shown in the second line of Fig. 6.10b. The computer then follows the instructions in lines 60 and 70 and prints

```
MINE WAS 2     YOURS WAS 2
YOU CALLED ODDS
```

Thus the computer won this round. The game is then played again, as shown in the table for Fig. 6.10a and in Fig. 6.10b. To end the program, we must hit the BREAK key. The program could have been written so that it also would decide who won; we will leave this for you to do as an exercise. Also, if one so desired, one could eliminate statement 20 and write statement 30 as

```
30   LET S=INT(2*RND(0))+1
```

Techniques of using random numbers to simulate a situation, as we did in this program, are called Monte Carlo methods. In general if one wishes to generate random integers from a minimum value of M to a maximum value of $M+N-1$ one would write

```
30   LET X=INT(N*RND(0))+M
```

6.4 TAB(X) and Graphical Displays

We now discuss a function used in the PRINT statement to control the positioning of the printing. It is called the TAB function, and its form is TAB(X) where X can be a number, a variable, an expression, or another function. It works as follows: the presence of TAB(X) in a PRINT statement positions the teletypewriter printing head at the column given by INT(X). The next item in the PRINT statement is printed starting in that column. For instance,

```
30   PRINT TAB(12.8);"X"
```

will print an X in column 12. The semicolon preceding the X has no effect here. On most systems it can be eliminated. Indeed, semicolons and commas that follow the TAB function and precede other items in the PRINT statement have no effect on the printed results.

On most systems the TAB function cannot position the printing head backward, only forward. Thus one has to be careful when placing the TAB function after another item in a PRINT statement. As an example, let us study the following:

```
30   PRINT TAB(20);12.6;TAB(10),"X"
```

Here, the TAB(20) instructs the computer to print 12.6 starting in column 20, then TAB(10) instructs the computer to print X starting in column 10. But backspacing on most systems is not allowed, so in this case, the computer prints X starting in the same column as it would if TAB(10) were not in the PRINT statement. In other words, the computer prints the same information as it would if the statement were

```
30   PRINT TAB (20);12.6;"X"
```

```
RUN
TYPE ODDS OR EVENS, COMMA, THEN 1 OR 2
?"ODDS",2
MINE WAS 2     YOURS WAS 2
YOU CALLED ODDS
TYPE ODDS OR EVENS, COMMA, THEN 1 OR 2
?"ODDS",2
MINE WAS 1     YOURS WAS 2
YOU CALLED ODDS
TYPE ODDS OR EVENS, COMMA, THEN 1 OR 2
?
READY
```

Figure 6.10b. Running the program of Fig. 6.10a. Execution of the program is ended by hitting the BREAK key.

Another example of a case in which the computer ignores the TAB function is

```
3Ø    PRINT 13.4,TAB(1Ø);196
```

The comma preceding TAB(10), positions the printing head to the 16th column. Since TAB(10) commands the computer to position the printing head back to column 10, it is ignored. The results are printed as though TAB(10) were not in the statement. Because of this, it is always a good idea to precede the TAB with a semicolon.

We now study the use of the TAB function in a program. The program shown in Fig. 6.11a, types a diagonal line across the page, as shown in Fig. 6.11b. It consists of a FOR–NEXT loop

```
2Ø    FOR I=1 TO 1Ø
3Ø    PRINT TAB(I);"X"
4Ø    NEXT I
```

in which the value of I in

```
3Ø    PRINT TAB(I);"X"
```

is increased by 1 for each execution of the loop. Thus for the fourth execution, the computer interprets this statement as

```
3Ø    PRINT TAB(4);"X"
```

and prints an X in column 4. If the statement were written ending with a semicolon

```
3Ø    PRINT TAB(I);"X";
```

all the X's would be printed on the same horizontal line.

Note: On many systems the first column is referred to as column zero. On these systems, the instruction   30 PRINT TAB(1); X would produce an X in the second column.

What happens if the value of I is 100? In answering this, we will assume that your teletypewriter has 75 columns. The computer, on many systems, subtracts 75 from 100, obtaining 25, then skips to the next line and prints an X in column 25.

USING THE TAB FUNCTION

needed for the last lab.

```
10    REM PRINTS A DIAGONAL LINE
20    FOR I=1 TO 10
30    PRINT TAB(I);"X"
40    NEXT I
50    END
```

Figure 6.11a. A program which uses the TAB function to print a diagonal line across the page, for example, when the value of I is 4 30 PRINT TAB (4) ; "X" instructs the teletypewriter to space to column 4 and type an X there. Semicolons and commas that follow the TAB and precede another item in the PRINT statement have no effect on the printed results.

```
RUN
  X
   X
    X
     X
      X
       X
        X
         X
          X
           X
READY
```

Figure 6.11b. Running the program of Fig. 6.11a.

If you wanted to write a program that would produce a table having a column width different from 15—the column width produced by commas—you would use the TAB function, as is shown in Fig. 6.12a. The statement

```
20      PRINT TAB(10);"X";TAB(20);"X SQUARED";TAB(35);"X CUBED"
```

produces the headings for the table. The X loop produces the numbers in the table. Because the arguments of the TAB function in

```
40      PRINT TAB(10);X;TAB(20);X↑2;TAB(35);X↑3
```

are identical to those in the corresponding TAB functions in the PRINT statement of line 20, the headings for the table and the numbers they label are in the same columns. This is shown in Fig. 6.12b.

USING THE TAB FUNCTION TO PRODUCE A TABLE

```
10      REM PRODUCES POWER OF X TABLE
20      PRINT TAB(10);"X";TAB(20);"X SQUARED";TAB(35);"X CUBED"
30      FOR X=1 TO 20
40      PRINT TAB(10);X;TAB(20);X↑2;TAB(35);X↑3
50      NEXT X
60      END
```

Figure 6.12a. The TAB is used to produce a table. Note both "X" and X are preceded in their respective PRINT statement by TAB(10); also "X SQUARED" and X ↑ 2 are preceded by TAB(20); and "X CUBED" and X ↑ 3 by TAB(35). Thus the heading for the table and the numbers they label are in the same columns, as we see in Fig. 6.12b.

```
RUN
    X               X SQUARED       X CUBED
    1               1               1
    2               4               8
    3               9               27
    4               16              64
    5               25              125
    6               36              216
    7               49              343
    8               64              512
    9               81              729
    10              100             1000
    11              121             1331
    12              144             1728
    13              169             2197
    14              196             2744
    15              225             3375
    16              256             4096
    17              289             4913
    18              324             5832
    19              361             6859
    20              400             8000
READY
```

Figure 6.12b. Running the program of Fig. 6.12a.

We now study the application of the TAB function to plotting graphs for trigonometric curves. The curve we will plot in the program shown in Fig. 6.13a is the sine curve. The program is similar to the one shown in Fig. 6.9a that produces a trigonometric table. The present program consists essentially of a FOR-NEXT loop starting with

30   FOR A=0 TO 360 STEP 15

As we see, the angle A varies from 0 to 360 degrees in steps of 15 degrees. The statement

40   LET R=C*A

converts the angle A (measured in degrees) to the angle R (measured in radians). Let us now investigate why we wrote the key statement of the program

50   PRINT A;"DEG";TAB(40+25*SIN(R));"X"

as we did. The first two entries in the statement print the angle and then the word DEG, as is shown in Fig. 6.13b, when the program is run. We see there that the first point of the program appears in the middle of the teletypewriter sheet. This is because for this point, A=0, R=0, and thus SIN(R)=0. Therefore, the computer interprets the TAB (and the string it precedes in the PRINT statement for this point) as

TAB(40+0);"X"

It thus prints the X in column 40. This is also shown in the first line of the table for Fig. 6.13a. If the 40 were not present in the TAB function, the first point in the curve would not be plotted at the center of the page—as it is plotted in Fig. 6.13b—but would be plotted at the left of the page. Thus there would be no room for the computer to plot the part of the curve for which the sine has negative values.

We see that the rightmost point in the curve of Fig. 6.13b corresponds to A=90. The second line of the table for Fig. 6.13a shows how the argument of the TAB function for this angle is evaluated.

Line no.	Time executed	A	R	SIN(R)	25*SIN(R)	40+25* SIN(R)	Column X is printed in
50	7th	90	1.571	1	25	65	65

USING THE TAB FUNCTION TO PLOT TRIGONOMETRIC CURVES

```
10    REM PRINTS A PLOT OF THE SIN CURVE
20    LET C=3.14159/180
30    FOR A=0 TO 360 STEP 15
40    LET R=C*A
50    PRINT A;"DEG";TAB(40+25*SIN(R));"X"
60    NEXT A
70    END
```

Figure 6.13a. Program plots a sine curve. The A loop plots X's in the appropriate place by using the TAB function; A is the angle measured in degrees, R is the angle measured in radians; in line 50, 25*SIN(R) determines that the maximum height and depth of curve is 25 columns; the 40 centers the curve at column 40.

Line no.	Time executed	A	R	SIN(R)	25*SIN(R)	40+25*SIN(R)	Column X is printed in
50	1st	0	0	0	0	40	40
50	7th	90	1.571	1	25	65	65
50	11th	150	2.618	0.5	12.5	52.5	52
50	13th	180	3.142	−1	−25	15	15

Table for Fig. 6.13a. The table shows how the argument of the TAB function TAB(40+25*SIN(R)) is evaluated for certain angles. At an angle of 90°, where the value of SIN is maximum, the X is plotted in column 65. At an angle of 180°, where the value of SIN is minimum, the X is plotted in column 15. When the argument of the TAB function has a fractional part, it is truncated; e.g., at 150° the argument is 52.5 and the X is printed in column 52.

We see that $SIN(R)=1$ here. In order to make our curve sufficiently wide, we have multiplied $SIN(R)$ by 25. We then add this to 40. The effect of all of this is to instruct the computer to print the X in column 65, as is shown in the table.

In order to see what happens when the value of $40+25*SIN(R)$ is nonintegral, we look at the third line of the table for Fig. 6.13a. Here its value is 52.5. The TAB function truncates 52.5—treats it as $INT(52.5)$—and obtains 52. So the computer prints the X in the 52nd column. If its value were 52.9, the computer would still print the X in the 52nd column. Thus the curve that this program produces is not as smooth as it could be. To obtain a more smoothly shaped curve, we would have to make the TAB function round the value of its argument: As we mentioned, the TAB function behaves like the INT function in truncating its argument before it positions the printing head. We remember that we could make the INT function round a number, X, by writing $INT(X+.5)$. Similarly —before it positions the printing head—we can make the TAB function round a number, X, by writing $TAB(X+.5)$. So in order to get a more smoothly shaped curve we would substitute

$$TAB(40.5+25*SIN(R))$$

for the TAB function presently in line 50.

Once we have written this program, it is very easy to write one that plots the cosine function. All we have to do is substitute $COS(R)$ for $SIN(R)$ in line 50.

In general the TAB function for plotting any curve $F(X)$ is

$$TAB \quad (M+.5+N*F(X))$$

where M is the number of the column in which you want the zero value of $F(X)$ to be printed, and $M+N*F(X)$ is the number of the column in which you want the maximum value of $F(X)$ to be printed. The purpose of the .5 is to round the value of the argument, thus enabling the computer to produce a smoother curve.

```
RUN
   0     DEG
  15     DEG
  30     DEG
  45     DEG
  60     DEG
  75     DEG
  90     DEG
 105     DEG
 120     DEG
 135     DEG
 150     DEG
 165     DEG
 180     DEG
 195     DEG
 210     DEG
 225     DEG
 240     DEG
 255     DEG
 270     DEG
 285     DEG
 300     DEG
 315     DEG
 330     DEG
 345     DEG
 360     DEG
READY
```

Figure 6.13b. Running the program of Fig. 6.13a.

We now discuss the program shown in Fig. 6.14a, which produces the triangle shown in Fig. 6.14b. This is an example of how to program the computer to plot a patern. If you are not interested in this aspect of programming, please skip to the next chapter. The program consists of an inner loop (the I loop) nested within an outer loop (the N loop). The statements

```
30    LET X=X-1
40    PRINT TAB(X);
```

in the outer loop determine in what column the printing of a line of Xs will begin, as we now explain. Since the value of X is originally 36 (in statement 10) the value of X−1 is 35. Thus the first line of Xs begins in column 35. The value of X is decreased by 1 each time statement 30 is executed. Thus each successive line of Xs in Fig. 6.14b starts one column to the left of where the preceding line of Xs began. *Note:* Statement 40 does not do any printing, it just positions the printing head to the column determined by the value of X. Since statement 40 ends with a semicolon, the printing done by the next PRINT statement executed (statement 60—it produces the lines of Xs), begins in the column at which the printing head was just positioned. We now see how the lines of Xs are printed.

The inner loop

```
50    FOR I=1 TO 2*N
60    PRINT "X";
70    NEXT I
```

produces the line of Xs. They are printed on a line because the PRINT statement in this loop ends with a semicolon. The number of Xs printed is twice the value of the index N, of the outer loop. Thus each successive line of Xs printed is longer than the preceding one. We now study the entire process in more detail.

The first time the outer loop (N loop) is executed, the value of N is 1. Thus the inner loops (I loop) is executed twice, as shown in the first two lines of the table for Fig. 6.14a.

Outer Loop		Inner Loop		
N	X	Line no.	I	Column X is printed in
1	35	60	1	35
		60	2	36

Since the value of X—the argument of the TAB function—is 35, the computer prints XX starting in column 35 as shown in Fig. 6.14b. The next statement executed after the inner loop is finished is

```
80    PRINT
```

This cancels the effect of the semicolon that ended the preceding PRINT statement. This means that, when the next PRINT statement is executed, the teletypewriter will start printing on the next line.

The outer loop is then executed a second time. Now the value of N is 2, so that the inner loop is executed four times as is shown in the next four lines of the table for Fig. 6.14a. Since the value of X is 34, the computer prints XXXX starting in column 34. The more times the outer loop is executed, the larger the printed triangle becomes.

HOW TO PROGRAM A COMPUTER TO PLOT A PATTERN

```
1    REM PLOTS TRIANGLE
10   LET X=36
20   FOR N=1 TO 10
30   LET X=X-1
40   PRINT TAB(X);
50   FOR I=1 TO 2*N
60   PRINT "X";
70   NEXT I
80   PRINT
90   NEXT N
100  END
```

Figure 6.14a. Program prints a triangle.

Outer loop		Inner loop		Column X is printed in
N	X	Line no.	I	
1	35	60	1	35
		60	2	36
2	34	60	1	34
		60	2	35
		60	3	36
		60	4	37

Table for Fig. 6.14a. The table shows in which column the X in line 60 is printed. The value of N (the index of the outer loop) determines in line 50 how many Xs are printed in a line.

```
RUN
                              XX
                             XXXX
                            XXXXXX
                           XXXXXXXX
                          XXXXXXXXXX
                         XXXXXXXXXXXX
                        XXXXXXXXXXXXXX
                       XXXXXXXXXXXXXXXX
                      XXXXXXXXXXXXXXXXXX
                     XXXXXXXXXXXXXXXXXXXX

READY
```

Figure 6.14b. Running the program of Fig. 6.14a.

PROBLEMS

1. Which of the following variables are legal string variables?

    $A   A$ B2$ Z10$ R$ L12$

2. Write a READ statement that will correctly read the data in the following DATA statement

    20   DATA ABC,12.36,CBA,13.6,17.23

3. What is printed by the following program?

    10   FOR I=1 TO 3
    20   READ A$,R
    30   PRINT A$,R
    40   NEXT I
    50   DATA CAT,123,DOG,456,HAT,789
    60   END

4. Given the DATA statement

    10   DATA ABC,DEF,GHI,JKL,MNO,PQR,STU,VWXYZ

5. Write a program that will use this DATA statement and write the letters of the alphabet in a horizontal line.

6. Write a program that, for a given number, calculates the square, cube, and square root of the number. Let the number vary from 1 to 10.

Lab 20

7. Rewrite the program of Fig. 5.18a using the SQR and EXP functions to write the formula for the normal curve.

8. The distance d, between two points whose coordinates are (X_1, Y_1) and (X_2, Y_2), respectively, is given by $d = \sqrt{(X_2 - X_1)^2 + (Y_2 - Y_1)^2}$. Using this formula, write a program that calculates the distance between two points whose coordinates are entered into the program using an INPUT statement.

9. What are the values of the following?
    (a) ABS(-13.2)   (b) ABS(13.2)   (c) INT(16.3) (d) INT(16.9)
    (e) INT(-16.3)   (f) INT(-16.9)

10. Write a program that will round a number to the nearest one-hundreth; i.e., a number like 3.143 would be rounded to 3.14 and a number like 3.148 would be rounded to 3.15.

Lab 21

11. The formula for the sine of the sum of two angles is
$$\sin(A+B) = \sin A \ \cos B + \cos A \ \sin B$$
Write a program to show the right-hand side of this equation equals the left-hand side for the following values of A and B

A	B
10°	20°
20°	30°
30°	40°
40°	50°

12. Rewrite the program of Fig. 6.10a which plays the game of choosing so that it determines whether you or the computer won.

13. Rewrite the program of Fig. 6.12a so that the numerical results are centered under the string that labels them.

14. Write a program that plots the parabola $Y = X^2$.

Lab 22 **15.** Write a program that produces the letter V. The output should look something like

```
    X         X
      X     X
       X  X
        XX
```

7

The STOP, Multiple Assignment, and ON-GO TO Statements and Subscripted Variables

7.1. The STOP Statement

Previously, if we wished to end the execution of a program at a given line (e.g., line 20) that was not the last line in the program, we would write

```
20  GO TO 80
```

where statement 80 would be

```
80 END
```

as is shown at the right of Fig. 7.1. This can be done more easily by simply writing

```
20 STOP
```

as we see at the left Fig. 7.1. The STOP statement ends the program's execution. We note here that every program must have one END statement in it. On the other hand, a program may have one or more STOP statements in it, but it also may have none.

STOP

The form of the STOP statement is: line number followed by STOP. Example:

```
70    STOP
```

USING THE STOP STATEMENT

Figure 7.1. You can stop the execution of a program anywhere in the program just by using the STOP statement. Thus 20   GO TO 80 (where 80 is the END statement) and 20   STOP are equivalent.

7.2. The Multiple Assignment Statement

You will find in writing programs that at times you may assign the same value to many variables. On most computers there is a space-saving way of doing this; for instance, if you wish to assign 1 to each of the variables X, Y, and Z you may write

$$20 \quad \text{LET} \quad X=Y=Z=1$$

as is shown in Fig. 7.2a. We see here an example of a multiple assignment statement. The number 1 in this statement is assigned to each of the variables to the left of it. Thus the values of X, Y, and Z are all 1, as is shown in line 20 of the table for Fig. 7.2a:

Line no.	X	Y	Z	U	V	A	L
20	1	1	1	Undef	Undef	Undef	Undef

Another example of a multiple assignment statement is shown in statement 30:

$$30 \quad \text{LET} \quad U=V=Y$$

Here the value of Y—which is 1, as we have seen in line 20—is assigned to U and V as is shown in the second line of the table for Fig. 7.2a:

Line no.	X	Y	Z	U	V	A	L
30	1	1	1	1	1	Undef	Undef

A third example is shown in

$$40 \quad \text{LET} \quad A=L=X*Y+2$$

Here the value of X*Y+2—which is $1*1+2$, or 3—is assigned to the variables L and A as is shown in the third line of the table for Fig. 7.2a:

Line no.	X	Y	Z	U	V	A	L
40	1	1	1	1	1	3	3

As with the ordinary assignment statement, only variables should appear to the left of an equals sign; a calculation or a number cannot. Thus a statement like

$$20 \quad \text{LET} \quad X=B*C+2=4$$

would be wrong since a calculation appears to the left of an equals sign. Similarly,

$$20 \quad \text{LET} \quad X=4=Y$$

would be wrong since a number appears to the left of an equals sign.

The program of Fig. 7.2a is run in Fig. 7.2b.

MULTIPLE ASSIGNMENT

> The form of the multiple assignment statement must be: statement number; followed by the word LET; followed by a variable; followed by an equals sign; followed by one or more variables (if there are more than one, they must be separated by equals signs); followed by what we wish to assign to the variable. Examples:
>
> $$10 \quad \text{LET} \quad A=B=C$$
> $$10 \quad \text{LET} \quad A=B=C=3+D1$$

THE MULTIPLE ASSIGNMENT STATEMENT

```
10    REM USE OF MULTIPLE ASSIGNMENT STATEMENT
20    LET X=Y=Z=1
30    LET U=V=Y
40    LET A=L=X*Y+2
50    PRINT X;Y;Z;U;V
60    PRINT A;L
70    END
```

Figure 7.2a. The program shows that one can assign in a statement the same value to many variables.

Line no.	X	Y	Z	U	V	A	L
20	1	1	1	Undef	Undef	Undef	Undef
30	1	1	1	1	1	Undef	Undef
40	1	1	1	1	1	3	3

Table for Fig. 7.2a. Status of the variables in the program of Fig. 7.2 given by line number.

```
RUN
 1      1      1      1      1
 3      3
READY
```

Figure 7.2b. Running the program of Fig. 7.2a.

7.3 **The** ON-GO TO **Statement**

The IF statement allows us to transfer the execution of the program to one of two statements in the program, depending on whether the condition in the IF statement is true or false. We now study a statement that permits the computer to transfer execution to one of many statements. It is called the ON-GO TO statement, an example of which is

50   ON X GO TO 90,70,110

In this statement, the truncated value of X—in other words, INT(X)—determines which one of many statements will be executed next. If the truncated value of X is 1, then the next statement executed is the one whose line number is the first number that appears after TO. In this case it will be line 90. If the truncated value of X is 2, then the next statement executed is the one whose line number is the second number that appears after TO. In this case it will be line 70. If the truncated value of X is 3, then the next statement executed is the one whose line number is the third number that appears after TO.* In this case it will be line 110. For this particular example of the statement, if the truncated value of X is either less than 1 or more than 3, an error occurs† during the program's execution.

If the program logic demands it, you can place as many line numbers after the TO as can fit on the teletypewriter line. Note that the numbers that follow the TO in this statement need not be in ascending order, as is shown here. Thus 40   ON Y GO TO 60,35,91,83,70 is an acceptable ON-GO TO statement. We will now study the use of this type of statement in the program of Fig. 7.3a.

In this program the computer reads a number from the data statement and then after executing

40   ON X GO TO 70,50,90,110

will execute one of the PRINT statements in lines 70, 50, 90, or 110, depending on the value of the number read.

First, the READ statement assigns one of the numbers in the DATA statement to X. Next, the computer executes line 40: 40   ON X GO TO 70,50,90,110. The table for Fig. 7.3a shows how this statement works. If the value of X is 1, line 70 is executed next and the number 1 is printed. If it is 2, line 50 is executed next and 2 is printed. If it is 3, line 90 is executed next and 3 is printed. If it is 4, then line 110 is executed next and 4 is printed.

Each of the PRINT statements except line 110 is followed by a GO TO statement, so that the statement executed after them will be the READ statement:

30   READ X

If these GO TO statements were omitted, only the first number in the DATA statement would be read, and then, since this number is 1, all the PRINT statements would be executed and then the program would end.

The program of Fig. 7.3a is run in Fig. 7.3b.

---

* On the HP 2000C, the form of this statement is GO TO X OF and the rounded value of X determines the next statement that will be executed.

† On some systems, an error does not occur; the computer simply executes the next statement in the program. This is the case on the HP 2000C.

USING THE ON-GO TO STATEMENT

```
10        REM SHOW USE OF ON-GO TO STATEMENT
30        READ X
40        ON X GO TO 70,50,90,110
50        PRINT "2,"
60        GO TO 30
70        PRINT "1,"
80        GO TO 30
90        PRINT "3,"
100       GO TO 30
110       PRINT "4"
120       DATA 1,2,2,1,3,3,4
130       END
```

Figure 7.3a. The program shows <u>how the ON-GO TO statement works</u>. In line 40, if the value of X is 1, line 70 is executed next. If it is 2, then line 50 is next. If it is 3, then line 90 is next. Finally, if it is 4, then line 110 is next.

Line no.	Time executed	X	Next statement
40	1st	1	70
40	2nd	2	50
40	3rd	2	50
40	4th	1	70
40	5th	3	90
40	6th	3	90
40	4th	4	110

Table for Fig. 7.3a. The table shows how 40 ON X GO TO 70,50,90,100 works.

```
RUN
 1,
 2,
 2,
 1,
 3,
 3,
 4
READY
```

Figure 7.3b. Running the program of Fig. 7.3a.

The reason we did not include a GO TO statement after line 110 is that we want the program to end here. Thus the next statement executed is the END statement. In general we have to use GO TO statements in conjunction with an ON–GO TO statement. An ON–GO TO statement can be replaced by a group of consecutive IF statements. We leave it for an exercise for you to rewrite this program using this fact.

We will now alter the program shown in Fig. 7.3a so that it will produce, as its result, a copy of the DATA statement in line 120. The altered program is shown in Fig. 7.3c. We have added the statement

           20   PRINT "120 DATA";

This reproduces the first part of the DATA statement in line 120. We have also ended each PRINT statement but the last with a semicolon. Thus when the program is run, everything is printed on one line and we obtain

           120   DATA 1,2,2,1,3,3,4

for the result, as is shown in Fig. 7.3d.

ON–GO TO

> The form of the ON–GO TO statement is: line number, followed by ON; followed by a variable or an expression involving a mathematical operation; followed by GO TO; followed by a list of line numbers that are separated by commas.
> Examples:
>   10   ON Z GO TO 20,15,10,25
>   40   ON X↑2 + Y↑2 GO TO 50,60,70,80
>   50   ON SQR(X) GO TO 60,65,70,75,80,85

So far, we have not used the fact that in an ON–GO TO statement the computer truncates the value of what is sandwiched between the ON and GO before it determines which will be the next statement it executes. In the next program we shall use this fact.

REPRODUCING A DATA STATEMENT

```
10      REM SHOW USE OF ON-GO TO STATEMENT
20      PRINT "120 DATA";
30      READ X
40      ON X GO TO 70,50,90,110
50      PRINT "2,";
60      GO TO 30
70      PRINT "1,";
80      GO TO 30
90      PRINT "3,";
100     GO TO 30
110     PRINT "4"
120     DATA 1,2,2,1,3,3,4
130     END
```

Figure 7.3c. Same as the program in Fig. 7.3a except that each PRINT statement (except line 110) ends with a semicolon. Thus all the numbers are printed on one line. Line 20 has been added to the program so that the results look like the DATA statement in line 120.

```
RUN
120 DATA1,2,2,1,3,3,4
READY
```

Figure 7.3d. Running the program of Fig. 7.3c. We see that the program duplicated the DATA statement which appears in line 120.

In Fig. 7.4a we show a program that determines a student's letter grade from his numerical mark. An A is given for marks ranging from 90 to 99, a B for marks from 80 to 89, and C for marks from 70 to 79. The program skips any mark that is not in this range. The names of six students and their examination marks are given in

```
20       DATA HAROLD,83,TED,64,MARY,81,RITA,92,HANK,71,SAM,80
```

Note: Since it is not necessary, we have not put the strings (i.e., the names) in quotation marks.

The heart of the program is a FOR-NEXT loop extending from line 30 to line 140, in which the statements are executed 6 times (once for each student). The statement

```
40       READ N$,M
```

assigns a student's name to N$ and that student's mark to M. We remind you here that a string can be assigned only to a string variable, and on most systems a number can be assigned only to a simple variable. Thus, given the DATA statement in line 20 we could have not written the READ statement as 40   READ M,N$, since that would mean, for instance, that we would be assigning the string HAROLD to the simple variable M.

In the ON-GO TO statement

```
70       ON M/10-6 GO TO 120,100,80
```

the mark is divided by 10, this quotient is then decreased by 6, the result is truncated,* and finally the statement corresponding to the truncated value of M/10-6 is executed.

The table for Fig. 7.4a shows how the letter grade is determined for each student. The first student processed is HAROLD. His name is assigned to N$ and his mark to M; the values of these variables at line 70 are shown in the table for Fig. 7.4a:

Line no.	N$	M	M/10	M/10-6	Next statement
70	HAROLD	83	8.3	2.3	100

His mark, 83, is divided by 10, giving 8.3. This is then decreased by 6, giving 2.3. This is truncated to 2, so line 100 (the second statement number after the TO) is executed next:

```
100      LET A$="B"
```

Here the string B is assigned to A$. Then because of the GO TO statement following line 80, the PRINT statement

```
130      PRINT N$;"'S MARK IS ";A$
```

is executed. Since N$ and A$ have (as we have seen) been defined, the following results are produced:

```
HAROLD'S MARK IS B
```

The remaining data except for the name TED and his mark, 64, are processed in a similar way, as shown in the table for Fig. 7.4a, and produces results similar to those shown in Fig. 7.4b. Since TED's mark is less than 64, when he is processed the expression in

```
60       IF M<70 THEN 140
```

is true. Thus the computer skips to line 140 and does not print any information about TED.

* On systems which round instead of truncate (like the HP 2000C), one should use M/10-6.5 in this statement.

ASSIGNING A LETTER GRADE TO A NUMERICAL GRADE

```
10        REM GRADES STUDENTS ACCORDING
15        REM TO MARKS
20        DATA HAROLD,83,TED,64,MARY,81,RITA,92,HANK,71,SAM,80
30        FOR J=1 TO 6
40        READ N$,M
50        IF M>99 THEN 140
60        IF M<70 THEN 140
70        ON M/10-6 GO TO 120,100,80
80        LET A$="A"
90        GO TO 130
100       LET A$="B"
110       GO TO 130
120       LET A$="C"
130       PRINT N$;"'S MARK IS ";A$
140       NEXT J
150       END
```

Figure 7.4a. The program assigns a letter grade to given numerical grade. The assignment is made on the basis of the truncated value of M/10-6 (this is the same as INT (M/10-6)) in the ON–GO TO statement.

Line no.	N$	M	M/10	M/10-6	Next statement
70	HAROLD	83	8.3	2.3	100
70	MARY	81	8.1	2.1	100
70	RITA	92	9.2	3.2	80
70	HANK	71	7.1	1.1	120
70	SAM	80	8	2	100

Table for Fig. 7.4a. The table shows how a student's mark, M, determines the next statement executed. It is in this next statement executed that a letter grade will be assigned to a student.

```
RUN
HAROLD'S MARK IS B
MARY'S MARK IS B
RITA'S MARK IS A
HANK'S MARK IS C
SAM'S MARK IS B
READY
```

Figure 7.4b. Running the program of Fig. 7.4a. The 'S at the end of each name, is produced by the string in line 130.

We now investigate a program shown in Fig. 7.5a that takes an inventory of different items in stock. The item number of each piece of stock is placed in a DATA statement

         30   DATA 1001,1002,1002,1003,1004,1003,1001

We see that there are four different types of items. These types are numbered 1001, 1002, 1003, and 1004. We will use the counters K1, K2, K3, and K4, respectively, to count the amount of each of these types. We use an ON-GO TO statement, in conjunction with the item number assigned to X, to determine which counter to use. In order to do this we have to subtract 1000 from X as shown in line 70

         70   ON X-1000 GO TO 80,100,120,140

Let us now see how the program works.

First, zero is assigned in a multiple assignment statement to each of the counters

         40   LET K1=K2=K3=K4=0

Then the statements in the FOR-NEXT loop are executed 7 times, once for each of the items in the DATA statement. In the loop, the item numbers are assigned to the variable X in

         60   READ X

The first item number read is 1001, and this is assigned to X. Since in line 70, X-1000 equals 1, execution is transferred to the first line number after the TO in this statement. This is line 80. There the value of the counter K1 is increased by 1, as is shown in the first line of the table for Fig. 7.5a:

X	K1	K2	K3	K4
1001	1	0	0	0

This table shows the status of the counters after each value of X (shown in the first column of the table) is processed. The next statement executed

         90   GO TO 160

transfers control to the last statement in the loop

         160   NEXT I

Thus the statements in the loop are executed again. The next number is read, and it is processed in the same way. Since its value is 1002, X-1000 equals 2, so the ON-GO TO statement transfers control to line 100 the second line number after the TO. There the value of K2 is increased by 1. After all the numbers in the DATA statement have been processed, the value of all the counters is shown in the last line of the table for Fig. 7.5a.

X	K1	K2	K3	K4
1001	2	2	2	1

These values of the counters are used when the PRINT statements in lines 170 to 200 are executed. Note: In this program 150   GO TO 160 is redundant, since the statement following it is line 160. However, it may make the program easier to read and hence easier to understand. The results are shown in Fig. 7.5b.

AN INVENTORY PROGRAM

```
10        REM INVENTORY PROGRAM FOR  4 CLASSES
20        REM K1,K2,K3,K4 ARE THE COUNTERS
30        DATA 1001,1002,1002,1003,1004,1003,1001
40        LET K1=K2=K3=K4=0
50        FOR I=1 TO 7
60        READ X
70        ON X-1000 GO TO 80,100,120,140
80        LET K1=K1+1
90        GO TO 160
100       LET K2=K2+1
110       GO TO 160
120       LET K3=K3+1
130       GO TO 160
140       LET K4=K4+1
150       GO TO 160
160       NEXT I
170       PRINT "ITEM 1001;";K1;"IN STOCK"
180       PRINT "ITEM 1002;";K2;"IN STOCK"
190       PRINT "ITEM 1003;";K3;"IN STOCK"
200       PRINT "ITEM 1004;";K4;"IN STOCK"
210       END
```

Figure 7.5a. Program determines how often a given number occurs in the DATA statement. Each number in the DATA statement represents an item in the inventory of a certain company. The value of X−1000 in the ON–GO TO statement, determines which statement will be executed next and thus determines the counter to be used for each inventory item.

X	1000-X	K1	K2	K3	K4
1001	1	1	0	0	0
1002	2	1	1	0	0
1002	2	1	2	0	0
1003	3	1	2	1	0
1004	4	1	2	1	1
1003	3	1	2	2	1
1001	1	2	2	2	1

Table for Fig. 7.5a. The table shows the value of each of the counters K1, K2, K3, and K4 after an item X is counted. The expression 1000−X in line 70 determines the appropriate counter to use for a given value of X.

```
RUN
ITEM 1001; 2     IN STOCK
ITEM 1002; 2     IN STOCK
ITEM 1003; 2     IN STOCK
ITEM 1004; 1     IN STOCK
READY
```

Figure 7.5b. Running the program of Fig. 7.5a. The results on each successive line here correspond to the last value of the counters K1, K2, K3, and K4, respectively.

7.4. Singly Dimensioned Variables; DIM Statement; Plotting Grade Distributions

In Fig. 7.6a we present a simple program that sums the numbers in the DATA statement. The table for Fig. 7.6a shows how the variables are assigned values in the program, and the results are shown in Fig. 7.6b. There is nothing new in this program. In fact, we could have written it after reading Chapter 4. At present, the variable names are themselves constant; i.e., the names cannot change during the execution of the program.

We now present a different way of representing variables. It will enable us to make part of the name itself a variable and thus allow us to change the name of a variable in a given statement during the execution of the program. We present three different versions of the program in Fig. 7.6a, which will help to explain this new technique. Each successive program will be somewhat more complicated then the preceding one. In Fig. 7.7a we show the simplest of the programs.

SUBSCRIPTED VARIABLES

```
10        DATA 11,12,15,6
20        READ B,D,C1,C2
30        LET A=B+D+C1+C2
40        PRINT A;B;D;C1;C2
50        END
```

Figure 7.6a. A simple program that reads four numbers and then calculates their sum.

Line no.	B	D	C1	C2	A
20	11	12	15	6	Undef
30	11	12	15	6	44
40	11	12	15	6	44

Table for Fig. 7.6a. The values assigned to the variables in the program of Fig. 7.6a.

```
RUN
44      11      12      15      6
READY
```

Figure 7.6b. Running the program of Fig. 7.6a.

In it, the variable C in the READ statement

```
30        READ C(1),C(2),C(3),C(4)
```

is called a subscripted or dimensioned variable. It consists of four parts, which are called the elements of the subscripted variable. They are: $C(1)$, $C(2)$, $C(3)$ and $C(4)$. Each of these elements acts as a separate variable. Only their names are related. In fact, each element usually has a different value. Thus after line 30 is executed, the element $C(1)$ has the value 11; $C(2)$ has the value 12, $C(3)$ has the value 15, and finally $C(4)$ has the value 6. This can be seen from the table for Fig. 7.7a. We see that part of the name of a subscripted variable— the part that appears between the parentheses—can be changed. We call that part the subscript. We see that in line 30 the subscript has the values 1, 2, 3, and 4.

In BASIC, the name of a subscripted variable can only be a letter of the alphabet. There are thus only 26 different subscripted variable names possible. Table 7.1 shows legal and illegal subscripted variable names. Thus $A1$ is not a possible name for a subscripted variable. The subscript can be a number, a simple variable, a subscripted variable, or an expression involving a calculation. The computer truncates * the value of the subscript before it assigns a value to the subscript variable. Thus the computer would interpret $C(2.6)$ as $C(2)$.

If we compare the program of Fig. 7.7a with that of 7.6a, we see that they are identical but for the fact that the places of B, D, $C1$, and $C2$ in the program of Fig. 7.6a have been taken by $C(1)$, $C(2)$, $C(3)$, and $C(4)$ in the program of Fig. 7.7a. For instance, 40   LET $A=C(1)+C(2)+C(3)+C(4)$ replaces 30   LET $A=B+D+C1+C2$. The values assigned to the four elements of the subscripted variable are the same as those assigned to the corresponding variables in the program of Fig. 7.6a, as can be seen by comparing the table for Fig. 7.7a with that for Fig. 7.6a. The results of running both programs are the same, as can be seen by comparing Fig. 7.7b with Fig. 7.6b.

---

* On some systems, the computer rounds the value of the subscript before it assigns a value to the subscripted variable. Thus C(2.6) would become C(3). This is the case on the HP 2000C.

SUBSCRIPTED VARIABLES

```
10      REM INTROD TO SUBSCRIPTED VARAIBLES
20      DATA 11,12,15,6
30      READ C(1),C(2),C(3),C(4)
40      LET A=C(1)+C(2)+C(3)+C(4)
50      PRINT A;C(1);C(2);C(3);C(4)
60      END
```

Figure 7.7a. Same as program in Fig. 7.6a. except that a subscripted variable C is used. It consists of four parts: C(1), C(2), C(3), C(4). Each of these is in effect a separate variable. They are called the elements of C. Only the names of these variables are related to each other. What distinguishes one variable name from the other is what appears in the parentheses. It is called the subscript.

Line no.	C(1)	C(2)	C(3)	C(4)	A
30	11	12	15	6	Undef
40	11	12	15	6	44
50	11	12	15	6	44

Table for Fig. 7.7a. The values assigned to the four parts—the elements—of the subscripted variable C are the same as the values assigned to the variables B, D, C1, and C2 in Fig. 7.6a, since the DATA statements in both programs are the same.

```
RUN
44      11      12      15      6
READY.
```

Figure 7.7b. Running the program of Fig. 7.7a. The results are the same as in Fig. 7.6b.

Legal names for subscripted variables	Illegal names for subscripted variables
A	A2
B	BB
R	#R

Table 7.1. The name of a subscripted variable can consist of one letter only.

The power of subscripted variables can be seen when the subscript is either a variable or an expression involving a mathematical operation. In Fig. 7.8a, the second version of the program that was shown in Fig. 7.7a, we have used variables as subscripts. We will explain this presently. Each of the four times the READ statement in the loop

```
30        FOR S=1 TO 4
40        READ C(S)
50        NEXT S
```

is executed, one of the numbers in the DATA statement is read. The first time line 40 is executed, the value of the subscript S is 1. The computer thus interprets this statement as

```
40    READ C(1)
```

and thus assigns 11 (the first number in the DATA statement) to the element C(1). The second time line 40 is executed, the computer interprets this line as

```
40    READ C(2)
```

and assigns 12 to the element C(2). This process continues until the loop is finished; the number assigned to C(S) for all values of the subscript S is given in the left half of the table for Fig. 7.8a. This table also shows how the computer interprets C(S) for each value of S. For instance, when S equals 3 the left half of the third line of the table for Fig. 7.8a

S	Form of C(S)	Value of C(S)
3	C(3)	15

shows us that the computer interprets C(S) here as C(3) and assigns it the value 15. We also see from the table that C(1), C(2), C(3), and C(4) have all been assigned numbers. Thus

```
60        LET A=C(1)+C(2)+C(3)+C(4)
```

can be evaluated without any difficulty—the value of A is $11+12+15+16$, or 44.

The execution of

```
80        FOR T=1 TO 4
90        PRINT C(T)
100       NEXT T
```

proceeds as follows. The first time the statements in the loop are executed, the value of the subscript T is 1. So the computer interprets line 90 as

```
90    PRINT C(1)
```

But C(1) has been defined. It has the value of 11, as we have seen. This is shown on the right half of the table for Fig.7.8a:

T	Form of C(T)	Value of C(T)
1	C(1)	11

Thus when the program is run, as shown in Fig. 7.8b, the computer prints this value. *Note:* It does not matter what variable is used as the subscript; what does matter, though, is the value of the variable. Consequently, when the values of S and T are the same, the values of C(S) and C(T) are the same. This is shown in the table for Fig. 7.8a.

WRITING THE SUBSCRIPT AS A VARIABLE

```
10      REM    VERSION 2
20      DATA 11,12,15,6
30      FOR S=1 TO 4
40      READ C(S)
50      NEXT S
60      LET A=C(1)+C(2)+C(3)+C(4)
70      PRINT A
80      FOR T=1 TO 4
90      PRINT C(T)
100     NEXT T
110     END
```

Figure 7.8a. Same as the program of Fig. 7.7a. except that in parts of the program, the subscripts are now variables—S and T. The value of C(S) when the value of S is 1, is the same as C(1).

S	Form of C(S)	Value of C(S)	T	Form of C(T)	Value of C(T)
1	C(1)	11	1	C(1)	11
2	C(2)	12	2	C(2)	12
3	C(3)	15	3	C(3)	15
4	C(4)	6	4	C(4)	6

Table for Fig. 7.8a. It does not matter which variable is used as the subscript. Thus when S and T have the same value, C(S) and C(T) have the same value.

```
RUN
44
11
12
15
6
READY
```

Figure 7.8b. The results of running Fig. 7.8a. They are the same as for Fig. 7.7a.

In the third version of the program, shown in Fig. 7.9a, the addition of the numbers is performed at line 60 in the FOR-NEXT loop:

```
40      FOR S=1 TO 4
50      READ C(S)
60      LET A=A+C(S)
70      NEXT S
```

We use A as an accumulator in line 60. The first time the statements in the loop are executed, the value of S is 1. Thus the computer interprets line 50 as

```
50    READ C(1)
```

and assigns 11, the first number in the DATA statement, to C(1). Similarly, it interprets line 60 as

```
60    LET A=A+C(1)
```

We see that A has been assigned the value zero in

```
30      LET A=0
```

before the loop begins. Thus the first time line 60 is executed, the value of A to the right of the equals sign is zero, and the value of A on the left of the equals sign is $0+11$, which is 11. This is shown in the first line of the table for Fig. 7.9a.

Line no.	Time executed	A to the right of =	S	C(S)	A to the left of =
60	1st	0	1	11	11

The second time the loop is executed, the value of S is 2. Thus the computer interprets line 50 now as

```
50    READ C(2)
```

and assigns 12, the second number in the DATA statement, to C(2). Similarly it interprets line 60 as

```
60    LET A=A+C(2)
```

The value of A to the right of the equals sign is now 11, and the value of A to the left of the equals sign is $11+12$, which equals 23. This is shown in the second line of the table for Fig. 7.9a:

Line no.	Time executed	A to the right of =	S	C(S)	A to the left of =
60	2nd	11	2	12	23

This procedure continues until the loop is finished. The last value assigned to A is 44. The results are then printed by the program. We see these when we run the program, as shown in Fig. 7.9b.

USING A SUBSCRIPTED VARIABLE WITH AN ACCUMULATOR

```
10      REM VERSION 3
20      DATA 11,12,15,6
30      LET ,A=0
40      FOR S=1 TO 4
50      READ C(S)
60      LET A=A+C(S)
70      NEXT S
80      PRINT A
90      FOR I=1 TO 4
100     PRINT C(I)
110     NEXT I
120     END
```

Figure 7.9a. Same as the program in Fig. 7.8a. except that the addition is done with an accumulator in a FOR–NEXT loop. In order to do the addition in this way, the subscript must be a variable—we have used S for the subscript's name—and must be the same as the index of the loop.

Line no.	Time executed	A to the right of equals sign	S	C(S)	A to the left of equals sign
60	1st	0	1	11	11
60	2nd	11	2	12	23
60	3rd	23	3	15	38
60	4th	38	4	6	44

Table for Fig. 7.9a. The table shows how 60 LET A=A+C(S) works. The variable A is the accumulator.

```
RUN
44
11
12
15
6
READY
```

Figure 7.9b. Running the program of Fig. 7.9a. The results are the same as for Fig. 7.8a.

In order for the computer to process a program that has subscripted variables, a location in its memory must be reserved for each of the elements of the subscripted variable. If the largest value of the subscript, for a given subscripted variable, is less than or equal to 10, the computer automatically leaves space for eleven elements. The subscript for these elements has the values: 0, 1, 2, 3, 4, 5, 6, 7, 8, 9, and 10. Thus in the programs shown in Figs. 7.7, 7.8, and 7.9 the computer automatically reserved space in its memory to accommodate the possible use of C(0), C(1), C(2), C(3), C(4), C(5), C(6), C(7), C(8), C(9), and C(10), although the largest value of the subscript actually used in these programs was 4. Some systems do not allow the subscript to have the value 0; for example, C(0) would be illegal. On these systems the computer automatically reserves 10 locations for a given subscripted variable. We will never assign a subscript the value 0 in any of the programs in this book. They can thus be run on any system.

If the largest value of the subscript is greater than 10, the programmer must use what is called the DIM—an abbreviation for DIMension—statement to instruct the computer to provide sufficient space for all the elements. The process is called dimensioning. In a DIM statement, we inform the computer what will be the largest value of the subscript of each subscripted variable used in the program. If we wanted the program in Fig. 7.9a to process 13 numbers, we would have to rewrite it—as shown in Fig. 7.10a—so that it also includes a DIM statement

$$30 \qquad DIM \ C(13)$$

If we do not use a DIM statement in this program, an error will result during the program's execution. On some systems the DIM statement must be placed in the program anywhere before the first occurrence of the subscripted variable, for example, in Fig. 7.10a before 60 READ C(S). On other systems, the DIM statement can be placed anywhere in the program. The results of the program in Fig. 7.10a are shown in Fig. 7.10b.

DIM

> The form of the DIM statement is: line number followed by DIM, followed by the name of a subscripted variable, followed by (, followed by the largest value of the subscript; followed by) . If there is more than one subscripted variable to be dimensioned, the variables must be separated by commas, for example, 20 DIM A(14), B(11), Z(20).

You are allowed to use a DIM statement to dimension variables whose subscript has a maximum value less than or equal to 10; for example, we could have included the statement 15 DIM C(4) in the programs of Figs. 7.7 to 7.9. The computer would then reserve space according to how the DIM statement instructs it; i.e., it would reserve space for only C(1), C(2), C(3), and C(4) in its memory. The effect is that the program uses less space in the memory. From now on, we will write all programs with DIM statements. We will now use

USING THE DIM STATEMENT

```
10        REM USE OF DIMENSION STATEMENT
20        DATA 11,12,15,6,3,7,84,21,6,1,9,8,2
30        DIM C(13)
40        LET A=0
50        FOR S=1 TO 13
60        READ C(S)
70        LET A=A+C(S)
80        NEXT S
90        PRINT "SUM=";A
100       FOR I=1 TO 13
110       PRINT C(I)
120       NEXT I
130       END
```

Figure 7.10a. Same as program in Fig. 7.9a. except that the maximum value of the subscript is 13. If the maximum value of a subscript is greater than 10, the appropriate subscripted variable must be placed in a DIM statement, with the maximum value of the subscripted appearing in parentheses. Thus 30 DIM C(13).

```
RUN
SUM= 185
 11
 12
 15
  6
  3
  7
 84
 21
  6
  1
  9
  8
  2
READY.
```

Figure 7.10b. Running the program of Fig. 7.10a.

dimensioned variables to rewrite the program of Fig. 7.5a, which took an inventory of different items in stock.

The DATA statement in the present program shown in Fig. 7.11a

    30   DATA 1001,1002,1002,1003,1004,1003,1001

is the same as the one shown in Fig. 7.5a. As you remember, the numbers represent the item numbers of each piece of merchandise in stock. We see that there are four different types in stock. They are numbered 1001, 1002, 1003, and 1004. We will use the subscripted variables $K(1)$, $K(2)$, $K(3)$, and $K(4)$, respectively, to count the amount of each of these types. The variables will thus be used as counters. We dimension the subscripted variable K in:

    20   DIM K(4)

At the beginning of the program, zeros are assigned to all four counters

    40   LET K(1)=K(2)=K(3)=K(4)=0

(in the next program we will do this in a more aesthetic way). The main part of the program is the loop extending from line 50 to line 90. In line 60

    60   READ X

the item numbers are assigned to X. In line 70

    70   LET S=X-1000

the item number is decreased by 1000 so that the subscript S assumes the value 1, 2, 3, or 4, depending on the value of X. This will indicate to the computer which counter to add 1 to. The addition for all the counters can now be done in one statement

    80   LET K(S)=K(S)+1

since the proper value of S has already been determined in line 70. For example, the first time the loop is executed, 1001 is assigned to X. Therefore, after line 70 is executed, the value of S is 1. Thus the computer interprets line 80 as

    80   LET K(1)=K(1)+1

and adds 1 to the counter $K(1)$. The values of the rest of the counters are still zero. All of this is shown in the first line of the table for Fig. 11a.

Time loop executed	X	S	K(1)	K(2)	K(3)	K(4)
1st	1001	1	1	0	0	0

The second time the loop is executed, X has the value 1002, and thus S has the value 2. Therefore the computer adds 1 to $K(2)$, so the value of $K(2)$ is now 1. All of this is shown in the second line of the table for Fig. 7.11a:

Time loop executed	X	S	K(1)	K(2)	K(3)	K(4)
2nd	1002	2	1	1	0	0

We see that the computer remembers that the value of $K(2)$ is 1. The third time the loop is executed, X has the value 1002, and thus S again has the value 2. Therefore the computer again adds 1 to the value of $K(2)$. The process continues as shown in the rest of the table.

REWRITING THE INVENTORY PROGRAM USING A SUBSCRIPTED VARIABLE

```
10   REM INVENTORY PROGRAM
20   DIM K(4)
30   DATA 1001,1002,1002,1003,1004,1003,1001
40   LET K(1)=K(2)=K(3)=K(4)=0
50   FOR I=1 TO 7
60   READ X
70   LET S=X-1000
80   LET K(S)=K(S)+1
90   NEXT I
100  PRINT "ITEM 1001:";K(1);"IN STOCK"
110  PRINT "ITEM 1002:";K(2);"IN STOCK"
120  PRINT "ITEM 1003:";K(3);"IN STOCK"
130  PRINT "ITEM 1004:";K(4);"IN STOCK"
140  END
```

Figure 7.11a. Same program as program of Fig. 7.5a. It determines how many of each item there are in the DATA statement. The subscripted variable K(S), represents all four counters. For instance, when the value of S is 1, K(S) is the same as K(1). Therefore the values of all the counters can be increased in one statement, i.e., line 80.

Time loop executed	X	S	K(1)	K(2)	K(3)	K(4)
1st	1001	1	1	0	0	0
2nd	1002	2	1	1	0	0
3rd	1002	2	1	2	0	0
4th	1003	3	1	2	1	0
5th	1004	4	1	2	1	1
6th	1003	3	1	2	2	1
7th	1001	1	2	2	2	1

Table for Fig. 7.11a. The value of each counter, after an item X is counted. The value of the subscript is determined from 70 LET S=X-1000.

When the loop is finished, the PRINT statements at the end of the program are executed, the first of which is

```
100    PRINT "ITEM 1001:"; K(1); "IN STOCK"
```

The value of K(1) here is the last value assigned to K(1) which, from the table, we see is 2. Thus when the program is run, as is shown in Fig. 7.11b, the first line of results is

```
ITEM 1001: 2       IN STOCK
```

The rest of the PRINT statements produce similar results, as we see by looking at the rest of Fig. 7.11b.

Statement 40

```
40    LET K(1)=K(2)=K(3)=K(4)=0
```

and the group of PRINT statements beginning with

```
100    PRINT "ITEM 1001:";K(1);"IN STOCK"
```

can be written in a more succinct way using FOR–NEXT loops. We do this in Fig. 7.12a. Let us now see how.

Statement 40 of the previous program can be rewritten as

```
40    FOR R=1 TO 4
42    LET K(R)=0
44    NEXT R
```

The first time this loop is executed, the value of K(1) is set equal to zero. The second time, the value of K(2) is set equal to zero, etc.

All four PRINT statements can be written as

```
100    FOR Q=1 TO 4
110    PRINT "ITEM 100";Q;":";K(Q);"IN STOCK"
120    NEXT Q
```

The first time this loop is executed, the value of Q is 1. The computer thus interpret line 110 as

```
110    PRINT "ITEM 100";1;":",K(1);"IN STOCK"
```

and prints

```
ITEM 100 1    : 2       IN STOCK
```

as is shown in the first line of results in Fig. 7.12b. Note that there is a space between the last zero in 100 and the 1 that follows it. This is the space the computer always leaves in case Q has a negative value. Each additional time the statements in this loop are executed another line of results is printed, as we see by looking at the rest of Fig. 7.12b.

```
RUN
ITEM 1001; 2     IN STOCK
ITEM 1002; 2     IN STOCK
ITEM 1003; 2     IN STOCK
ITEM 1004: 1     IN STOCK
READY
```

Figure 7.11b. Running the program of Fig. 7.11a. The results on each successive line here correspond to the last value of the counters K(1), K(2), K(3), and K(4),respectively.

A MORE EFFICIENT WAY OF WRITING THE PREVIOUS PROGRAM

```
10    REM VERSION 2 OF INVENTORY PROGRAM
20    DIM K(4)
30    DATA 1001,1002,1002,1003,1004,1003,1001
40    FOR R=1 TO 4
42    LET K(R)=0
44    NEXT R
50    FOR I=1 TO 7
60    READ X
70    LET S=X-1000
80    LET K(S)=K(S)+1
90    NEXT I
100   FOR Q=1 TO 4
110   PRINT "ITEM 100";Q;";";K(Q);"IN STOCK"
120   NEXT Q
130   END
```

Figure 7.12a. Same as program of Fig. 7.11a. except that the assignment of zeros to the counters K(R) is now done in a loop—the R loop—and the results are printed in a loop—the Q loop.

```
RUN
ITEM 100 1     : 2     IN STOCK
ITEM 100 2     : 2     IN STOCK
ITEM 100 3     : 2     IN STOCK
ITEM 100 4     : 1     IN STOCK
READY
```

Figure 7.12b. Running the program of Fig. 7.12a. The computer leaves a space within the item number because the last digit of this number corresponds to a variable—the variable Q—which could conceivably be negative.

We will now use subscripted variables in a program to determine the distribution of grades in a class of students; i.e., we will determine how many students received grades between 63 and 69, between 70 and 79, between 80 and 89, and finally between 90 and 99. The program is shown in Fig. 7.13a. The elements B(1), B(2), B(3), and B(4), respectively, are the counters for the four categories of grades. The grades are placed in the statements

```
30      DATA 78,84,96,75,81,68,72,78
35      DATA 91,73,82,61,74,-1
```

The −1 at the end of the data is a trailer, indicating that it is the last piece of data. In the program we will use the fact that, when the subscript of a subscripted variable has a non-integral value, it is truncated before the subscripted variable is further processed by the computer. Thus B(7.8) would become B(7). Let us now investigate the program in more detail.

The loop

```
40      FOR L= 1 TO 4
50      LET B(L)=0
60      NEXT L
```

assigns zeros to all four counters. The grade is read in statement 70 and assigned to the variable X. The computer tests whether the grade is the last in the DATA statement

```
80      IF X=-1 THEN 120
```

If it is, then the results are printed. If the grade is not the last, the computer determines which counter should be increased by 1, in

```
90      LET J=X/10-5
```

Let us now seee how. The first grade is 78. Thus X/10 is 7.8, and the value of J is 2.8 Therefore the computer interprets line 100 as

```
100    LET B(2.8)=B(2.8)+1
```

Before the computer processes this statement any further, it truncates * 2.8 to 2. The computer interprets this statement now as

```
100    LET B(2)=B(2)+1
```

It has thus ascertained that this grade is between 70 and 79 and has added 1 to the proper counter. The value of B(2) is therefore now 1, and the values of the remaining counters are still zero. All of this is shown in the first line of the table for Fig. 7.13a.

X	X/10	J	B(1)	B(2)	B(3)	B(4)
78	7.8	2.8	0	1	0	0

The second grade is 84, so the value of J is 3.4. This means that the computer adds 1 to B(3). The value of B(2) is still 1, and that of B(1) and B(4) are still zero, all of which is shown in the second line of the table. The rest of the table shows how the third, fourth, fifth, and last grades are processed.

---

* On systems which round instead of truncate (like the HP 2000C), one should write line 90 as 90 LET J=X/10−5.5.

DETERMINING A GRADE DISTRIBUTION

```
10      REM DETERMINES GRADE DISTRIBUTION
20      DIM B(4)
30      DATA 78,84,96,75,81,68,72,78
35      DATA 91,73,82,61,74,-1
40      FOR L= 1 TO 4
50      LET B(L)=0
60      NEXT L
70      READ X
80      IF X=-1 THEN 120
90      LET J=X/10-5
100     LET B(J)=B(J)+1
110     GO TO 70
120     FOR L=1 TO 4
130     PRINT B(L);"GRADES FROM";50+10*L;"TO";50+10*L+9
140     NEXT L
150     END
```

Figure 7.13a. The program determines the distribution of grades stored in the DATA statement. Lines 90 and 100 determine what interval—60 to 69, 70 to 79, 80 to 89, or 90 to 99—the marks are in. The value of a subscript is always truncated. All of this is shown in the table for Fig. 7.13a. The number of grades in each interval are stored in the appropriate counter: B(1), B(2), B(3) or B(4).

Grade processed	X	X/10	J	B(1)	B(2)	B(3)	B(4)
1st	78	7.8	2.8	0	1	0	0
2nd	84	8.4	3.4	0	1	1	0
3rd	96	9.6	4.6	0	1	1	1
4th	75	7.5	2.5	0	2	1	1
5th	81	8.1	3.1	0	2	2	1
.	.	.	.	.	.	.	.
.	.	.	.	.	.	.	.
.	.	.	.	.	.	.	.
13th	74	7.4	2.4	2	6	3	2

Table for Fig. 7.13a. How 90 LET J=X/10–5 and 100 B(J)=B(J)+1 determine what interval a given grade, X, is in.

The loop

```
120    FOR L=1 TO 4
130    PRINT B(L);"GRADES FROM";50+10*L;"TO";50+10*L+9
140    NEXT L
```

at the end of the program, prints the results. The first time line 130 is executed, the value of L is 1. The computer thus interprets line 130 as

```
130    PRINT B(1);"GRADES FROM";50+10*1;"TO";50+10*1+9
```

or

```
130    PRINT B(1);"GRADES FROM";60;"TO";69
```

Since the last value of B(1) is 2, the statement produces the results

```
2      GRADES FROM 60    TO 69
```

as shown in the first line of results in Fig. 7.13b. Each successive time this statement is executed, the value of L is increased by 1 and the number of grades in the next grade range is printed as seen in the rest of Fig. 7.13b. If you examine the DATA statement, you will see that these results are correct.

Had we wished to, we could have eliminated line 90 and written line 100 as

```
100   LET B(X/10-5)=B(X/10-5)+1
```

since the subscript would be an expression. However, it is easier to write this as two statements, as we did in Fig. 7.13a.

```
RUN
2     GRADES FROM 60    TO 69
6     GRADES FROM 70    TO 79
3     GRADES FROM 80    TO 89
2     GRADES FROM 90    TO 99
READY
```

Figure 7.13b. Running the program of Fig. 7.13a. The results are produced by the loop from line 120 to 140. Thus when $L=1$, the computer interprets the last part of line 130 as: $50+10*1$; `"TO"`; $50+10*1+9$ or 60; `"TO"`; 69.

We will now investigate how to produce a graph of the results obtained in the last program. We will first describe a simple program that produces two consecutive horizontal lines of X's on the teletypewriter, as shown in Fig. 7.14b.

```
XX
XXXXXX
```

The length of each line is determined by a number in the program. The program is shown in Fig. 7.14a.

Each line is produced by a FOR-NEXT loop. The first line is produced by

```
20      FOR W=1 TO 2
30      PRINT "X";
40      NEXT W
```

Because statement 30 ends with a semicolon, this loop produces two Xs on the same line. The statement immediately following the loop is

```
50      PRINT
```

Therefore, the next PRINT statement executed will produce results on the next line. The next PRINT statement appears in the second loop

```
60      FOR W=1 TO 6
70      PRINT "X";
80      NEXT W
```

Thus this loop prints 6 Xs on the next line, as shown in the second line of results in Fig. 7.14b

In Fig. 7.15a we vary this program slightly by assigning the numbers (which determine the lengths of the lines) to a subscripted variable B. Thus 2 is assigned to B(1) and 6 to B(2) in

```
14      LET B(1)=2
16      LET B(2)=6
```

respectively. The two elements of the subscripted variable replace the appropriate two numbers in the FOR statements of the last program, i.e., statement 20 of Fig. 7.14a

```
20      FOR W=1 TO 2
```

becomes

```
20      FOR W=1 TO B(1)
```

in this program, and statement 60 in the program of Fig. 7.14a

```
60      FOR W=1 TO 6
```

becomes

```
60      FOR W=1 TO B(2)
```

in this program. Thus the first loop (which produces a line consisting of 2 Xs) is now

```
20      FOR W=1 TO B(1)
30      PRINT "X";
40      NEXT W
```

MAKING A BAR GRAPH

```
10      REM GIVES TWO LINES OF X'S
20      FOR W=1 TO 2
30      PRINT "X";
40      NEXT W
50      PRINT
60      FOR W=1 TO 6              RUN
70      PRINT "X";               XX
80      NEXT W                   XXXXX
90      END                      READY
```

Figure 7.14a. The program produces two consecutive lines of Xs. If 50 PRINT were not in the program, the program would produce one line of Xs.

Figure 7.14b. The results of running Fig. 7.14a.

```
10      REM GIVES TWO LINES OF X'S
11      REM VERSION 2
12      DIM B(2)
14      LET B(1)=2
16      LET B(2)=6
20      FOR W=1 TO B(1)
30      PRINT "X";
40      NEXT W
50      PRINT
60      FOR W=1 TO B(2)          RUN
70      PRINT "X";               XX
80      NEXT W                   XXXXX
90      END                      READY
```

Figure 7.15a. The program produces two lines of X's. Same as Fig. 7.14a except that the maximum value of the index W for the two loops—in lines 20 and 60—is given by B(1) and B(2), respectively.

Figure 7.15b. Results of running Fig. 7.15a. As we expect, they are the same as is shown in Fig. 7.14b.

Statement 50 is still needed for the production of two lines of Xs. The second loop is now

```
60        FOR W=1 TO B(2)
70        PRINT "X";
80        NEXT W
```

and produces a new line consisting of 6 Xs. The results of this program are shown in Fig. 7.15b. As we expect they are the same as the ones for the last program. When we compare the two FOR-NEXT loops in Fig. 7.15a, we see that they are identical except for the subscript of B. This suggests that we write the two loops as one loop, as shown in Fig. 7.16a,

```
40        FOR W=1 TO B(G)
50        PRINT "X";
60        NEXT W
```

by replacing the subscripts 1 and 2 with the variable G. Since G will assume the values 1 and 2, we place this loop (henceforth called the W loop) in an outer loop in which G is the index, i.e., the G loop. We insert the statement

```
70        PRINT
```

directly after the W loop, so the program will produce more than one line of Xs. The results, as shown in Fig. 7.16b, are identical to those of the last two programs.

We now take this program and make it a part of the program we studied in Fig. 7.13a, which produced the distribution of students' grades. The combined program shown in Fig. 7.17a will produce a bar graph, or histogram, of the distribution of the students' grades using the counters B(1), B(2), B(3), and B(4) to determine the length of the lines of Xs in the results.

In order to combine the two programs (Fig. 7.16a and Fig. 7.13a), we first eliminate the part of Fig. 7.13a that did the printing (lines 120 to 140). We then take the statements from the last program (Fig. 7.16a) that did the printing (lines 30 to 80) and number them so they are executed at the appropriate time in the program, i.e., when the trailer, −1, is read. We must also rewrite the FOR statement that began the last program (Fig. 7.16a), so that now four lines are printed. These four lines will correspond to the four categories of grades. Thus the FOR statement executed when the trailer is read is

```
120      FOR G= 1 TO 4
```

In order to label each line of Xs, we have included the following statement in the program

```
130      PRINT 50+10*G;"TO";50+10*G+9;
```

The first time the G loop (lines 120 to 180) is executed, the value of G is 1, so the computer interprets statements 130 to 170 in it as

```
130      PRINT 50+10*1;"TO";50+10*1+9;
140      FOR W=1 TO B(1)
150      PRINT "X";
160      NEXT W
170      PRINT
```

The computer first performs the calculation in line 130 and prints

```
60    TO 69
```

```
10        REM GIVES TWO LINES OF X'S
11        REM VERSION 3
12        DIM B(2)
14        LET B(1)=2
16        LET B(2)=6
30        FOR G=1 TO 2
40        FOR W=1 TO B(G)
50        PRINT "X";
60        NEXT W
70        PRINT
80        NEXT G
90        END
```

```
RUN
XX
XXXXXX
READY
```

Figure 7.16a. We have rewritten the program of Fig. 7.15a so that the two W loops are now one W loop. The maximum value of W in line 40 is given by B(G). The values of G are specified by the index of the outer or G loop.

Figure 7.16b. Running the program of Fig. 7.16a. As we expect, the results are the same as those shown in Figs. 7.15b and 7.14b.

PRODUCING A BAR GRAPH OF GRADE DISTRIBUTIONS

```
10        REM GRAPH OF GRADE DISTRIBUTION
20        DIM B(4)
30        DATA 78,84,96,75,81,68,72,78
35        DATA 91,73,82,61,74,-1
40        FOR L= 1 TO 4
50        LET B(L)=0
60        NEXT L
70        READ X
80        IF X=-1 THEN 120
90        LET J=X/10-5
100       LET B(J)=B(J)+1
110       GO TO 70
120       FOR G= 1 TO 4
130       PRINT 50+10*G;"TO";50+10*G+9;
140       FOR W=1 TO B(G)
150       PRINT "X";
160       NEXT W
170       PRINT
180       NEXT G
190       END
```

Figure 7.17a. This program combines Fig. 7.13a and Fig. 7.16a; it produces a bar graph (or histogram) of the distribution of grades given in the DATA statement. B(1), B(2), B(3), and B(4) are the counters. In statement 140, they determine how many Xs will appear in a line.

```
RUN
60    TO 69    XX
70    TO 79    XXXXXX
80    TO 89    XXX
90    TO 99    XX
READY
```

Figure 7.17b. Running the program of Fig. 7.17a.

We see from the table for Fig. 7.13a that the last value of B(1) is 2. Thus the computer interprets line 140 as

140   FOR W=1 TO 2

and executes the W loop twice, thereby printing two Xs. Since the PRINT statement in line 130 ends with a semicolon, the two Xs appear on the same line as 60 TO 69. Thus we obtain

60   TO 69   XX

The two X correspond to the fact that there are two grades betwen 60 and 60.

The second time the G loop is executed, B(G) in line 140 becomes B(2). Since its value is 6, the computer prints

70   TO 79   XXXXXX

the 6 Xs correspond to the fact that there are 6 grades between 70 and 79. Since the outer loop is executed 4 times, there are 4 lines of results in Fig. 7.17b.

PROBLEMS

1. Which of these multiple assignment statements are illegal in BASIC?

    a. 10   LET A=B=C+D+2
    b. 10   LET A=B+2=C=D
    c. 10   LET A=2=B2=3
    d. 10   LET A=B=C=D2

2. (a) Write a statement that will transfer control to statement 130 if the value of X equals 101; to statement 134 if the value of X is 102; and to statement 138 if the value of X is 103.
    (b) Alter the program in Fig. 7.4a so that a student who has a mark of 100 will will receive an A.
    (c) Rewrite the program of Fig. 7.3a using IF statements instead of the ON-GO TO statement.

3. Given the following DATA statement
    DATA 1,3,4,2,3,7,2,4,3
    and using an ON-GO TO statement, write a program that determines how many 1s, 2s, 3s, and 4s there are in the DATA statement.

4. Which of the following are illegal subscripted variable names?
    X   A2   A10   RA   B

5. What is printed by the following program?

```
10    FOR I=1 TO 6
20    LET N(I)=I
30    NEXT I
40    PRINT N(3),N(4),N(5)
60    END
```

6. What is printed by the following program?

```
5     DIM X(3),Y(3)
10    DATA 1,2,3,4,5,6
20    FOR I=1 TO 3
30    READ X(I),Y(I)
40    NEXT I
50    FOR L=1 TO3
60    PRINT Y(L),X(L)
70    NEXT L
80    END
```

7. Use a dimensioned variable to do problem 3.

8. Given a DATA statement that contains 8 numbers, write a program that calculates the sum of these 8 numbers and the fraction each of these numbers is of the sum.

9. Given the following DATA statement
```
15    DATA 10,11,6,15,33,21,6
```
Write a program that will print the numbers in the DATA statement in the reverse order, i.e.:

6   21   33   15   6   11   10

10. Alter the inventory program of Fig. 7.12a so that it will produce a bar graph (histogram) of the results.

11. Alter the histogram program of Fig. 7.17a so that it also prints the number of grades in each category.

8

Subscripted String Variables, Subroutines and User-Defined Functions

8.1. Subscripted String Variables

In Chapter 7 we saw that the use of subscripted variables made the writing of programs somewhat easier. We can apply this same technique to string variables by subscripting them. For instance, if we use A$, as a subscripted variable, we can assign one string to A$(1), a second string to $A(2), a third string to A$(3), etc. If the maximum value of the subscript is greater than 10, we have to dimension the string variable in a DIM statement, as is the case with nonstring subscripted variables; otherwise, we do not have to dimension it. We will, however, dimension all subscripted string variables. The subscript can be a number, a variable, or an expression involving a calculation. Also, if the subscript has a nonintegral value, the computer truncates it. Thus A$(2.2) becomes A$(2).

The name of a subscripted string variable must consist of a letter followed by a dollar sign. We will now rewrite the program of Fig. 7.4a using a subscripted string variable. This program determined a student's letter grade from his numerical grades. The new program is shown in Fig. 8.1a. An A is given for marks ranging from 90 to 99, a B for marks from 80 to 89, and a C for marks from 70 to 79. In order to simplify the program, we assume that there are no grades below 70 nor any above 99. We have thus changed TED's mark from 64 (its value in the previous program) to 74. The three letter grades are assigned to the subscripted variable A$ in*

```
40      LET  A$(1)="C"
50      LET  A$(2)="B"
60      LET  A$(3)="A"
```

The main part of the program is a FOR–NEXT loop (lines 70 to 110) in which the student's letter mark is determined. The statements in the loop are executed 6 times, once for each student. The first thing done in the loop is to read in the student's name and numbered grade.

---

*On the HP 2000C we would eliminate lines 40 to 60 and replace them with 40   LET A$ = "CBA", replace line 90 with LET I = M/10 − 6.5, and replace the A$ (I) in line 100 with A$(I,I).

276

SUBSCRIPTED STRING VARIABLES

```
10       REM CONVERTS NUMBER GRADE TO LETTER GRADE
20       DIM A$(3)
30       DATA HAROLD,83,TED,74,MARY,81,RITA,92,HANK,71,SAM,80
40       LET A$(1)="C"
50       LET A$(2)="B"
60       LET A$(3)="A"
70       FOR J=1 TO 6
80       READ N$,M
90       LET I=M/10-6
100      PRINT N$;"'S MARK IS ";A$(I)
110      NEXT J
120      END
```

Figure 8.1a. Program assigns a student's letter grade on the basis of his numerical grade. The computer makes this assignment by first converting (in line 90) the mark into the number 1, 2, or 3 and assigning it to I. Then it truncates the value of I in A$($I$) (in line 100). The value of A$($I$) is given by either line 40, 50, or 60.

This is done in

        80   **READ N$,M**

Here his name is assigned to N$ and his mark to M.

    Then in

        90   **LET I=M/10-6**

the subscript that will determine the student's letter grade is calculated. The first student processed is HAROLD. The status of the variable in the program at line 100 is shown in the table for Fig. 8.1a. We see from the first line

Line no.	N$	M	I	Element of A$ used	Mark
100	HAROLD	83	2.2	A$(2)	B

that HAROLD is assigned to N$ and 83 to M; and that the value of I is 2.2. Since I is a subscript, the computer then truncates it to 2. This is indicated by the fact that A$(2) appears under the column labeled "Element of A$ used." Thus the computer interprets line 100 as

    100   PRINT N$;" 'S MARK IS";A$(2)

Again, since the value of N$ is HAROLD and, since we see from line 50 that the value of A$(2) is B, the computer prints

    HAROLD'S MARK IS B

when line 100 is executed. This is shown in Fig. 8.1b.

    The second time the statements in the loop are executed, the computer assigns TED to N$ and 74 to M. In line 90, the computer calculates the value of I. We see from the second line of table that it is 1.4:

Line no.	N$	M	I	Element of A$ used	Mark
100	TED	74	1.4	A$(1)	C

Because I appears as a subscript, the computer truncates its value to 1. The computer now interprets line 100 as

    100   PRINT N$;" 'S MARK IS";A$(1)

Since the value of N$ is TED and that of A$(1) is C, the computer prints

    TED'S MARK IS C

when line 100 is executed, as is shown in Fig. 8.1b. When the other student's names and marks are processed by the computer, it produces the remaining lines of results shown in Fig. 8.1b.

Line no.	N$	M	I	Element of A$ used	Mark
100	HAROLD	83	2.3	A$(2)	B
100	TED	74	1.4	A$(1)	C
100	MARY	81	2.1	A$(2)	B
100	RITA	92	3.2	A$(3)	A
100	HANK	71	1.1	A$(1)	C
100	SAM	80	2	A$(2)	B

Table for Fig. 8.1a. The table shows how a student's mark, M, determines which element of A$, the computer will use, and thus which letter mark the student will receive.

```
RUN
HAROLD'S MARK IS B
TED'S MARK IS C
MARY'S MARK IS B
RITA'S MARK IS A
HANK'S MARK IS C
SAM'S MARK IS B
READY
```

Figure 8.1b. Running the program of Fig. 8.1a.

8.2.   More on Comparing Strings

Each character that appears on a teletypewriter key has been assigned a number in the compiler. The computer uses these numbers when it processes the characters in strings. The letters of the alphabet have been assigned higher numbers than the digits. Each successive letter of the alphabet has been assigned a higher number than the preceding letter. The blank is assigned the lowest number. Table 8.1 lists the characters in columns in the order given by the American Standard Code for Information Interchange (ASCII), starting with the one that has the lowest numerical equivalent—the blank—and proceeding to the one that has the highest numerical equivalent—the ↑ (some systems may use a different scheme, so we advise you to check the appendix of your manual for details). This feature of BASIC will enable us to compare strings in an IF statement.

Using Table 8.2, let us now investigate what happens when line 30 of the following two-line sequence

```
30    IF "B">"A" THEN 80
40    STOP
```

is executed. Since the number internally assigned to B in the computer is greater than that assigned to A, the condition in the IF statement is true. Thus the next statement that will be executed is line 80.

The relational operators $>=$ and $<=$ can also be used with strings. Thus after line 30 of the following two-line sequence

```
30    IF "B">="A"    THEN 80
40    STOP
```

is executed, the next statement executed would be line 80. The reason for this is that the $>$ part of the condition in line 30 is true. Similarly after line 30 of the following two-line sequence

```
30    IF"A"<="A" THEN 80
40    STOP
```

is executed, the next statement executed would be line 80. The reason for this is that the $=$ part of the condition in line 30 is true.

We see from Table 8.1 that each successive digit in ascending numerical order has been assigned a higher number. Thus when line 30 of the following two-line sequence

```
30    IF"2">"3" THEN 80
40    STOP
```

is executed, since the number internally assigned to the string "2" is smaller than the one assigned to the string "3," the condition in the IF statement is false. Thus the next line executed will be line 40.

The blank, i.e., "   ", has been assigned the lowest number of all the characters, thus when line 30 in the following two-line sequence

```
30    IF " "<"2" THEN 80
40    STOP
```

is executed, since the number internally assigned to "   " is smaller than the one assigned to the string "2", the condition in the IF statement is true. Thus the next line executed would be line 80.

A LIST OF CHARACTERS IN THE ORDER GIVEN BY ASCII

Lowest	space	5	J
	!	6	K
	"	7	L
	#	8	M
	$	9	N
	%	:	O
	&	;	P
	'	<	Q
	(	=	R
	)	>	S
	*	?	T
	+	@	U
	,	A	V
	-	B	W
	.	C	X
	/	D	Y
	Ø	E	Z
	1	F	[
	2	G	\
	3	H	]
	4	I	↑ *Highest*

Table 8.1. The teletypewriter characters that appear on the teletypewriter key listed in columns according to the order given by the American Standard Code for Information Interchange (ASCII). This is the order that is used when strings are compared. As you proceed down a column, the characters have higher values; as you proceed to the right (along a row), the characters have higher values. How this is used in an IF statement is shown in Table 8.2.

The computer compares strings consisting of more than one character in the same way as you would compare two words when alphabetizing them in a dictionary. Thus the condition

$$\texttt{"THINK">"THAT"}$$

is considered true since THINK would follow THAT in a dictionary. Similarly

$$\texttt{"THINKS">"THINK"}$$

is also considered true. On some systems, such as the CDC 6600 series, blanks included at the end of a string before the quotation marks—they are called trailing blanks—are considered significant. Thus

$$\texttt{"THINK ">"THINK"}$$

is considered true. All of this is summarized in Table 8.2. On some systems, trailing blanks are not considered significant, so

$$\texttt{"THINK "="THINK"}$$

is considered true.

COMPARING STRINGS IN IF STATEMENTS

Statements	Next statement
30 IF "B">"A" THEN 80 40 STOP	80
30 IF "2">"3" THEN 80 40 STOP	40
30 IF" "<"2" THEN 80 40 STOP	80
30 IF "B">="A" THEN 80 40 STOP	80
30 IF "A"<="A" THEN 80 40 STOP	80
30 IF "THINK">"THAT" THEN 80 40 STOP	80
30 IF"THINKS">"THINK" THEN 80 40 STOP	80

Table 8.2. Comparing strings in IF statements. The truth value of the comparisons is determined by how the numerical equivalents of the strings compare. The computer compares strings consisting of more than one character in the same way as you would compare two words when alphabetizing them in a dictionary.

We will now learn how to write a program that alphabetizes words. We will do this in two steps. The first step is to write a program shown in Fig. 8.2a which, if given a DATA statement consisting of a list of strings

```
20        DATA TED, JOE, BOB, BILL
```

will start by taking the first two strings in the list and, if necessary, will switch them so they will be in alphabetical order. Thus JOE would be switched with TED. Therefore, the modified list is JOE, TED, BOB, BILL. Then the program will take the second and third strings in the modified list (in this case they would now be TED and BOB and, if necessary, switch them so they too will be in alphabetical order. This process continues until the string with the highest alphabetical value is at the end of the list. Before we begin the switching, we assign all the strings in the DATA statement to the subscripted string variable W$.
This is done in

```
30        FOR R=1 TO 4
40        READ W$(R)
50        NEXT R
```

Therefore the value of W$(1) is TED, W$(2) is JOE, W$(3) is BOB and W$(4) is BILL. The alphabetizing is done in the loop

```
60        FOR I=1 TO 3
70        IF W$(I)<W$(I+1) THEN 110
80        LET S$=W$(I)
90        LET W$(I)=W$(I+1)
100       LET W$(I+1)=S$
110       NEXT I
```

The first time this loop is executed, the value of I is 1. Therefore the computer interprets line 70 as

```
70   IF W$(1)<W$(2)   THEN 110
```

The strings assigned to W$(1) and W$(2) at this point are given in the left side of the first line of the table for Fig. 8.2a:

Line no.	I	W$(I)	W$(I+1)
70	1	TED	JOE

Since W$(1) is TED and W$(2) is JOE, the condition in line 70 is false. Therefore, the computer next executes line 80 where it performs the first step in interchanging the subscripts of TED and JOE. It interprets line 80 as

```
80   LET S$=W$(1)
```

and since the value of W$(1) is TED, it stores TED in S$. It interprets line 90 as

```
90   LET W$(1)=W$(2)
```

and thus stores JOE, which was originally stored in W$(2), in W$(1). It interprets line 100 as

```
100 LET W$(2)=S$
```

and thus stores TED the value of S$ in W$(2). The strings assigned to W$(1) and W$(2) now are given in the right side of the first line of the table for Fig. 8.2a:

Line no.	I	W$(I)	W$(I+1)
110	1	JOE	TED

SORTING STRINGS (FIRST STEP)

```
10      REM STEP 1 IN SORTING NAMES
20      DATA TED,JOE,BOB,BILL
30      FOR R=1 TO 4
40      READ W$(R)
50      NEXT R
60      FOR I=1 TO 3
70      IF W$(I)<W$(I+1) THEN 110
80      LET S$=W$(I)
90      LET W$(I)=W$(I+1)
100     LET W$(I+1)=S$
110     NEXT I
120     FOR T=1 TO 4
130     PRINT W$(T)
140     NEXT T
150     END
```

Figure 8.2a. Program interchanges adjacent strings in the DATA statement according to their alphabetical order. The interchanging is done toward the right of the list of strings so that the order of the final list is: JOE, BOB, BILL, TED. This program is the first step in a two-step sequence that will alphabetize the strings.

Original List: TED, JOE, BOB, BILL

Line no.	I	W$(I)	W$(I+1)	Line no.	I	W$(I)	W$(I+1)
70	1	TED	JOE	110	1	JOE	TED
70	2	TED	BOB	110	2	BOB	TED
70	3	TED	BILL	110	3	BILL	TED

Final List: JOE, BOB, BILL, TED

Table for Fig. 8.2a. The table shows how adjacent strings are alphabetized. In 70 IF W$(I)<W$(I+1) THEN 110 the strings are compared. At line 110, adjacent strings have already been alphabetized.

The order of the names in W\$ is now JOE, TED, BOB, BILL. Therefore the positions of TED and JOE have been interchanged. The second time the loop is executed the value of I is 2. Thus in line 70 W\$(2) and W\$(3) (ie., TED and BOB), are compared. Since the alphabetical value of TED is greater than that of BOB, the two strings are interchanged. Thus the order of the names in W\$ at the end of this execution of the statements in the loop is: JOE, BOB, TED, BILL. The third time the loop is executed, W\$(3) and W\$(4) (i.e., TED and BILL) are compared. Since the value of TED is greater than the value of BILL, the two strings are interchanged. Thus the order of the names in W\$ at the end of this execution of the statements in the loop is: JOE, BOB, BILL, TED.

This final order of the words in W\$ is printed when

```
120     FOR T=1 TO 4
130     PRINT W$(T)
140     NEXT T
```

are executed. It is JOE, BOB, BILL, TED as is shown in Fig. 8.2b.

Notice that although there were four strings in the DATA statement, we only had to execute the statements in the loop three times. The reason for this is that it takes only three interchanges to make the first word the last.

When a beginner writes a program like this, often he is tempted to write the interchange shown in lines 80 to 100 in two lines instead of three, i.e.,

```
90   LET W$(I)=W$(I+1)
100 LET W$(I+1)=W$(I)
```

This is wrong, as we will now show. Let us assume that the value of W\$(I+1) is JOE and W\$(I) is TED before these lines are executed. When line 90 is executed, JOE is assigned to W\$(I). When line 100 is executed, W\$(I) (which is now JOE) is assigned to W\$(I+1). Now, not only is the value of W\$(I), JOE, but the value of W\$(I+1) is also JOE. For this reason, we had to use another variable, S\$, to enable us to make the interchange correctly.

```
RUN
JOE
BOB
BILL
TED
READY
```

Figure 8.2b. Results of running the program of Fig. 8.2a. We see that TED has been placed (by three interchanges) at the end of the list.

At the end of the program shown in Fig. 8.2a, we have not alphabetized the names in the DATA statement. All we succeeded in doing was to place TED, the name which has the "highest value" at the end of the list. How do we alphabetize the entire list? The most natural way to do this is to repeat the entire comparison and interchanging procedure to our final list until all the strings are in alphabetical order. We can do this by simply placing the I loop of the present program in an outer loop, so that the entire I loop is itself executed 3 times. We do this in the program of Fig. 8.3a. The outer loop (the K loop) starts in line 55 and ends in line 115 as is shown in Fig. 8.3a. Other than this outer loop, the programs shown in Figs. 8.2a and 8.3a are identical. Let us now see how the program in Fig. 8.3a works.

After the first time the inner loop is executed, the order of the names in the list is the same as it was at the end of the last program:

JOE,BOB,BILL,TED

Thus the last name is in the correct position for the entire list to be in alphabetical order. Therefore, the second time the inner loop is executed, we really have to compare only two sets of names: JOE and BOB, then JOE and BILL. However, in order to make the program easier to understand, we have written the FOR statement in the inner loop as FOR I = 1 TO 3, so that it compares all three sets of names each time the inner loop is executed. After the second time the inner loop is executed, the order of the names in the list is

BOB,BILL,JOE,TED

Thus the last two names are in the correct positions for the entire list to be in alphabetical order. Therefore the third time the inner loop is executed we have only to compare the first set of names: BOB and BILL. But, as we have mentioned before, we have written the program so that it compares all three sets of names. After the inner loop has been executed for the third time, the names are in alphabetical order. We see that this is so, when we run the program, as is shown in Fig. 8.3b.

The same procedure we just followed to place strings in alphabetical order can be used to place a set of numbers in ascending order. In fact, once you have rewritten the DATA statement so that it contains numbers instead of strings, all you have to do is remove all the dollar signs from the program in Fig. 8.3, and, presto, you have the required program.

SORTING STRINGS (SECOND STEP)

```
10          REM SORTS NAMES IN ALPHABETICAL ORDER
20          DATA TED,JOE,BOB,BILL
30          FOR R=1 TO 4
40          READ W$(R)
50          NEXT R
55          FOR K=1 TO 3
60          FOR I=1 TO 3
70          IF W$(I)<W$(I+1) THEN 110
80          LET S$=W$(I)
90          LET W$(I)=W$(I+1)
100         LET W$(I+1)=S$
110         NEXT I
115         NEXT K
120         FOR T=1 TO 4
130         PRINT W$(T)
140         NEXT T
150         END
```

Figure 8.3a. This program alphabetizes the strings in the DATA statement. The I loop of the last program (here lines 60 to 110) is executed three times, so that the final order of the strings in the list is alphabetized.

```
RUN
BILL
BOB
JOE
TED
READY
```

Figure 8.3b. Running the program of Fig. 8.3a. The names are now in alphabetical order.

8.3. Substrings

There is another system in use for processing strings. One computer it is used on is the HP 2000C.

This system allows you to refer not only to the entire string, but also to only parts of the string—called substrings. This feature is very useful, as we shall see. However, it has a major drawback in that it is very difficult to use different strings as components of one subscripted string variable as we did quite simply in the preceding string programs.*

A requirement of this system is that one *must* dimension each string variable to which a string containing more than one character has been assigned. The dimension must be greater than or equal to the number of characters in the string. Thus if we write

$$30 \quad \text{LET A\$="JOHN"}$$

as is shown in Fig. 8.4a since JOHN has 4 characters in it, we must dimension A$ in a DIM statement as DIM A$(4), as is shown in line 20 of this figure. If your computer does not use this system you may wish to skip this discussion and proceed to Section 8.4.

When A$ is subscripted, e.g., A$(2), as in 40   PRINT A$(2), it refers to the substring consisting of the second character to the last character of A$. Thus this statement produces the substring OHN as shown in Fig. 8.4b. Similarly the statement 50   PRINT A$(3) produces the substring consisting of the third character to the last character of A$. Thus it produces the substring HN, as is also seen in Fig. 8.4b.

If you use a second subscript you can reference substrings that do not end with the last character of the string. Just as the first subscript determines what the first character will be in the substring, the second subscript determines what the last character will be in the substring. Thus A$(1,3) references JOH. If you want to refer to only one character, e.g., the second one, you must write A$(2,2). We can now see why 60   PRINT A$(1,3), A$(2,2), A$(1,1), A$(2,4) produces

        JOH   O   J   OHN

as is shown in Fig. 8.4b.

---

* BASIC on the **XEROX** Sigma 5–9 computers, however, allows you to use substrings, and also to use different strings as components of a given subscripted string variable.

SUBSTRINGS

```
10    REM USE OF SUBSTRINGS
20    DIM A$(4)
30    LET A$="JOHN"
40    PRINT A$(2)
50    PRINT A$(3)
60    PRINT A$(1,3),A$(2,2),A$(1,1),A$(2,4)
70    END
```

Figure 8.4a. This program shows use of substrings on the HP 2000C. A$(2) is the substring. consisting of the characters of A$ from the second character to the last character. A$(2,4) is the substring consisting of the characters of A$ from the second to the fourth. A$(2,2) is the second character of A$. All strings that have more than one character must be dimensioned.

```
RUN
OHN
HN
JOH              O              J              OHN
READY
```

Figure 8.4b. Running the program of Fig. 8.4a.

We now employ this system in a program shown in Fig. 8.5a. This program, if given a person's name, will print his weight. Thus once you supply this program with a person's name in

```
50   INPUT B$
```

the program searches the DATA statements

```
30   DATA "JOHN 165","MARY 125","JILL 119"
35   DATA "MIKE 165","BILL 160"
```

(which are composed of strings that contain a person's name and weight, e.g. JOHN 165) for the person's name. It then prints the person's name and weight.

The person's name and weight are assigned to A$ in

```
70   READ A$
```

Since the person's name constitutes the first four letters of the string, it is referred to as A$(1,4). Since the weight is represented by the sixth to the last characters in the string, it can be referred to as A$(6). The statement in the R loop

```
80   IF B$=A$(1,4) THEN 120
```

tests for the person's name you wish to find. If the name is in the DATA statement the computer next executes

```
120   PRINT A$(1,4);"'S WEIGHT IS ";A$(6);" LBS."
```

where, as you recall, A$(6) is the weight. If the name is not there, then the computer executes line 100, thereby printing

```
CAN'T FIND NAME
```

When we run the program, we type the name JILL (as is shown in Fig. 8.5b). This is assigned to B$. On the third execution of the loop, A$(1,4) also equals JILL as seen in the third line of the table for Fig. 8.5a

Line no.	B$	A$	A$(1,4)	A$(6)	Next line
80	JILL	JILL 119	JILL	119	120

The condition in the IF statement   80 IF B$=A$ THEN 120 is therefore true. So the next statement executed is line 120. Since A$(6) is the string 119, line 120 produces the result

```
JILL'S WEIGHT IS 119 LBS.
```

as is seen in Fig. 8.5b. The punctuations in the result are produced by the strings in the PRINT statement (line 120). The next statement executed after the PRINT is the RESTORE statement. This enables the program to search for more names, as we see in Fig. 8.5b. We end the program by hitting the BREAK key.

USING SUBSTRINGS

```
10    REM FINDS PERSON'S WEIGHT
20    DIM A$(8),B$(4)
30    DATA "JOHN 165","MARY 125","JILL 119"
35    DATA "MIKE 165","BILL 160"
40    PRINT "TYPE NAME TO FIND WEIGHT";
50    INPUT B$
60    FOR R=1 TO 5
70    READ A$
80    IF B$=A$(1,4) THEN 120
90    NEXT R
100   PRINT "CAN'T FIND NAME"
110   GOTO 130
120   PRINT A$(1,4);"'S WEIGHT IS ";A$(6);" LBS."
130   RESTORE
140   GOTO 40
150   END
RUN
```

Figure 8.5a. Each string in the DATA statement contains a person's name and weight. A$(1,4) contains the person's name; A$(6) contains the person's weight. Program searches DATA statement for a person's name. If it is found, the program prints the person's weight.

Line no.	B$	A$	A$(1,4)	A$(6)	Next line
80	JILL	JOHN 165	JOHN	165	90
80	JILL	MARY 125	MARY	125	90
80	JILL	JILL 119	JILL	119	120

Table for Fig. 8.5a. How 80 IF B$=A$ (1,4) THEN 120 works. Also shown are A$(1,4) and A$(6), two substrings of A$. When B$=A$(1,4) the computer leaves the R loop. This is the case when B$=JILL and A$=JILL 119.

```
TYPE NAME TO FIND WEIGHT?JILL
JILL'S WEIGHT IS 119 LBS.
TYPE NAME TO FIND WEIGHT?JOHN
JOHN'S WEIGHT IS 165 LBS.
TYPE NAME TO FIND WEIGHT?SAM
CAN'T FIND NAME
TYPE NAME TO FIND WEIGHT?MARY
MARY'S WEIGHT IS 125 LBS.
TYPE NAME TO FIND WEIGHT?
READY
```

Figure 8.5b. Running the program of Fig. 8.5a. The program, after being given a person's name—the first name given is JILL—finds the person's weight. You stop the program by pressing the appropriate key on the teletypewriter. For instance, on the HP 2000C you must press the CTRL and the C keys simultaneously.

8.4. Subroutines

Sometimes it is necessary to perform the same calculation many times in a program. instead of doing this, it is more convenient to perform the calculation at one part of the program and then transfer the execution to that part of the program whenever the calculation is required. The part of the program just discussed is called a subroutine. The GO SUB statement changes the ordinary order in which the statements in the program are executed and transfers the execution to the subroutine. Another way of saying this is that the GO SUB statement "transfers control" to the subroutine; the process is called "calling a subroutine." GO SUB is an abbreviation for GO TO SUBroutine.

GO SUB

> The form of the GO SUB statement is: line number; followed by the words GO SUB; followed by the line number at which the subroutine starts. Example GO SUB 40.

If the subroutine ends with a RETURN statement, control is automatically transferred back to the statement that follows the GO SUB statement which called the subroutine. If the subroutine does not end with a RETURN, the next statement executed is the statement that follows the subroutine in the program.

RETURN

> The form of the RETURN statement is: statement number; followed by the word RETURN. Example: 60 RETURN.

In Fig. 8.6a we present a program that calculates the product of the integers from 1 to M, where M is a number given by the READ statement. This product, as you remember, is called M!. This program could have been written without using subroutines; however, we will use it as an example of how the GO SUB and RETURN statements work. The subroutine calculates the product of the numbers from 1 to M and thus consists of the statements

```
90    LET P=1
100   FOR J=1 TO M
110   LET P=P*J
120   NEXT J
130   PRINT "M=";M;"M!=";P
140   RETURN
```

USING THE GO SUB STATEMENT

```
10    REM SHOWS USE OF GO SUB
20    READ N
30    LET M=N
40    GOSUB 90
50    READ L
60    LET M=L
70    GOSUB 90
80    STOP
90    LET P=1
100   FOR J=1 TO M
110   LET P=P*J
120   NEXT J
130   PRINT "M=";M;"M!=";P
140   RETURN
150   DATA 4,8
160   END
```

Figure 8.6a. Program calculates the product N! using the GO SUB and the RETURN statements. The GO SUB 90 transfers control to line 90. The RETURN transfers control to the statement that follows GO SUB, i.e., line 50 and then later line 80.

Line no.	Time executed	Next line
140	1st	50
140	2nd	80

Table for Fig. 8.6a. The statement 140 RETURN transfers control to the statement that follows the GO SUB statement that last called the subroutine.

After, 4, the first number read by the program, is assigned to N in 20   READ N, we must assign it to M before the subroutine is called. We do this in   30 LET M=N. The next statement,   40 GO SUB 90, transfers control to line 90, the first statement in the subroutine. Since we have already assigned the number 4 to M, the computer has no difficulty evaluating 100 FOR J=1 TO M. The product 4! is calculated and then printed in line 130

$$M= \ 4 \qquad M! = \ 24$$

as is shown in Fig. 8.6b. Then   140 RETURN, transfers control to   50 READ L, the statement after the GO SUB that called the subroutine. This is indicated in the table for Fig. 8.6a. In line 50, the number 8 is assigned to L. Again we must reassign the value of L just read, to M, before the subroutine is called. We do this in   60 LET M=L (if we did not do this, the value of M in the subroutine would be the previous one and thus the subroutine would calculate 4! again). Then   70 GO SUB 90, transfers control again to the subroutine. Now it calculates 8!, and the result is printed by line 130

$$M= \ 8 \qquad M! = \ 40320$$

as is shown in Fig. 8.6b. This time the RETURN statement transfers control to   80 STOP, and the program stops.

We will now use the same subroutine in a program that calculates the binominal coefficient

$$\binom{N}{R} = \frac{N!}{(N-R)! \cdot R!}$$

The symbol $\binom{N}{R}$ is also called a combination symbol. It tells us how many different ways we can choose R objects from a total of N objects, regardless of the order in which we choose the R objects. Thus we can use this symbol to determine how many different 5-card hands we can obtain from a desk of 52 cards. Here $R=5$ and $N=52$ so $\binom{N}{R} = \binom{52}{5} = \frac{52!}{47! \times 5!}$ or approximately 2,600,000.

```
RUN
M= 4      M!= 24
M= 8      M!= 40320
READY
```

Figure 8.6b. Running the program of Fig. 8.6a.

In evaluating $\binom{N}{R}$, we calculate the same type of product—a factorial—3 times. It is in cases like this that subroutines are invaluable.* The program shown in Fig. 8.7a calculates the binominal coefficient $\binom{10}{4}$. Because we are limited in the program to writing expressions on one line, we will write $\binom{10}{4}$ as (10,4). The three products (or factorials) are all calculated in the same subroutine we used in the preceding program. In the present program, this subroutine extends from line 150 to line 190

```
150   LET P=1
160   FOR J=1 TO M
170   LET P=P*J
180   NEXT J
190   RETURN
```

In the beginning of the program, a number is assigned to N and one to R in:

```
30   READ N,R
```

Since the subroutine is written to calculate the product of the numbers from 1 to M, we must assign the value of N to M. This is done in   40 LET M=N. Then control is transferred to the subroutine. Since the value of M is now the same as the value of N, the subroutine actually calculates N factorial. It assigns it to P. Then the statement, 190 RETURN, automatically transfers control to   60 LET N1=P, as is shown in the table for Fig. 8.7a. Here N ! is stored in N1 for later use in calculating the binominal coefficient. Now the program is ready to calculate R !. Again, since the subroutine is written to calculate the product of the numbers from 1 to M, the value of R is assigned to M in   70 LET M=R. Control is then transferred to the subroutine. The subroutine calculates R ! and assigns it to P. Control is then transferred to line 90, where the value of R ! is assigned to N2 for later use in the calculation. The program is now ready to calculate (N−R) !. In statement 100, the value of N−R is assigned to M in   100 LET M=N−R, and control is transferred to subroutine for the last time. The subroutine calculates (N−R) ! and assigns it to P. Since the binomial coefficient will be calculated next, there is no need to store the value of P in another variable. We will use P directly in the next statement executed

```
120   PRINT "(";N;",";R;")=";N1/(N2*P)
```

When the program is run, as shown in Fig. 8.7b it produces the results:

```
( 10    , 4    )= 210
```

At first glance it might seem that the statements connected with using a subroutine are purely camouflage; i.e., it might appear that the GO SUB and RETURN statements could be replaced by two GO TO statements. After a little thought, we realize that this is wrong. The RETURN statement in line 190 first returns control to line 60, then to line 90, and finally to line 120, as is indicated in the table for Fig. 8.7a. One GO TO statement could never do that.

* There is a more efficient way of evaluating $\binom{N}{R}$, but it does not demonstrate the power of a subroutine, so we will not discuss it here.

CALCULATING THE BINOMIAL COEFFICIENT

```
10    REM CALCULATES BINOMIAL
15    REM COEFFICIENT (N,R)
20    DATA 10,4
30    READ N,R
40    LET M=N
50    GOSUB 150
60    LET N1=P
70    LET M=R
80    GOSUB 150
90    LET N2=P
100   LET M=N-R
110   GOSUB 150
120   PRINT "(";N;",";R;")=";N1/(N2*P)
130   STOP
140   REM FACTORIAL SUBROUTINE*****
150   LET P=1
160   FOR J=1 TO M
170   LET P=P*J
180   NEXT J
190   RETURN
200   END
```

Figure 8.7a. Program calculates $N!/(N–R)!R!$
The <u>subroutine</u> is the same as in the last program. It is called three times: once to calculate $N!$; once to calculate $R!$ and finally to calculate $(N–R)!$. The statement 190 RETURN, transfers control to the statement that follows the GO SUB statement that just called the subroutine.

Line no.	Time executed	M	P (or $M!$)	Next line
190	1st	10	10!	60
190	2nd	4	4!	90
190	3rd	6	6!	120

Table for Fig. 8.7a. The table shows which statement is executed after 190 RETURN. It also shows the values of M and P (which equals $M!$) after each time the subroutine is executed.

```
RUN
( 10  , 4   )= 210
READY
```

Figure 8.7b. Running the program of Fig. 8.7a.

Other facts about subroutines are as follows:

1. You may use more than one RETURN statement in a subroutine if you wish to leave the subroutine from one of many points.

2. One subroutine may call another. This is called "nesting" subroutines.

3. On most systems a subroutine may not call itself. Another way of saying this is that a subroutine may not be called recursively.*

4. On most systems, if the subroutine starts with a nonexecutable statement, e.g., a REM, the first statement executed will be the one that follows the nonexecutable statement. Also, if the RETURN statement transfers control to a nonexecutable statement, the statement executed will be the one that follows this nonexecutable statement. We will see examples of this in the next program.

Subroutines are sometimes used to facilitate the reading of programs by dividing a program into easy to read sections, or modules. This process is called the modularization of program. We now use subroutines to modularize the program shown in Fig. 7.12a. That program took an inventory of different items in stock. The modularized program appears in Fig. 8.8a. We have divided the program into three subroutines.

The first subroutine is called in line 50. It assigns zeros to all the counters: it begins in line 110. The RETURN statement in line 140 of this subroutine transfers control to line 60, but since this is a REM statement, the next statement executed is

```
70   GOSUB 160
```

which is obviously another GO SUB statement. This calls the second subroutine.

The second subroutine, which begins in line 160, reads all the items and then determines which counter to use. The RETURN statement at the end of this subroutine transfers control to line 90, which is another GO SUB statement:

```
90   GOSUB 230
```

This statement calls the third subroutine.

The third subroutine prints the results. Since the program ends at the end of this subroutine we have not ended this subroutine with a RETURN but have simply terminated it with an END. We have altered the PRINT statement that was in Fig. 7.12a, so that in this subroutine it appears as

```
240   PRINT "ITEM";1000+Q;":";K[Q];"IN STOCK"
```

The expression $1000+Q$ will print the item number so that there is no space in it. This is shown in Fig. 8.8b when the program is run.

---

* On the CDC 6600 series, however, subroutines may call themselves.

REWRITING THE INVENTORY PROGRAM USING SUBROUTINES

```
10    REM TAKES AN INVENTORY OF
20    REM ITEMS IN STOCK
30    DATA 1001,1002,1002,1003,1004,1003,1001
40    REM  CALL SUBROUTINE WHICH ZEROES COUNTERS
50    GOSUB 110
60    REM CALL SUBROUTINE WHICH READS ITEMS AND THEN
65    REM DETERMINES WHICH COUNTER TO USE
70    GOSUB 160
80    REM CALL SUBROUTINE WHICH PRINTS THE AMOUNT OF
85    REM EACH ITEM IN STOCK
90    GOSUB 230
100   REM******************************************
110   FOR R=1 TO 4
120   LET K(R)=0
130   NEXT R
140   RETURN
150   REM*******************************************
160   FOR I=1 TO 7
170   READ X
180   LET S=X-1000
190   LET K[S]=K(S)+1
200   NEXT I
210   RETURN
220   REM********************************************
230   FOR Q=1 TO 4
240   PRINT "ITEM";1000+Q;":";K(Q);"IN STOCK"
250   NEXT Q
260   END
```

Figure 8.8a. Program takes an inventory of items in stock. It is the same as the program of Fig. 7.12a, but we have divided it into three parts by using subroutines. In line 240, first we print the item number by calculating 1000+Q. This means that the item number will be printed without any spaces in it (as opposed to Fig. 7.12b). Then the value of the counter $K(Q)$ is printed.

```
RUN
ITEM 1001    : 2     IN STOCK
ITEM 1002    : 2     IN STOCK
ITEM 1003    : 2     IN STOCK
ITEM 1004    : 1     IN STOCK
READY
```

Figure 8.8b. Results of Fig. 8.8a are the same as those of Fig. 7.12a, as we see.

8.5.   User-Defined Functions

The functions that we used until now were built into the system and were called library functions. Each library function activates a program that does a specific task. In this section we will show how programmers can write their own functions. To facilitate defining the terms associated with a function and describing how to use a function we will briefly discuss the square root function.

In algebra we could define the square root function as

$$S(X) = X^{1/2}$$

Subsequently, we would replace $S(X)$, everytime we saw it in an expression, with $X^{1/2}$ before we evaluated the expression. Thus if we saw the following expression

$$Y = 3 \cdot S(X) + Z \cdot S(X)$$

We would interpret it as

$$Y = 3 \cdot X^{1/2} + Z \cdot X^{1/2}$$

If we had wished to, we could have called the square root function, F. The function F would be defined as $F(X) = X^{1/2}$. We would then replace $F(X)$ by $X^{1/2}$ everytime we saw $F(X)$ in an expression. Thus given

$$Y = 2 \cdot F(X) + 3 \cdot F(X)$$

we would interpret it as

$$Y = 2 \cdot X^{1/2} + 3 \cdot X^{1/2}$$

We learn from this that the name we give a function is immaterial; what is important is how we define the function. Once we have named a function we must always refer to the function by that name.

We now define the terms associated with the use of a function. Given

$$F(X) = X^{1/2}$$

the expression, $X^{1/2}$ is called the function; X, as we remember, is called the **argument** of the function, and F is called the **function name**.

We now define another function

$$G(X) = X + 4$$

Here, $X + 4$ is the function, G is the function name, and X is the argument of the function. If we replace the argument in the function name with another argument, the argument is changed in the function as well. Thus when we replace X with Y in this function [i.e., write $G(Y)$], then the function is defined in terms of Y

$$G(Y) = Y + 4$$

User-defined functions in BASIC are used the same way as functions are used in algebra. However, there is one difference: The function name in BASIC must consist of three characters. The first two are the letters FN. The third character in the name must be a letter. Thus the BASIC programmer has 26 function names to chose from, and thus can define 26 different functions. In a program, the argument of the function does not have to be a variable. It could be a number, an expression involving a calculation, a subscripted variable, or another function. For example, if we define `FNB(X)=X+4`, then `FNB(3)=3+4`, or 7, and `FNB(SQR(T))=SQR(T)+4`. If we wish to use a function in a program, we must define it in a DEF statement.

DEF

The form of the DEF statement is: line number; followed by DEF, followed by the function name; followed by (; followed by a variable; followed by) = ; followed by the function written in terms of that variable. Functions may be defined in terms of other user-defined functions which have been previously defined or in terms of library functions. The DEF statement in most systems must be placed in a line that precedes the line where the function is used. Each function must be defined in a different DEF statement. Examples:

```
10    DEF FNA(T)=T↑2+2
20    DEF FNR(L)=SIN(L)+2*COS(L)
30    DEF FNX(A)=SQR(A)+FNR(A)
```

In Fig. 8.9a we present a program in which we use the function FNR to calculate the area of a square. The function is defined in

$$20 \quad DEF \ FNR(L)=L*L$$

The DEF statement is not executed, it is referred to when the function is used later in the program.

In statement 30

$$30 \quad PRINT \ FNR(6),6$$

the computer evaluates FNR(6). It does this by referring to line 20, where the function FNR(L) is defined.It substitutes 6 for L in L*L and thus determines that FNR(6)=6*6 or 36. It then prints the result in line 30. Then in the loop

```
40    FOR I=1 TO 5
50    PRINT FNR(I),I
60    NEXT I
```

the computer calculates and then prints the area of squares the sides of which are 1, 2, 3, 4, and 5. The first time line 50 is executed, since the value of I is 1 the computer interprets the function as FNR(1). It then evaluates FNR(1) as 1*1. All of this is shown in the first line of the table for Fig. 8.9a.

Line no.	Time executed	I	Format FNR(I)	Value of FNR(I)
50	1st	1	FNR(1)	1*1 or 1

Each time line 50 is executed, the computer evaluates FNR(I) for the current value of I and and prints the results. The results are shown in Fig. 8.9b.

USING FUNCTIONS

```
10    REM USE OF FUNCTION
15    PRINT "AREA OF SQUARE","LENGTH OF SIDE"
20    DEF FNR(L)=L*L
30    PRINT FNR(6),6
40    FOR I=1 TO 5
50    PRINT FNR(I),I
60    NEXT I
70    END
```

Figure 8.9a. The function FNR, is defined in statement 20. Whenever FNR appears in the program, the computer refers to line 20 and evaluates the function for the given argument. A function name must begin with the letters FN followed by a letter of the alphabet.

Line no.	Time executed	I	Form of FNR(I)	Value of FNR(I)
50	1st	1	FNR(1)	1*1 or 1
50	2nd	2	FNR(2)	2*2 or 4
50	3rd	3	FNR(3)	3*3 or 6
50	4th	4	FNR(4)	4*4 or 16
50	5th	5	FNR(5)	5*5 or 25

Table for Fig. 8.9a. How FNR(I) is evaluated in line 50 for different values of I. The computer refers to line 20 for the definition of FNR.

```
RUN
AREA OF SQUARE  LENGTH OF SIDE
   36              6
    1              1
    4              2
    9              3
   16              4
   25              5
READY
```

Figure 8.9b. Running the program of Fig. 8.9a.

In Fig. 8.10a we show a program in which the same function we used to calculate the area of a square in the last program is now itself used in a calculation. The program calculates the value of a rectangular prism which has a 3×3 square for a base and a height of 10. The volume of the prism is calculated in

$$30 \quad \text{LET V=10*FNR(3)}$$

When the program is run, we obtain the results shown in Fig. 8.10b.

USING A FUNCTION IN A CALCULATION

```
10    REM CALCULATES VOLUME OF PRISM
20    DEF FNR(L)=L*L
30    LET V=10*FNR(3)
40    PRINT "VOLUME=";V;"FOR 3*3*10 PRISM"
50    END
```

Figure 8.10a. The function FNR (which calculates the area of a square) <u>is now used in line 30 in a calculation of the volume of a prism.</u>

```
RUN
VOLUME= 90    FOR 3*3*10 PRISM
READY
```

Figure 8.10b. Running the program of Fig. 8.10a.

We now use a function, in writing the program shown in Fig. 8.11a, that produces a table of values for any function that the user defines. The program begins at line 30 by typing

```
TO DEFINE A NEW FUNCTION TYPE Y; ELSE TYPE N.
```

You type Y. The program then executes lines 60 to 90 and prints:

```
TYPE YOUR FUNCTION AS A FUNCTION OF X, AFTER YOU TYPE
20 DEF FNA(X)=
THEN HIT THE RETURN KEY AND FINALLY TYPE THE COMMAND RUN
```

All of this is shown in Fig. 8.11b when the program is run. The program then terminates at line 100 and **READY** is typed. Anything you type now which starts with a line number will be considered to be a statement in a program. Let us say you want the table for the function $F(X) = X^2$. Following the computer's instructions, you would type

```
20   DEF FNA(X)=X↑2
```

as is shown at the top of Fig. 8.11c. What you have just done is to replace the old line 20 in the program of figure 8.11a with a new line that defines your function.

PRODUCING A TABLE OF VALUES FOR ANY FUNCTION

```
10    REM PRINTS A TABLE OF VALUES FOR ANY FUNCTION
20    DEF FNA(X)=X
30    PRINT "TO DEFINE A NEW FUNCTION TYPE Y; ELSE TYPE N."
40    INPUT A$
50    IF A$="N" THEN 110
60    PRINT "TYPE YOUR FUNCTION AS A FUNCTION OF X, AFTER YOU TYPE"
70    PRINT "20 DEF FNA(X)="
80    PRINT "THEN HIT THE RETURN KEY AND FINALLY";
90    PRINT " TYPE THE COMMAND RUN"
100   STOP
110   PRINT "WHAT ARE THE MINIMUM,MAXIMUM AND INCREASE IN X"
120   INPUT X1,X2,D
130   FOR I=X1 TO X2 STEP D
140   PRINT "X=";I;"F(X)=";FNA(I)
150   NEXT I
160   END
```

Figure 8.11a. The program prints a table of values for any function. The user types the function after the program stops at line 100. Since the user first types 20 DEF FNA(X) = and then the function, the definition of the function becomes part of the program.

```
RUN
TO DEFINE A NEW FUNCTION TYPE Y; ELSE TYPE N.
?Y
TYPE YOUR FUNCTION AS A FUNCTION OF X, AFTER YOU TYPE
20 DEF FNA(X)=
THEN HIT THE RETURN KEY AND FINALLY TYPE THE COMMAND RUN
READY
```

Figure 8.11b. The program asks whether we want to define a new function, we type Y for YES. It instructs us how to do this, stops and then types READY.

```
20 DEF FNA(X)=X↑2
```

Figure 8.11c. In response to these instruction, we type: 20 DEF FNA(X) = X $\uparrow$ 2. This becomes part of our program—it replaces the previous function in line 20.

You then type the command RUN and the program starts again and types in Fig. 8.11d:

TO DEFINE A NEW FUNCTION TYPE Y; ELSE TYPE N.

This time, since you already have defined your function, you type N and the program skips to line 110, where it prints

WHAT ARE THE MINIMUM,MAXIMUM AND INCREASE IN X

You type in -10, 10, 2. These are assigned to $X1$, $X2$, and D, respectively, in line 120. The computer then interprets line 130 as

130   FOR I=-10 TO 10 STEP 2

and executes the FOR-NEXT loop. The first time line 140 is executed, the computer interprets it as

140   PRINT "X";-10;"F(X)=";FNA(-10)

It refers to line 20 for the definition of FNA and determines that $FNA(-10)$ is $(-10)^2$ or 100. It types the results as shown in the first line of the tabulation of results shown in Fig. 8.11d. Each additional time line 140 is executed, the computer prints a new line of results, as is shown in the rest of Fig. 8.11d.

```
RUN
TO DEFINE A NEW FUNCTION TYPE Y; ELSE TYPE N.
?N
WHAT ARE THE MINIMUM,MAXIMUM AND INCREASE IN X
?-10,10,2
X=-10    F(X)= 100
X=-8     F(X)= 64
X=-6     F(X)= 36
X=-4     F(X)= 16
X=-2     F(X)= 4
X= 0     F(X)= 0
X= 2     F(X)= 4
X= 4     F(X)= 16
X= 6     F(X)= 36
X= 8     F(X)= 64
X= 10    F(X)= 100
READY
```

Figure 8.11d. This time when the program asks whether we want to define a new program, we type N for NO. The next line executed in the program is line 110, and the computer produces the results for the function we typed in.

8.6.   Monte Carlo Techniques: Simulating a Shuffled Deck of Cards

We now discuss a program that will use the random number generator to produce a shuffled deck of cards. We shall write this program in two steps. The first step will produce the integers (whole numbers) from 1 to 52 in random order. The second step will contain the first as a subroutine, but instead of producing random numbers, it will produce cards in a random order, i.e., produce a shuffled deck of cards. The method we describe here is efficient only when it generates the first few random numbers (cards). However, we present this method here because students have found this method relatively easy to understand. Let us now investigate the first step, which is shown in Fig. 8.12a.

We use two subscripted variables in this program, each of which has a dimension of 52. One of them, $X(I)$, ensures that none of the 52 random numbers generated will be the same. Thus, none of the 52 cards in the shuffled deck will be the same. $X(I)$ has the value 1 if the number represented by I has already been generated. It has the value of 0, if the number represented by its subscript has not yet been generated. For example, if 14 were the number just generated, then $X(14)$ would equal 1 if 14 has been previously generated; and would equal 0, if 14 has not been previously generated.

The other subscripted variable, $M(I)$, at the completion of the program will contain 52 numbers in random order, it will thus contain the equivalent of the shuffled cards.

The program works as follows. All the components of $M(I)$ and $X(I)$ are set equal to zero in

```
130     FOR I=1 TO 52
140     LET M(I)=X(I)=0
150     NEXT I
```

The random integers from 1 to 52 are generated in

```
170     LET R=INT(RND(0)*52)+1
```

The next statement uses the subscripted variable X to check whether R, the random number just generated, has been generated before

```
180     IF X(R)=1 THEN 170
```

If it has, then $X(R)$ would equal 1. The computer would then return to line 170 and generate another number. If it has not been generated before, then $X(R)$ equals 0 and 190   LET $X(R)=1$, is executed. This statement records the fact that this new number, R, has been generated by setting $X(R)$ equal to 1. The next statement executed determines how many new numbers have been generated

```
200     LET K=K+1
```

The first time a random number, R, is generated the value of K is 1. Then R is placed in the first location of M in

```
210     LET M(K)=R
```

The computer interprets this as   210 LET $M(1)=R$. Thus the random number R corresponds to the first card dealt.

PRODUCING 52 RANDOM INTEGERS TO CORRESPOND TO 52 CARDS IN A SHUFFLED DECK

```
110     REM PRODUCES 52 UNIQUE RANDOM NUMBERS
120     DIM M(52),X(52)
130     FOR I=1 TO 52
140     LET M(I)=X(I)=0
150     NEXT I
160     LET K=0
170     LET R=INT(RND(0)*52)+1
180     IF X(R)=1 THEN 170
190     LET X(R)=1
200     LET K=K+1
210     LET M(K)=R
220     IF K<>52 THEN 170
230     FOR J=0 TO 12
240     FOR I= 1 TO 4
250     PRINT M(I+4*J);
260     NEXT I
270     PRINT
280     NEXT J
290     END
```

Figure 8.12a. The program produces 52 unique random integers from 1 to 52. If the value of X(R) is 1, the integer has already been generated. if it is 0, the integer has not previously been generated. The 52 elements M(K) store the 52 unique random integers.

The first line of the table for Fig. 8.12a traces the sequence of events up to this point in the program, assuming the first number generated is 4

Line no.	R	X(4)	X(21)	X(48)	X(10)	K	M(K)
210	4	1	0	0	0	1	4

The other elements of X correspond to the next 3 random numbers which the author knows will be generated, because he has run the program. We see that X(4) is set equal to 1. This will prevent our having more than one number 4 in the deck. The value of K is 1, indicating that the first number has been generated. The variable M(K) is thus interpreted as M(1) by the computer and its value is 4 (thus the number 4 is the first nonrepeated number generated or the first card dealt). The rest of the table indicates how the next four numbers generated are treated by the program.

Line no.	R	X(4)	X(21)	X(48)	X(10)	K	M(K)
210	21	1	1	0	0	2	21
210	48	1	1	1	0	3	48
210	21	1	1	1	0	3	48
210	10	1	1	1	1	4	10

The second number generated is 21. Since it has not been previously generated, X(21) is set equal to 1, K is set equal to 2, and M(2) is set equal to 21, indicating that the second non-repeated number generated is 21. The third number generated, 48, is treated the same way. The fourth number generated, 21, has been generated before, so the value of X(21) is already 1. Line 180 is interpreted by the computer as

```
180   IF X(21)=1 THEN 170
```

Since the expression in this IF statement is true, the number 21 is skipped and a new random number will be generated in its place. Thus the value of K is not increased, by 1 and 21 does not become the equivalent of the fourth card. If we did not do this, we would have two 21s in our "deck" at this point.

This process continues until 52 unique numbers have been generated. When this has happened, the statement

```
220      IF K<>52 THEN 170
```

determines that the generating process should cease. The next set of statements executed

```
230      FOR J=0 TO 12
240      FOR I= 1 TO 4
250      PRINT M(I+4*J);
260      NEXT I
270      PRINT
280      NEXT J
```

prints the 52 random numbers, 4 to a line. These statements consist of an I loop nested in a J loop. The first value of J is zero, so the computer interprets line 250 as

```
250      PRINT M(I)
```

and it prints the values of M(1) to M(4), i.e., the first 4 random numbers. The second time the I loop is executed, J = 1, so the computer interprets line 250 as

```
250      PRINT M(I+4)
```

and it prints the value of M(5) to M(8), i.e., the second 4 random numbers. This process continues until all 52 random numbers are printed. The results are shown in Fig. 8.12b.

Line no.	R	X(4)	X(21)	X(48)	X(10)	K	M(K)
210	4	1	0	0	0	1	4
210	21	1	1	0	0	2	21
210	48	1	1	1	0	3	48
210	21	1	1	1	0	3	48
210	10	1	1	1	1	4	10

Table for Fig. 8.12a. The status of the elements of X after a random number, R, has been generated. For each new value of R, the value of K (the variable that indicates how many unique random integers have been generated) is increased by 1, and the value of R is assigned to the appropriate element of M (the subscripted variable that stores the random numbers). Note that when the number 21 is generated for the second time, the value of K is not increased by 1.

```
RUN
4      21     48     10
43     46     36     23
52     27     42     17
40     15     14     7
41     1      13     49
24     30     18     47
39     45     20     5
8      3      25     19
28     34     29     33
50     26     12     51
35     37     44     9
22     38     2      11
16     32     6      31
READY
```

Figure 8.12b. The 52 unique random numbers produced by Fig. 8.12a.

The second step of the program, as shown in Fig. 8.13a, uses the first step (Fig. 8.12a) to generate 52 unique numbers from 1 to 52, and then translates every fourth number so that it corresponds to a card in a suit. We have dimensioned all the subscripted variables in the program in one DIM statement, i.e.,

```
5          DIM C$(13),S$(4),M(52),X(52)
```

The strings in the DATA statement

```
10          DATA CLUBS,DIAMONDS,HEARTS,SPADES
```

area assigned to S$(1), S$(2), S$(3), and S$(4), respectively, in

```
25          FOR K=1 TO 4
30          READ S$(K)
35          NEXT K
```

Then the strings in the other DATA statements, i.e., ACE, TWO, THREE, etc. are assigned to C$(1), C$(2), C$(3), etc., respectively, in

```
40          FOR L=1 TO 13
45          READ C$(L)
50          NEXT L
```

The part of the program that generates the 52 unique numbers are the statements in the program that appeared in Fig. 8.12a. We have made these statements into a subroutine of the present program. They begin at line 130. Since they now constitute a subroutine, we have ended them with

```
290          RETURN
```

This part of the program is called when

```
55          GO SUB 130
```

is executed.

The statements

```
60          FOR I=1 TO 52 STEP 4
65          LET S=INT((M(I)-1)/13)+1
70          LET C=M(I)-13*(S-1)
75          PRINT C$(C);" OF ";S$(S)
80          NEXT I
```

converts every fourth number stored in the subscripted variable M to card terms and then prints them. We now investigate how this is done.

PRODUCING A SHUFFLED DECK

```
2         REM   SIMULATES A SHUFFLED DECK OF CARDS
5         DIM C$(13),S$(4),M(52),X(52)
10        DATA CLUBS,DIAMONDS,HEARTS,SPADES
15        DATA ACE,TWO,THREE,FOUR,FIVE,SIX,SEVEN
20        DATA EIGHT,NINE,TEN,JACK,QUEEN,KING,
25        FOR K=1 TO 4
30        READ S$(K)
35        NEXT K
40        FOR L=1 TO 13
45        READ C$(L)
50        NEXT L
55        GO SUB 130
60        FOR I=1 TO 52 STEP 4
65        LET S=INT((M(I)-1)/13)+1
70        LET C=M(I)-13*(S-1)
75        PRINT C$(C);" OF ";S$(S)
80        NEXT I
90        STOP
130       FOR I=1 TO 52
140       LET M(I)=X(I)=0
150       NEXT I
160       LET K=0
170       R=INT(RND(0)*52)+1
180       IF X(R)=1 THEN 170
190       LET X(R)=1
200       LET K=K+1
210       LET M(K)=R
220       IF K<>52 THEN 170
230       FOR J=0 TO 12
240       FOR I= 1 TO 4
250       PRINT M(I+4*J);
260       NEXT I
270       PRINT
280       NEXT J
290       RETURN
300       END
```

Figure 8.13a. This program uses that of Fig. 8.12a. as a subroutine (lines 130 to 290) to generate 52 unique random interests. It then converts these integers to a suit and card number.

For I equals 1; then $M(I) = 4$, assuming that the subroutine produces the same random numbers as did the previous program. We see from Part 1 of the table for Fig. 8.13a how statement 65

$$65 \qquad LET\ S = INT((M(I)-1)/13)+1$$

calculates the proper suit:

I	M(I)	M(I) − 1	(M(I) − 1)/13	INT(M(I) − 1)/13	S	S$(S)
1	4	3	3/13	0	1	CLUBS

Since the value of S is 1, the value of S$(S) is CLUBS. We see from Part 2 of the table for Fig. 8.13a how statement 70

$$70 \qquad LET\ C = M(I)-13*(S-1)$$

calculates the proper card number:

I	M(I)	S	13*(S−1)	C	C$(C)
1	4	1	0	4	FOUR

(The value of S is obtained from line 65.) Since the value of C is 4 the value of C$(C) is FOUR. At this point in the program, the computer interprets line 75 as

$$75 \qquad PRINT\ C\$(4); "OF"; S\$(1)$$

and therefore prints

FOUR OF CLUBS

As we mentioned before, because of the STEP 4 in line 60, the program converts only every fourth number to card terms. Therefore, only the 13 numbers that form the first column of the results in Fig. 8.13b are converted to card terms. The 13 cards are listed after all the numbers have been listed.

I	M(I)	M(I)−1	(M(I)−1)/13	INT((M(I)−1)/13	S	S$(S)
1	4	3	3/13	0	1	CLUBS
2	21	20	20/13	1	2	DIAMONDS
3	48	47	47/13	3	4	SPADES
4	10	7	7/13	0	1	CLUBS

Table for Fig. 8.13a, Part 1. How the suit is calculated in line 65.

I	M(I)	S	13*(S−1)	C	C$(C)
1	4	1	0	4	FOUR
2	21	2	13	8	EIGHT
3	48	4	39	9	NINE
4	10	1	0	10	TEN

Table for Fig. 8.13a, Part 2. How the card number is calculated in line 70.

```
RUN
 4    21    48    10
43    46    36    23
52    27    42    17
40    15    14     7
41     1    13    49
24    30    18    47
39    45    20     5
 8     3    25    19
28    34    29    33
50    26    12    51
35    37    44     9
22    38     2    11
16    32     6    31
FOUR OF CLUBS
FOUR OF SPADES
KING OF SPADES
ACE OF SPADES
TWO OF SPADES
JACK OF DIAMONDS
KING OF HEARTS
EIGHT OF CLUBS
TWO OF HEARTS
JACK OF SPADES
NINE OF HEARTS
NINE OF DIAMONDS
THREE OF DIAMONDS
READY.
```

Figure 8.13b. Running the program of Fig. 8.13a. After the programs prints the 52 random integers, it prints the card value of every fourth card.

PROBLEMS

1. Given the DATA statement

   20   DATA JOHN, JILL, JACK, JOE, JANE

   and using the subscripted string variable R$(I), write a program that reads all of the names in the DATA statement in one FOR-NEXT loop; then prints the first, third, and fifth name in another FOR-NEXT loop; and finally prints the second and fourth names in the last FOR-NEXT loop.

2. Given A$(1)=CAT, A$(2)=DOG. What statement is executed after the IF statement in each of the following is executed?

   a. 20   IF A$(1)>A$(2)   THEN 80
       30   PRINT A$(1)

   b. 20   IF A$(1)<A$(2)   THEN 80
       30   PRINT A$(1)

   c. 20   IF A$(1)<>A$(2)   THEN 80
       30   PRINT A$(1)

   d. 20   IF A$(1)>=A$(2)   THEN 80
       30   PRINT A$(1)

3. Given the DATA statement

   20   DATA JOHN, JILL, JACK, JOE, JANE

   write a program that prints the strings in the reverse order that they appear in the DATA statement.

4. Write a program that prints the names in the DATA statement

   20   DATA 5,JOHN, JILL, JACK, JOE, JANE

   in reverse alphabetical order. Use the number in the DATA statement to indicate how many names follow.

5. Write a program that prints the names in the DATA statement

   20   DATA JOHN, JILL, JACK, JOE, JANE, TRAILER

   in reverse alphabetical order. The string TRAILER should not be alphabetized, but should only serve to indicate that it is the last string in the DATA statement.

6. Given the following two DATA statements

```
10   DATA FOUR, KING, THREE, QUEEN
20   DATA SPADES, DIAMONDS, CLUBS, HEARTS
```

write a program that uses subscripted string variables to print:
FOUR OF SPADES, KING OF DIAMONDS, THREE OF CLUBS and
QUEEN OF HEARTS.

7. What does the following program print?

```
10   FOR I=1 TO 5
20   GO SUB 50
30   NEXT I
40   STOP
50   PRINT I;
60   RETURN
70   END
```

8. Write a program that does the following:
   a. Uses a subroutine to read a group of numbers from a DATA statement.
   b. Uses another subroutine to place these numbers in ascending order.
   c. Uses a third subroutine to print the results.

9. Which of the following function names are illegal?
FNA   FNC2   FNR   FNT$ FN2
What does the following program do?

```
10   DEF FNA(I)=INT(I*RND(0)+1)
20   FOR I=1 TO 100
30   PRINT FNA (3)
40   NEXT I
50   END
```

10. Define a function FNS whose argument is an angle defined in degrees and whose value is the sine of that angle. Define a similar function FNC for the cosine. Write a program which uses FNS and FNC to produce a trigonometric table.

11. Write a program that will simulate the tossing of a coin and print the result `HEAD` or `TAILS` randomly.

12. Write a program that uses a Monte Carlo technique to simulate the throwing of of a pair of dice.

13. Knowing that the area of a circle with unit radius is π and that the area of the square in which the circle is circumscribed is 2^2 or 4, we can find the value of π by dividing the area of the circle by the area of the square and multiplying by 4. The same argument applies if we apply this procedures to the quarter of a circle which is in the first quadrant of the $X - Y$ plane and the unit square in which the quarter of a circle is inscribed

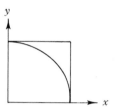

By generating two random numbers between 0 and 1 corresponding to the values of X and Y coordinates of the point, knowing that the formula of the circle is $X^2 + Y^2 = 1$, we can then count the number of points falling within the quarter of a circle. If we generate a total of 1000 points in the unit square, the value of π would be given by the algebraic equation

$$\pi = \frac{4 \times \text{(number of points falling within the quarter circle)}}{1000}$$

Write a program that uses this technique to find the value of π.

9
Doubly Subscripted Variables and Matrices

9.1. Doubly Subscripted Variables; Chi-Squared

We now explain the use of variables that have two subscripts by using a doubly subscripted variable in the program shown in Fig. 9.1a. This program enables the programmer to determine whether there is any connection between the result of throwing one die—which is red for identification purposes—and the result of throwing a second die—which is white—in a game in which two dice are thrown (the word die is the singular of dice). The pair of dice are thrown 360 times.

The doubly subscripted variable $X(F,S)$ is used as a counter to record the results each time the two dice are thrown. The first subscript, F, refers to the results when the first die is thrown. The second subscript, S, refers to the results when the second die is thrown. Thus if the results of throwing the first die is a 3, and of throwing the second die is a 4, then the value of $X(3,4)$ is increased by 1. If these results occurred in the opposite order, then $X(4,3)$ is increased by 1.

Since there are 6 numbers on each die, there are 36 possible combinations that can occur when the two dice are thrown. We thus need 36 counters to record the results. The loops

```
30    FOR S=1 TO 6
40    FOR F=1 TO 6
50    LET X(F,S)=0
60    NEXT F
70    NEXT S
```

assign zeros to all the 36 counters, $X(S,F)$, in line 50. In this line, F assumes the values 1 to 6 for each value of S. Thus when S equals 1, the computer in successive executions of line 50 interprets $X(F,S)$ as: $X(1,1)$, $X(2,1)$, $X(3,1)$, $X(4,1)$, $X(5,1)$ and $X(6,1)$. When S equals 2, the computer interprets $X(F,S)$ as: $X(1,2)$, $X(2,2)$, $X(3,2)$, $X(4,2)$, $X(5,2)$ and $X(6,2)$. This process continues until all 36 counters $X(F,S)$ are assigned zeros.

USING DOUBLY SUBSCRIPTED VARIABLES

```
10    REM SIMULATES DICE THROW
20    DIM X(6,6)
30    FOR S=1 TO 6
40    FOR F=1 TO 6
50    LET X(F,S)=0
60    NEXT F
70    NEXT S
80    FOR I=1 TO 360
85    LET R=INT(RND(0)*6)+1
90    LET W=INT(RND(0)*6)+1
100   LET X(R,W)=X(R,W)+1
110   NEXT I
120   FOR F=1 TO 6
130   FOR S=1 TO 6
140   PRINT X(F,S);
150   NEXT S
160   PRINT
170   NEXT F
180   END
```

Figure 9.1a. Program simulates throwing of a pair of dice 360 times. The numbers on the first and second die are generated in lines 85 and 90, respectively. The results of the throws are recorded in the 36 counters $X(R,W)$, which are set equal to zero in the nested loops (lines 30 to 70). When the program prints the results we can see whether there is any relation between the first and second throw. The subscript F determines the row (horizontal line) in the result. The subscript S determines the column (vertical line) in the results.

The statements

```
85   LET R=INT(RND(Ø)*6)+1
90   LET W=INT(RND(Ø)*6)+1
```

produce a pair of random numbers each of which represents one of the six numbers on a die. The result of throwing the first die (the red one) is assigned to the variable R (for red); the results for the second die (the white one) is assigned to the variable W (for white). These two statements, which simulate the throwing of the dice, as well as a statement that records the results (line 100) are executed 360 times in the I loop

```
80   FOR I=1 TO 360
85   LET R=INT(RND(Ø)*6)+1
90   LET W=INT(RND(Ø)*6)+1
100   LET X(R,W)=X(R,W)+1
110   NEXT I
```

once for each simulated throw of the two dice. If the first two numbers generated are 4 and 2, the computer would interpret line 100 as

```
100   LET X(4,2)=X(4,2)+1
```

Since the original value of $X(4,2)$ is 0 (from line 50) its value after line 100 is executed is 1. Each time a 4 and 2 are thrown in that order, the value of $X(4,2)$ is increased by 1. Since the results of each throw should be random, we would expect to obtain approximately the same amount of each of the 36 combinations. Thus after the program is finished, there should be approximately equal numbers in each of the X counters. Since there are 36 counters and 360 throws, we would expect, on the average, the value of each counter to be 360/36, or 10. If the results are drastically different, i.e., $X(1,3)=25$, $X(3,4)=1$, then there is something wrong with the dice or the way they were thrown. This would actually mean that our random number generator is not producing truly random numbers.*

The statements

```
120   FOR F=1 TO 6
130   FOR S=1 TO 6
140   PRINT X(F,S);
150   NEXT S
160   PRINT
170   NEXT F
```

print the numbers stored in each counter at the end of the program The first time the statements in the F loop are executed, the value of F is 1, therefore the computer interprets line 140 as

```
140   PRINT X(1,S);
```

and as the computer executes the (nested) S loop, it prints the values of $X(1,1)$, $X(1,2)$, $X(1,3)$, $X(1,4)$, $X(1,5)$, and $X(1,6)$ on the first line of results. The second time the statements in the F loop are executed, the computer interprets line 140 as

```
140   PRINT X(2,S);
```

and, as the computer executes the (nested) S loop for the second time, it prints the values of $X(2,1)$, $X(2,2)$, $X(2,3)$, $X(2,4)$, $X(2,5)$, and $X(2,6)$ on the next line of results (because of line 160). When the program is complete, it has produced a table consisting of 6 lines of results, as shown in Fig. 9.1b.

---

* Malfunctions in random number generators that may not be apparent when the numbers are generated one at a time, may become apparent when the numbers are generated in pairs as they are here.

```
RUN
     9      10      10      11      13      10
     7      11       7      16       4      12
     8      14       9       9      13       9
     7       9       9       9      13      11
    13       5      11      11       7      18
     9      10      10       7       8      11
READY
```

Figure 9.1b. Running the program of Fig. 9.1a. The first row, i.e., 9, 10, 10, 11, 13, 10, corresponds to X(1,1), X(1,2), X(1,3), X(1,4), X(1,5), and X(1,6). We expect each counter X(F,S) to contain approximately 10. We see that in general, this is true.

Later in the chapter, we will refer to the horizontal lines of tables such as this as rows, and to the vertical lines as columns; we will refer both to subscripted variables and their contents as matrices. The doubly subscripted ones will be two-dimensional matrices; and the singly subscripted ones will be one-dimensional matrices—we will call these vectors. We will refer to the locations in a subscripted variable as the elements of the matrix. In contrast to this, we will call simple variables and the numbers assigned to them scalars.

We see from the results that the number assigned to each counter (matrix element) is approximately 10. Therefore, our judgment is that there is no relation between the throwing of the first die and the second die.

We now discuss the dimensioning of doubly subscripted variables. If the maximum value of both the subscripts is less than 11, the doubly subscripted variable does not have to be dimensioned. Space is automatically reserved in the computer's memory for all the elements of a subscripted variable both of whose subscripts have a maximum value of 10. If the maximum value of *either* of the subscripts is 11 or more, the subscripted variable must be dimensioned. Although in this program, the maximum value of both subscripts is 6, we have dimensioned X in line 20 in order to save space in the computer's memory.

The reader can skip to Section 9.2 if he is not interested in the mathematical analysis of the results of the last program.

There is a statistical test for determining whether the dice in the last program were honest dice, that is, whether our random number generator is producing truly random numbers. It is called the chi-square test and it involves calculating the quantity χ^2 (chi-squared) which is defined as*

$$\chi^2 = \text{sum of all} \frac{(\text{observed} - \text{expected})^2}{\text{expected}}$$

The values of each of the 36 counters $X(F,S)$ at the end of the preceding program, corresponds to each of the "observed" terms in the summation called for in this formula. The expected value of each of the 36 counters, as we showed, is 10. This corresponds to "expected" in this formula.

From the results of the last program, we observe that $X(1,1)=9$, $X(1,2)=10$, $X(1,3)=10$, $X(1,4)=11$, etc. These are the observed results. If we begin to calculate χ^2 by hand for the results of that program, χ^2 would look like

$$\chi^2 = \frac{(9\text{-}10)^2}{10} + \frac{(10\text{-}10)^2}{10} + \frac{(10\text{-}10)^2}{10} + \cdots$$

The final equation would be the sum of 36 terms. If the student attempts to do this calculation by hand, he will find it extremely tedious. Fortunately, we can do calculations like this quite simply in BASIC, as shown in Fig. 9.2a, using our old friend the accumulator. As we see, the equation that defines χ^2, is just the sum of the like terms

$$\frac{(\text{observed-expected})^2}{\text{expected}}$$

* Mathematically it is written $\chi^2 = \Sigma \dfrac{(\text{observed} - \text{expected})^2}{\text{expected}}$

CALCULATING CHI-SQUARED

```
10    REM CHI-SQUARED FOR
15    REM SIMULATED DICE THROW
20    DIM X(6,6)
30    FOR S=1 TO 6
40    FOR F=1 TO 6
50    LET X(F,S)=0
60    NEXT F
70    NEXT S
80    FOR I=1 TO 360
85    LET R=INT(RND(0)*6)+1
90    LET W=INT(RND(0)*6)+1
100   LET X(R,W)=X(R,W)+1
110   NEXT I
120   FOR F=1 TO 6
130   FOR S=1 TO 6
140   PRINT X(F,S);
150   NEXT S
160   PRINT
170   NEXT F
180   LET K2=0
190   FOR F=1 TO 6
200   FOR S=1 TO 6
210   LET K2=K2+(X(F,S)-10)↑2/10
220   NEXT S
230   NEXT F
240   PRINT "CHI-SQUARED IS";K2
250   END
```

Figure 9.2a. This program is the same as that for Fig. 9.1a, but it determines by using the chi-squared test whether there is any relation between the first and second throw of the die. $\chi^2 = \Sigma$ (expected-observed)^2/observed, is calculated in line 210; $X(F,S)$ is the observed frequency of throws in which F is the number on the first die and S is the number on the second. The expected frequency is 10. $K2$ is used as the accumulator to form the summation in the calculation of χ^2. The summation is done by placing line 210 in the F loop and (nested) S loop.

These terms are represented in the program by

$$(X (F , S) - 10) \uparrow 2 / 10$$

By adding this to the accumulator K2 in

$$210 \quad LET \; K2 = K2 + (X (F , S) - 10) \uparrow 2 / 10$$

and then placing this statement in the F loop and (nested) S loop, we calculate χ^2. Thus the final value of K2 is the value of χ^2. We place these loops preceded by a statement that zeroes the accumulator K2 at the end of the program shown in Fig. 9.1a. We ran this program on a system that produces a different set of random numbers each time the program is run. We obtained the results shown in Fig. 9.2b. In order to interpret the chi-squared of 33.2 shown here, we must first calculate what is called the degrees of freedom. For this type of problem, the degrees of freedom is defined as the number of counters minus one. In our case this would be $36 - 1$ or 35. Knowing that our chi-squared is 33.2 and our degrees of freedom is 35, we refer to statistical tables and find that there is a probability of approximately 35% of obtaining a chi-squared greater than the one we obtained. This means that our chi-squared is acceptable and that there is no relationship between the throw of the first die and that of the second.

```
RUN
  7        8       13       12        8        5
 19       13        7       14       11        8
 13        7        9       11       13        9
 12       14        8       13        8        7
  5       11       11        7        7       12
  9       10        5       11       12       11
CHI-SQUARED IS 33.2
READY
```

Figure 9.2b. Running the program of Fig. 9.2a. We see that the value of chi-squared is 33.2. For 35 degrees of freedom, this means that there is no connection between the first and the second throws of the dice. The final values of the counters are different in this program as compared with the program of Fig. 9.1a because the system on which we ran the programs produces a different set of random numbers each time the program is run.

9.2 MAT PRINT and the ZER Matrix

There is a set of instructions that will greatly facilitate your use of matrices. They all begin with the letters MAT (which is an abbreviation of matrix). Before we explain the use and meaning of all the MAT instructions, we will use two different MAT instruction, to greatly shorten the program of Fig. 9.1a. Although we did not define it as such then, X(F,S) in that program was a matrix. The altered program is shown in Fig. 9.3a. Statement 30

```
30   MAT X=ZER
```

replaces statements 30 to 70 in Fig. 9.1a. This statement thus assigns zeros to the locations in the matrix X. In other words, the values of all the counters X(F,S) are set equal to zero. The ZER is an abbreviation for zero. From now on, we can use this instruction to assign zeros to all the locations in any matrix.

Statement 120 in this program

```
120   MAT   PRINT X;
```

replaces statements 120 to 170 in Fig. 9.1a:

```
120   FOR F=1 TO 6
130   FOR S=1 TO 6
140   PRINT X(F,S);
150   NEXT S
160   PRINT
170   NEXT F
```

It thus prints the contents of each of the locations of the matrix X. They are printed row by row as is shown in Fig. 9.3b. Since a semicolon follows the X, the spacing between the elements in a row is the same as that produced by the PRINT statement in line 140 of Fig. 9.1. If a comma follows the X, the columns of numbers in the matrix are printed starting in columns 1, 16, 31, 46, 61, etc.

On most systems, the computer skips a line between each row printed.

USING THE ZER MATRIX

```
10    REM SIMULATES DICE THROW
15    REM USING MAT STATEMENTS
20    DIM X(6,6)
30    MAT X=ZER
80    FOR I=1 TO 360
85    LET R=INT(RND(0)*6)+1
90    LET W=INT(RND(0)*6)+1
100   LET X(R,W)=X(R,W)+1
110   NEXT I
120   MAT  PRINT X;
180   END
```

Figure 9.3a. Same program as that of Fig. 9.1a; it simulates the throwing of a pair of dice 360 times. The MAT X=ZER assigns zeros to all the counters. It replaces lines 30 to 70 in Fig. 9.1a. The counters X(R,W) are now considered to be the elements of the Matrix X. The statement MAT PRINT X; prints all the elements of the matrix X and thus replaces lines 120 to 170 of Fig. 9.1a.

```
RUN
 7      10      11       8       7      14

 7       9      13      12      11      15

11      13       6       5      14       7

 9      13       6      14      11       6

11      14      12      10       7      15

11       8      11       6       9       7
READY
```

Figure 9.3b. Running the program of Fig. 9.3a.

9.3   MAT READ, MAT **Multiplication, Inverse, Transpose, Addition, and Subtraction**

Matrix multiplication is much different from regular (or scalar) multiplication as is shown in Fig. 9.4a. In it we show how the multiplication in the matrix equation

$$C = A * B$$

is evaluated, where the matrices A and B are specified as

$$
\overset{\textstyle A}{\begin{pmatrix} 1 & 2 & 3 \\ 4 & 5 & 6 \end{pmatrix}}
\qquad
\overset{\textstyle B}{\begin{pmatrix} 7 \\ 8 \\ 9 \end{pmatrix}}
$$

The elements are always enclosed in parentheses to show that they constitute a matrix. To simplify the calculation, we have made all of the elements integers; they could, in actuality, be any type of number. The elements of the matrix C will be evaluated from the matrix product, so at this point we represent them as the unknowns X and Y as is shown in Fig. 9.4a.

In order to facilitate explaining matrix multiplication we have depicted it pictorially as shown in Fig. 9.4a, in five steps.

Step 1.   The matrix B, in this case

$$\begin{pmatrix} 7 \\ 8 \\ 9 \end{pmatrix}$$

in which the elements are in a vertical line, is physically turned so that the elements are in a horizontal line: (7 8 9) and is placed on top of the matrix A so that each of the numbers in A lines up with the columns of B.

Step 2.   The matrix B descends on matrix A.

Step 3.   When B reaches the first row of A, each element of B multiplies its corresponding element in the first row of A, i.e., 7 multiplies 1, 8 multiplies 2, and 9 multiplies 3. Then each element of B multiplies its corresponding element in the second row of A.

Step 4.   The products in the first row of our new matrix are added together. They equal 50. The products in the second row of our new matrix are added together. They equal 122.

Step 5.   If two matrices are equal to each other, their elements are equal, so X = 50 and Y = 122. Therefore C is the matrix

$$\begin{pmatrix} 50 \\ 122 \end{pmatrix}$$

MATRIX MULTIPLICATION

$$\underset{\left(\begin{smallmatrix} X \\ Y \end{smallmatrix}\right)}{\overset{C}{=}} \quad \underset{\left(\begin{smallmatrix} 1 & 2 & 3 \\ 4 & 5 & 6 \end{smallmatrix}\right)}{\overset{A}{}} \quad * \quad \underset{\left(\begin{smallmatrix} 7 \\ 8 \\ 9 \end{smallmatrix}\right)}{\overset{B}{}}$$

Figure 9.4a. Multiplying the matrix A times the matrix B:

Terms used to describe a matrix:
The rows are the horizontal lines of numbers.
The columns are the vertical lines of numbers.
The numbers are called the elements of the matrix. Thus for matrix A

	First column	Second column	Third column
First row	1	2	3
Second row	4	5	6

$$(7 \quad 8 \quad 9) \leftarrow$$

$$\underset{C}{\left(\begin{smallmatrix} X \\ Y \end{smallmatrix}\right)} \quad \underset{A}{=} \quad \left(\begin{smallmatrix} 1 & 2 & 3 \\ 4 & 5 & 6 \end{smallmatrix}\right) \quad \underset{B}{*} \quad \left(\begin{smallmatrix} 7 \\ 8 \\ 9 \end{smallmatrix}\right)$$

Step 1. Rotate the matrix B a quarter turn to the left and place on top of A as shown.

$$(7 \quad 8 \quad 9) \; B$$
$$\downarrow \quad \downarrow \quad \downarrow$$
$$\underset{C}{\left(\begin{smallmatrix} X \\ Y \end{smallmatrix}\right)} = \underset{A}{\left(\begin{smallmatrix} 1 & 2 & 3 \\ 4 & 5 & 6 \end{smallmatrix}\right)}$$

Step 2. The matrix B descends on A.

$$\left(\begin{matrix} X \\ Y \end{matrix}\right) = \left(\begin{matrix} 1*7 & 2*8 & 3*9 \\ 4*7 & 5*8 & 6*9 \end{matrix}\right)$$
$$C \quad = \quad A*B$$

Step 3. Each element of B multiplies the corresponding element in the first row of A, then the corresponding element in the second row of A.

$$\left(\begin{matrix} X \\ Y \end{matrix}\right) = \left(\begin{matrix} 7 + 16 + 27 \\ 28 + 40 + 54 \end{matrix}\right) = \left(\begin{matrix} 50 \\ 122 \end{matrix}\right)$$
$$C \quad = \quad A*B$$

Step 4. Add the products in the first row, then add the products in the second row

$$X = 50$$
$$Y = 122$$

Step 5. If two matrices are equal their elements are equal.

It is important to note that the matrix multiplication B*A, is not the same as the matrix multiplication A*B, since in B*A the matrix A is to the *right* of B as is shown in Fig. 9.4b, whereas in A*B, the matrix A is to the *left* of matrix B. For the matrices given for A and B, the matrix multiplication B*A cannot occur. This is because after the matrix A is turned, as is shown in the Fig. 9.4b, half of the turned matrix A has no corresponding elements to multiply in B. Thus for any two matrices A and B, you can perform the matrix multiplication A*B only when the number of rows in B equals the number of columns in A. We will see how to do matrix multiplication in general later on in the chapter.

ILLEGAL MATRIX MULTIPLICATION

$$C = \quad B \quad * \quad A$$

$$\begin{pmatrix} 7 \\ 8 \\ 9 \end{pmatrix} \begin{pmatrix} 1 & 2 & 3 \\ 4 & 5 & 6 \end{pmatrix}$$

$$\begin{pmatrix} 3 & 6 \\ 2 & 5 \\ 1 & 4 \end{pmatrix} \leftarrow$$

STEP 1

$$\begin{pmatrix} 7 \\ 8 \\ 9 \end{pmatrix} \begin{pmatrix} 1 & 2 & 3 \\ 4 & 5 & 6 \end{pmatrix}$$
$$B \qquad\qquad A$$

$$\begin{pmatrix} 3 & 6 \\ 2 & 5 \\ 1 & 4 \end{pmatrix} A$$
$$\downarrow \quad \downarrow$$
$$\begin{pmatrix} 7 \\ 8 \\ 9 \end{pmatrix} B$$

STEP 2

Figure 9.4b. Why B*A for the matrices given is not allowed: At Step 2 half of the turned matrix A has no corresponding elements to multiply in B.

You can perform the matrix multiplication B*A only when the number of columns in B equals the number of rows in A.

338 *Doubly Subscripted Variables and Matrices*

We will now write a program that will do the matrix multiplication A*B we have just performed, and assign the result to the matrix C. The program is shown in Fig. 9.5a. The matrices are dimensioned in line 20

20 DIM A(2,3),B(3,1),C(2,1)

In the dimensioning of matrices, the first subscript indicates the number of rows the matrix has, and the second subscript indicates the number of columns the matrix has. Thus the fact that A is dimensioned as A(2,3) indicates that it has 2 rows and 3 columns; the fact that B is dimensioned as B(3,1) indicates that it has 3 rows and 1 column; and finally the fact that C is dimensioned as C(2,1) indicates that it has 2 rows and 1 column. The reader might now ask, "How does one determine the dimension of C before he has performed the matrix multiplication?" An easy way of determining it is to place the dimensioned matrix A to the left of the dimensioned matrix B (i.e., in the same order in which they appear in the matrix equation C=A*B):

A(2,3) B(3,1)

We see that the second subscript of A (which is 3) equals the first subscript of B (which is also 3). This must be true in any matrix multiplication.* The remaining subscripts (2 and 1) are the dimensions of C. Thus the number of rows in C equals the number of rows in A; and the number of columns in C equals the number of columns in B.

On many systems you do not have to dimension the matrix that is the result of a matrix calculation if none of the dimensions of the matrix are greater than 10, e.g., here the matrix C. However on many systems, you must dimension all matrices; consequently we have followed this procedure for all the programs in this chapter.

On all systems, matrices whose elements are to be read by the computer must be dimensioned in the program so that the computer will read them correctly. We will now see why.

In statement 40

40 MAT READ A,B

we assign the appropriate numbers in the DATA statement

30 DATA 1,2,3,4,5,6,7,8,9

to the matrices A and B. It is done in the following way: the numbers in the DATA statement are assigned by row, to the matrix A first. Since the DIM statement specifies that A has 3 columns (i.e., there are 3 elements in each row), the numbers 1, 2, and 3 become the elements of the first row of A and 4, 5, 6 become the elements of the second row of A. The matrix A is now complete. The computer then assigns the remaining numbers in the DATA statement to B in accordance with the dimensions of B. Since the DIM statement specifies that B has 3 rows and 1 column, the number 7 becomes the element of the first row of A; 8, the second row; and 9, the third row.

* This corresponds to the fact that the numbers of columns in A must equal the number of rows in B.

PROGRAMMING A MATRIX MULTIPLICATION

```
10    REM MATRIX MULTIPLICATION
20    DIM A(2,3),B(3,1),C(2,1)
30    DATA 1,2,3,4,5,6,7,8,9
40    MAT    READ A,B
50    MAT C=A*B
60    PRINT "MATRIX A"
70    MAT    PRINT A;
80    PRINT "MATRIX B"
90    MAT    PRINT B
100   PRINT "MATRIX C=A*B"
110   MAT    PRINT C;
120   END
```

Figure 9.5a. Program performs the matrix operation A*B where A and B are as defined in Fig. 9.4a. The matrices are read in row by row from the DATA statement. All matrices, regardless of their size, must be dimensioned somewhere in the program. The dimensions of A, which are A(2,3), inform the computer that A has 2 rows; each row has 3 elements, i.e., A has 3 columns. Thus 1,2,3, are the elements of the first row of A; and 4,5,6 are the elements of the second row; the dimensions of B, which are B(3,1) inform the computer that B has 3 rows; each row has 1 element. Thus 7,8,9 are the first, second, and third rows of B. All matrix operations must be preceded by the word MAT.

$$C = \quad A \quad * \quad B$$

$$\begin{pmatrix} 1 & 2 & 3 \\ 4 & 5 & 6 \end{pmatrix} \begin{pmatrix} 7 \\ 8 \\ 9 \end{pmatrix}$$

A matrix M is dimensioned as M(number of rows, number of columns). Thus since A has 2 rows and 3 columns, we dimension it as A(2,3). Since B has 3 rows and 1 column, it is dimensioned as B(3,1).

To check that the numbers were properly assigned to the matrices A and B, we first instruct the computer to print the elements of A

70   MAT   PRINT A;

We see that its elements are printed by row and, as we expect, are

1	2	3
4	5	6

as shown in Fig. 9.5b. We then instruct it to print the elements of B

90   MAT   PRINT B

We see that its elements are also printed by row and as we expect, they are

7
8
9

as is also shown in Fig. 9.5b. We remind you at this point that the first subscript indicates the row and the second indicates the column that the element is in. Thus, for the matrix A: $A(1,1)=1, A(1,2)=2, A(1,3)=3, A(2,1)=4, A(2,2)=5$ and $A(2,3)=6$. For the matrix B: $B(1,1)=7, B(2,1)=8$ and $B(3,1)=9$.

In most other languages, a matrix multiplication requires many lines of programing. In BASIC we can perform this operation in one statement

50   MAT C=A*B

When we run the program we find that the results are as we calculated in Fig. 9.4a, i.e., the elements of C are

$$\begin{pmatrix} 50 \\ 122 \end{pmatrix}$$

Remembering Fig. 9.4b, we see that we could not perform the matrix multiplication B*A. Thus if we wrote statement 50 as

50   MAT C=B*A

we would obtain an error during the execution of the program.

```
RUN
MATRIX A
   1      2      3
   4      5      6
MATRIX B
   7
   8
   9
MATRIX C=A*B
   50
   122
READY
```

Figure 9.5b. The `MAT PRINT` statement prints the elements of the matrix row by row. If a semicolon follows this statement, the elements will be printed more closely together than if this statement is followed by a comma. The results are the same as in Fig. 9.4b.

We now discuss the application of matrix multiplication to the calculation of total weekly sales for each of four car dealers. The number of cars of a given make that each of four dealers sells per week is shown in Fig. 9.6a. Thus dealer 1 sold 7 Chryslers, 8 Dodges, and 11 Plymouths in one week, etc. In Fig. 9.6b we show the matrix S, which represents the weekly sales of the four dealers.

In Fig. 9.7a we show the selling price of each car and in Fig. 9.7b we show the matrix P representing these prices. To repeat, the problem is to calculate the total sales for each dealer. We can do this easily by performing the matrix multiplication S*P. We set the result equal to the total sales matrix, T whose elements are unknown until the matrix multiplcation is performed. We will refer to these elements as T_1, T_2, T_3 and T_4. When we perform the matrix multiplication shown in Fig. 9.8a, we obtain as an intermediate result what is shown in Fig. 9.8b. When we sum the numbers in each row, we get the results shown in Fig. 9.8c. The total sales for dealer 1, T_1, equals 122,000 dollars; T_2 equals 117,000, etc. We see that matrices are convenient when the same operation—here multiplication—must be performed on all the elements of a group.

APPLICATION OF MATRIX MULTIPLICATION

Dealer	Chrysler	Dodge	Plymouth
1	7	8	11
2	4	10	13
3	2	7	3
4	8	8	4

Figure 9.6a. The number of cars each of four dealers sells per week.

Make	Price
Chrysler	7000
Dodge	5000
Plymouth	3000

Figure 9.7a. The price of each car.

$$S$$
$$\begin{pmatrix} 7 & 8 & 11 \\ 4 & 10 & 13 \\ 2 & 7 & 3 \\ 8 & 8 & 4 \end{pmatrix} \quad \text{SALES MATRIX}$$

Figure 9.6b. Matrix for sales shown in Fig. 9.6a.

$$P$$
$$\begin{pmatrix} 7000 \\ 5000 \\ 3000 \end{pmatrix} \quad \text{PRICE MATRIX}$$

Figure 9.7b. Price matrix for Fig. 9.7a.

$$\text{TOTAL} = \text{SALES} * \text{PRICE}$$

$$T \qquad\qquad S \qquad\qquad P$$
$$\begin{pmatrix} T_1 \\ T_2 \\ T_3 \\ T_4 \end{pmatrix} \begin{pmatrix} 7 & 8 & 11 \\ 4 & 10 & 13 \\ 2 & 7 & 3 \\ 8 & 8 & 4 \end{pmatrix} \begin{pmatrix} 7000 \\ \\ 5000 \\ \\ 3000 \end{pmatrix}$$

Figure 9.8a. The matrix multiplication needed to obtain the total sales for each dealer; e.g., T_1 is the total sales for dealer no. 1.

$$\begin{pmatrix} T_1 \\ T_2 \\ T_3 \\ T_4 \end{pmatrix} = \begin{pmatrix} 49000 + 40000 + 33000 \\ 28000 + 50000 + 39000 \\ 14000 + 35000 + 9000 \\ 56000 + 40000 + 12000 \end{pmatrix}$$

Figure 9.8b. An intermediate result in the matrix multiplication shown in Fig. 9.8a.

$T_1 = 122000$
$T_2 = 117000$
$T_3 = 58000$
$T_4 = 108000$

Figure 9.8c. The final results of the matrix multiplication shown in Fig. 9.8a. These are the elements of the total sales matrix T.

It is quite easy to write a program to do this matrix calculation. The program is shown in Fig. 9.9a. The dimension statement is

```
20    DIM  S(4,3),P(3,1),T(4,1)
```

The statement

```
50    MAT    READ  S,P
```

reads the first three numbers—7, 8, and 11—in the DATA statement

```
30    DATA  7,8,11,4,10,13,2,7,3
```

and assigns them to the elements in the first row of S. It assigns the second three numbers—4, 10, and 13—to the second row; and the third three numbers—2, 7, and 3—to the third row. It then refers to the next DATA statement

```
40    DATA  8,8,4,7000,5000,3000
```

and assigns the first three numbers to the fourth row of S. It finally assigns the last three numbers—7000, 5000, and 3000—to the elements of P. To check that these numbers were assigned correctly we instruct the computer in

```
70    MAT    PRINT  S;
```

and in statement 90

```
90    MAT    PRINT  P;
```

to print these matrices. When the program is run, as shown in Fig. 9.9b, we see that the assignments were made correctly. The matrix multiplication is performed in

```
100    MAT  T=S*P
```

The results are shown when statement 120 is executed. They are the same results as those shown in Fig. 9.8c.

PROGRAMMING THE APPLICATION OF MATRIX MULTIPLICATION

```
10    REM CALCULATES TOTAL SALES
15    REM USING MATRICES
20    DIM S(4,3),P(3,1),T(4,1)
30    DATA 7,8,11,4,10,13,2,7,3
40    DATA 8,8,4,7000,5000,3000
50    MAT   READ S,P
60    PRINT "SALES MATRIX"
70    MAT   PRINT S;
80    PRINT "PRICE MATRIX"
90    MAT   PRINT P;
100   MAT T=S*P
110   PRINT "TOTAL SALES MATRIX"
120   MAT   PRINT T
130   END
```

$$T = \begin{matrix} & S & \\ \begin{pmatrix} 7 & 8 & 11 \\ 4 & 10 & 13 \\ 2 & 7 & 3 \\ 8 & 8 & 4 \end{pmatrix} & \begin{matrix} P \\ \begin{pmatrix} 7000 \\ 5000 \\ 3000 \end{pmatrix} \end{matrix} \end{matrix}$$

Figure 9.9a. The program calculates the total sales matrix T using the matrix multiplication in line 100.

```
RUN
SALES MATRIX
   7      8      11
   4     10      13
   2      7       3
   8      8       4
 PRICE MATRIX
 7000
 5000
 3000
TOTAL SALES MATRIX
 122000
 117000
 58000
 108000
READY
```

Figure 9.9b. Running the program of Fig. 9.9a. We see the two inputs to the program: the sales matrix and the price matrix. They are followed by the resulting total sales matrix. The results are as we calculated them in Fig. 9.8c.

We now solve this problem in reverse: Given the fact that we want the total sales for each dealer to be $100,000 and given the sales matrix, what should be the price per car of a Chrysler, a Dodge, and a Plymouth? In solving this problem, we will consider only three dealers. The matrices are shown in Fig. 9.10a; please note that we are using a new sales matrix S. Now the total sales matrix is known, but the price matrix is unknown. We indicate its elements by P_1, P_2, and P_3. When we do the matrix operation indicated by T=S*P we get three equations shown in Fig. 9.10b.

$$100000 = 7*P_1 + 8*P_2 + 11*P_3$$
$$100000 = 4*P_1 + 10*P_2 + 13*P_3$$
$$100000 = 8*P_1 + 8*P_2 + 8*P_3$$

We must solve them for P_1, P_2, and P_3. If we do not use matrix notation, this is a fairly tedious task since it involves solving 3 simultaneous equations. Let us now set about solving this problem using matrices. We must find the elements of the matrix P. We first multiply both sides of the equation T=S*P by (1/S). We thus obtain

$$(1/S)*T = (1/S)*S*P$$

but (1/S)*(S)=1 so

$$(1/S)*T = 1*P = P \text{ or } P = (1/S)*T$$

Thus, we can easily obtain the elements of P by simply performing the matrix multiplication (1/S)*P. The term (1/S) is called the inverse of S. In BASIC we obtain the inverse of a matrix such as S by writing INV(S). This can only be done for matrices that have the same number of rows as columns—these are called square matrices. If we set A equal to INV(S) in the equation P=(1/S)*T, we obtain the equation

$$P = A*T$$

We thus solve for the elements of P by multiplying the matrix A by the matrix T. In most computer languages you would need a host of statements to calculate the inverse of a matrix. the fact that this can be done in only one statement in BASIC makes calculations involving the inverse of matrices, very simple to perform.

MATRIX REPRESENTATION OF SIMULTANEOUS EQUATIONS

TOTAL SALES   SALES   PRICE
   MATRIX   MATRIX   MATRIX

$$
\begin{array}{c}
T \\
\begin{pmatrix} 100000 \\ 100000 \\ 100000 \end{pmatrix}
\end{array}
=
\begin{array}{c}
S \\
\begin{pmatrix} 7 & 8 & 11 \\ 4 & 10 & 13 \\ 8 & 8 & 8 \end{pmatrix}
\end{array}
\begin{array}{c}
P \\
\begin{pmatrix} P_1 \\ P_2 \\ P_3 \end{pmatrix}
\end{array}
$$

Figure 9.10a. We now solve the problem in reverse. If we want the total sales for each dealer to be $100,000. For the sales matrix S given here, what should the price matrix P be?

$$100000 = 7*P_1 + 8*P_2 + 11*P_3$$
$$100000 = 4*P_1 + 10*P_2 + 13*P_3$$
$$100000 = 8*P_1 + 8*P_2 + 8*P_3$$

Figure 9.10b. The three equations obtained from the matrix multiplication in Fig. 9.10a. We must solve three simultaneous equations for P_1, P_2, and P_3. This can be done rather easily using the MAT statements shown in Fig. 9.11a.

We now write a program, shown in Fig. 9.11a, that determines what the price per car should be in order to obtain $100,000 in total sales for each dealer. The statement.

40   MAT   READ S,T

assigns the proper numbers in the DATA statement to the matrices S and T. We obtain the inverse of the matrix S and assign it to the matrix A in

50   MAT A=INV(S)

The inverse of a matrix has the same dimensions as the matrix itself. Since S is dimensioned as S(3,3), therefore A is dimensioned as A(3,3).

The required matrix P is obtained from 60   MAT P=A*T. When the program is run, as shown in Fig. 9.11b, we see the values of the matrix S, its inverse A, the total sales matrix T, and the solution to the problem, the matrix P. Thus each dealer should charge $5000 for a Chrysler, $5833.34 for a Dodge, and $1666.67 for a Plymouth if he wants his total to be $100,000. If you check these results you will see that, remarkably enough, they are correct.

We would like to make two remarks here.

1. The elements of the total sales matrix T do not all have to be the same in order to permit us to use this method. The elments could have had any value.

2. The method used in Fig. 9.11 could be used to solve any set of simultaneous equations.

SOLVING SIMULTANEOUS EQUATIONS USING MATRICES

```
10   REM USES INVERSE MATRIX TO CALCULATE
15   REM PRICE MATRIX
17   DIM A(3,3),P(3,1),T(3,1),S(3,3)
20   DATA 7,8,11,4,10,13,8,8,8
30   DATA 100000.,100000.,100000.
40   MAT  READ S,T
50   MAT A=INV(S)
60   MAT P=A*T
70   PRINT "SALES MATRIX"
80   MAT  PRINT S;
90   PRINT "INVERSE OF SALES MATRIX"
100  MAT  PRINT A
110  PRINT "TOTAL SALES  (IN $) MATRIX"
120  MAT  PRINT T;
130  PRINT "REQUIRED PRICE MATRIX"
140  MAT  PRINT P;
150  END
```

Figure 9.11a. One can solve the matrix equation T = S*P for P by multiplying both sides of the equation by (1/S). We thus get (1/S)*T = (1/S)*S*P. But (1/S*S) = S/S = 1 so (1/S*T = P. In BASIC (1/S) is called INV(S) or the inverse of S. Thus P = INV(S)*T. We get A, the inverse of the sales matrix, S, in 50 MAT A = INV (S). Using this we obtain the price matrix in 60 MAT P = A*T.

```
RUN
SALES MATRIX
 7       8      11
 4      10      13
 8       8       8
INVERSE OF SALES MATRIX
 .2            -.2           .05
-.6             .266667      .391667
 .4            -6.66667E-02  -.316667
TOTAL SALES   (IN $) MATRIX
 100000
 100000
 100000
REQUIRED PRICE MATRIX
 5000
 5833.34
 1666.67
READY
```

Figure 9.11b. Running the program of Fig. 9.11a. We see the input matrices: the sales and total sales matrix. We also see the inverse of the sales matrix. (One can calculate the inverse of a square matrix only.) We finally see the resulting price matrix.

In the problem of Fig. 9.11a all the elements of the matrix T are the same. In cases such as this, the matrix does not have to be read into the program. We can create the matrix by multiplying the appropriate scalar (number) by the matrix CON (the abbreviation for constant), a matrix whose elements are all ones. In Fig. 9.12a we rewrite the program of Fig. 9.11a using the CON matrix in line 55

55   MAT T=CON

The dimensions of CON in this case are determined by the dimensions of T. The dimenson of T are given in the DIM statement

20   DIM A(3,3),S(3,3),P(3,1),T(3,1)

Thus the CON matrix in this case looks like

$$\begin{pmatrix} 1 \\ 1 \\ 1 \end{pmatrix}$$

as is shown in Fig. 9.12b. In statement 57 we multiply T by 100000 and thus obtain the desired matrix* for T. One thing to note in statement 57 is that whenever a scalar multiplies any matrix, the scalar must appear in parentheses. When the program is run as shown in Fig. 9.12c, it produces the same results as the previous one did.

* It would have been simpler to perform statements 55 and 57 in one statement, e.g., **55 MAT T=(100000)*CON**. However, on most systems this is forbidden.

USING THE CON MATRIX

```
10    REM TOTAL SALES MATRIX CALCULATED
15    REM USING THE CON MATRIX
20    DIM A(3,3),S(3,3),P(3,1),T(3,1)
30    DATA 7,8,11,4,10,13,8,8,8
40    MAT   READ S
50    MAT A=INV(S)
55    MAT T=CON
57    MAT T=(100000.)*T
60    MAT P=A*T
70    PRINT "SALES MATRIX"
80    MAT   PRINT S;
90    PRINT "INVERSE OF SALES MATRIX"
100   MAT   PRINT A
110   PRINT "TOTAL SALES (IN$) MATRIX"
120   MAT   PRINT T;
130   PRINT " REQUIRED PRICE MATRIX"
140   MAT   PRINT P;
150   END
```

Figure 9.12a. We rewrite the program of Fig. 9.11a. Instead of reading in the matrix T, since all the elements in it are the same, we can create the T matrix in the program itself by using the CON matrix. The CON matrix consists of all ones. The dimension of the CON matrix is determined by the dimensions of T when 55 MAT T = CON is executed.

$$T = CON = \begin{pmatrix} 1 \\ 1 \\ 1 \end{pmatrix} \quad T = (100000)*T = \begin{pmatrix} 100000 \\ 100000 \\ 100000 \end{pmatrix}$$

Figure 9.12b. Since T is dimensioned as T(3,1), the CON matrix appears as shown here. In 57 MAT T = (100000.)*T we obtain the desired matrix T. When you multiply a matrix by a scalar, the scalar must appear in parentheses.

```
RUN
SALES MATRIX
 7        8        11
 4        10       13
 8        8        8
INVERSE OF SALES MATRIX
 .2               -.2             .05
-.6                .266667        .391667
 .4               -6.66667E-02   -.316667
TOTAL SALES (IN$) MATRIX
 100000
 100000
 100000
 REQUIRED PRICE MATRIX
 5000
 5833.34
 1666.67
READY
```

Figure 9.12c. Running the program of Fig. 9.12a. We obtain the same results we obtained when we read the matrix T in Fig. 9.11a.

In the program of Fig. 9.13a, we demonstrate matrix addition and subtraction. An example of matrix addition is given in

80   MAT C=A+B

The dimensions of A and B must be the same. They are specified in the DIM statement

20   DIM A(2,3),B(2,3),C(2,3)

The process of addition works as folows: the elements of A are added to the corresponding elements of B, giving the elements of C. Thus the results of adding the matrices A and B

$$\begin{pmatrix} 1 & 2 & 3 \\ 4 & 5 & 6 \end{pmatrix} + \begin{pmatrix} 2 & 3 & 4 \\ 5 & 6 & 7 \end{pmatrix}$$

where A is the matrix on the left and B is the one on the right, is the matrix C

$$\begin{pmatrix} 3 & 5 & 7 \\ 9 & 11 & 13 \end{pmatrix}$$

as is shown in Fig. 9.13b. An example of matrix subtraction is also given in Fig. 9.13a.

110   MAT C=A-B

Again the dimensions of A and B must be the same. The process of subtraction works as follows: the elements of B are subtracted from the corresponding element of A, giving the elements of C.

Thus the result of subtracting B from A is

$$\begin{matrix} -1 & -1 & -1 \\ -1 & -1 & -1 \end{matrix}$$

as we see in Fig. 9.13b. In both addition and subtraction, the dimensions of C are the same as those of A or B.

MATRIX ADDITION AND SUBTRACTION

```
10        REM MATRIX ADDITION AND SUBTRACTION
20        DIM A(2,3),B(2,3),C(2,3)
30        MAT READ A,B
40        PRINT "MATRIX A"
50        MAT PRINT A;
60        PRINT "MATRIX B"
70        MAT PRINT B;
80        MAT C=A+B
90        PRINT "MAT C=A+B"
100       MAT PRINT C;
110       MAT C=A-B
120       PRINT "MAT C=A-B"
130       MAT PRINT C;
140       DATA 1,2,3,4,5,6
150       DATA 2,3,4,5,6,7
160       END
```

Figure 9.13a. Program performs the matrix addition A+B and the matrix substraction A−B. For both of these operations, the dimensions of A and B must be the same.

```
RUN
PROGRAM TRANSFERRED TO COMPILER
MATRIX A
 1        2        3
 4        5        6
MATRIX B
 2        3        4
 5        6        7
MAT C=A+B
 3        5        7
 9       11       13
MAT C=A-B
-1       -1       -1
-1       -1       -1
READY
```

Figure 9.13b. Running the program of Fig. 9.13a. In matrix addition, the elements of A are added to the corresponding ones in B, giving the elements of C. For subtraction the elements of B are subtracted from the corresponding elements of A, producing the elements of C. Thus the dimension of C in both these processes is the same as the dimensions of A or B.

We now explain matrix multiplication in general with the example

$$
\overset{\mathbf{A}}{\begin{pmatrix} 1 & 2 & 3 \\ 4 & 5 & 6 \end{pmatrix}} \quad * \quad \overset{\mathbf{B}}{\begin{pmatrix} 1 & 2 & 3 \\ 4 & 5 & 6 \\ 7 & 8 & 9 \end{pmatrix}}
$$

in the equation $C = A*B$. As we see A is the matrix on the left and B, the matrix on the right. C is the resulting matrix. As we have previously mentioned, the number of rows in B must equal the number of columns in A. In our example, this condition is satisfied since A has 3 columns, B has 3 rows.

As we see in Fig. 9.14, each of the three columns in matrix B separately multiplies matrix A. The result of each of these products is a column in matrix C. Thus when the column

$$
\begin{matrix} 1 \\ 4 \\ 7 \end{matrix}
$$

in B multiplies A it produces the elements in the first column of C, when the column

$$
\begin{matrix} 2 \\ 5 \\ 8 \end{matrix}
$$

multiplies B it produces the elements in the second column of C, and when

$$
\begin{matrix} 3 \\ 6 \\ 9 \end{matrix}
$$

multiplies B, it produces the elements in the third column of C. This is shown in Fig. 9.14. In all matrix multiplications the number of rows in resultant matrix C equals the number of rows in A. The number of columns in C equals the number of columns in B. Thus in our case, since A has 2 rows and B has 3 columns, C has 2 rows and 3 columns.

MATRIX MULTIPLICATION IN GENERAL

$$C = \quad A \quad * \quad B$$

$$\begin{pmatrix} 1 & 2 & 3 \\ 4 & 5 & 6 \end{pmatrix} \begin{pmatrix} 1 & 2 & 3 \\ 4 & 5 & 6 \\ 7 & 8 & 9 \end{pmatrix}$$

Step 1 of multiplying the matrix A times the matrix B

$$A \qquad\qquad B$$

$$\begin{pmatrix} 1 & 2 & 3 \\ 4 & 5 & 6 \end{pmatrix} \begin{pmatrix} 1 \\ 4 \\ 7 \end{pmatrix} \begin{pmatrix} 2 \\ 5 \\ 8 \end{pmatrix} \begin{pmatrix} 3 \\ 6 \\ 9 \end{pmatrix}$$

Step 2. We treat each column of B as a column matrix

$$C = \begin{pmatrix} 1*1 + 2*4 + 3*7 & 1*2 + 2*5 + 3*8 & 1*3 + 2*6 + 3*9 \\ 4*1 + 5*4 + 6*7 & 4*2 + 5*5 + 6*8 & 4*3 + 5*6 + 6*9 \end{pmatrix}$$

Step 3. When we multiply A by each of the columns of B, we get three columns of results.

$$C = \begin{pmatrix} 30 & 36 & 42 \\ 66 & 81 & 96 \end{pmatrix}$$

Step 4. We perform the addition in step 3 and obtain these results for the matrix C.

Figure 9.14. Performing the matrix multiplication A*B.

We now write a program, shown in Fig. 9.15a, that will multiply the matrices A and B and obtain the matrix C. Both matrix A and B are read in line 30. There the numbers in the DATA statement in line 110 are assigned to the matrix A and the numbers in the DATA statement in line 120 are assigned to the matrix B. We check this by including 50   MAT PRINT A ; and 70   MAT PRINT B ; in the program. When these two statements are executed, as shown in Fig. 9.15b , the matrices are printed. We see that they are the same as the matrices A and B which were shown in Fig. 9.14 and are now shown to the right of Fig. 9.15a. The matrix multiplication is performed in 90   MAT C $=$ A ∗B. The results of this multiplication are shown at the end of Fig. 9.15b under the heading MATRIX C and they agree with what we calculated in Fig. 9.14.

PROGRAMMING THE GENERAL MATRIX MULTIPLICATION

```
10    REM GENERAL MATRIX MULTIPLICATION
20    DIM A(2,3),B(3,3),C(2,3)
30    MAT  READ A,B
40    PRINT "MATRIX A"
50    MAT  PRINT A;
60    PRINT "MATRIX B"
70    MAT  PRINT B;
80    PRINT "MATRIX C"
90    MAT C=A*B
100   MAT  PRINT C;
110   DATA 1,2,3,4,5,6
120   DATA 1,2,3,4,5,6,7,8,9
130   END
```

$$C = \begin{pmatrix} 1 & 2 & 3 \\ 4 & 5 & 6 \end{pmatrix} * \begin{pmatrix} 1 & 2 & 3 \\ 4 & 5 & 6 \\ 7 & 8 & 9 \end{pmatrix}$$

Figure 9.15a. The program performs the matrix operation A*B which was done manually in Fig. 9.14.

```
RUN
MATRIX A
   1      2      3
   4      5      6
MATRIX B
   1      2      3
   4      5      6
   7      8      9
MATRIX C
  30     36     42
  66     81     96
 READY
```

Figure 9.15b. Running the program of Fig. 9.15a. The results are the same as those we obtained in Fig. 9.14.

In mathematics and physics, the student is often required to perform the dot product of two vectors. The dot product of the vector $\mathbf{A} = 3\mathbf{i} + 2\mathbf{j} - 4\mathbf{k}$ and the vector $\mathbf{B} = 6\mathbf{i} + 0\mathbf{j} + 7\mathbf{k}$ is shown in Fig. 9.16a. The symbols $\mathbf{i}$, $\mathbf{j}$ and $\mathbf{k}$ represent the unit vectors along the X, Y, and Z axes, respectively. The dot product is given by $\mathbf{A} \cdot \mathbf{B} = 3*6 + 2*0 - 4*7$: i.e., the coefficient of $\mathbf{i}$ in $\mathbf{A}$ multiplies the coefficient of $\mathbf{i}$ in $\mathbf{B}$; the coefficient of $\mathbf{j}$ in $\mathbf{A}$ multiplies the coefficient of $\mathbf{j}$ in $\mathbf{B}$; and the coefficient of $\mathbf{k}$ in $\mathbf{A}$ multiplies the coefficient of $\mathbf{k}$ in $\mathbf{B}$. We then add these three products and get our answer: -10. This is also called the scalar product because the result is a scalar. In order to do this calculation with matrices, we have to write one of the vectors as a 1 by 3 matrix (1 row and 3 columns), called a row vector, and the other one as a 3 by 1 matrix, which we now call a column vector. Originally, the vectors $\mathbf{A}$ and $\mathbf{B}$ are represented as the column vectors

$$\begin{pmatrix} 3 \\ 2 \\ -4 \end{pmatrix} \text{ and } \begin{pmatrix} 9 \\ 0 \\ 7 \end{pmatrix}$$

respectively. We then make the vector $\mathbf{A}$ into a row vector and obtain $(3 \quad 2 \quad -4)$ as is shown in Fig. 9.16b. We then do the matrix multiplication and obtain the same answer as before, -10.

PERFORMING THE DOT PRODUCT

$$\mathbf{A} = 3\mathbf{i} + 2\mathbf{j} - 4\mathbf{k}$$
$$\mathbf{B} = 6\mathbf{i} + 0\mathbf{j} + 7\mathbf{k}$$
$$\mathbf{A} \cdot \mathbf{B} = 18 - 28 = 10$$

Figure 9.16a. Taking the dot product of the vectors A and B. The vectors **i**, **j**, and **k** are unit vectors along the X, Y, and Z axes, respectively. In matrix notation, the vectors are, as usual, column matrices.

$$\mathbf{A} = \begin{pmatrix} 3 \\ 2 \\ -4 \end{pmatrix} \qquad \mathbf{B} = \begin{pmatrix} 6 \\ 0 \\ 7 \end{pmatrix}$$

Transpose of **A**   **B**

$$(3 \quad 2 \quad -4) \begin{pmatrix} 6 \\ 0 \\ 7 \end{pmatrix} = (18 + 0 - 28) = (-10)$$

Figure 9.16b. In order to perform the dot product using matrix multiplication, we must make one of the vectors a row matrix. This is an example of taking the transpose of a matrix. Thus we have taken the transpose of the vector **A** and have obtained (3 2 −4). When the indicated matrix multiplication is performed, we obtain the same answer as in Fig. 9.16a.

There is a matrix operation which, when applied to vectors, changes a column vector to a row vector and vice versa. It is called the transpose. We will use it to change the column vector **A** into a row vector **D,** in the program shown in Fig. 9.17a, which calculates the dot product. The transpose of

$$\begin{pmatrix} 3 \\ 2 \\ -4 \end{pmatrix}$$

is (3   2 -4).   If we want the matrix A to be the transpose of the matrix A, we write, as is shown in line 60,

        60   MAT D=TRN(A)

Since we will use the transpose to change the column vector A into the row vector D, we will dimension both A and B as column vectors in the DIM statement and read them in

        50   MAT   READ A,B

Since D, the transpose of A, is a row vector we can now write the dot product as

        70   MAT C=D*B

Since the answer is a scalar, the matrix C has only one element C(1,1); we instruct the computer to print the answer in

        120   PRINT "DOT PRODUCT OF TRN(A)*B=";C(1,1)

The result is -10, as we see when the program is run in Fig. 9.17b.

USING THE TRANSPOSE TO FIND THE DOT PRODUCT

```
10    REM FINDING THE DOT PRODUCT
20    REM USING THE TRANSPOSE
30    DIM C(1,1),D(1,3),A(3,1),B(3,1)
40    DATA 3,2,-4,6,0,7
50    MAT   READ A,B
60    MAT D=TRN(A)
70    MAT C=D*B
80    PRINT "MATRIX A"
90    MAT   PRINT A;
100   PRINT "TRANSPOSE OF A"
110   MAT   PRINT D;
115   PRINT "MATRIX B"
117   MAT   PRINT B;
120   PRINT "DOT PRODUCT OF TRN(A)*B=";C(1,1)
130   END
```

Figure 9.17a. Program calculates the dot product of the vectors **A** and **B**. These vectors are read in as usual. The statement 60   MAT D = TRN(A) converts the vector **A** into a row vector **D**. This is a special case of taking the transpose of a matrix. The dot product is then performed in 70   MAT C = D*B.

```
RUN
MATRIX A
 3
 2
-4
TRANSPOSE OF A
 3      2     -4
MATRIX B
 6
 0
 7
DOT PRODUCT OF TRN(A)*B=-10
READY
```

Figure 9.17b. Running the program of Fig. 9.17a. The transpose of A is a row vector.

In general the transpose of an M by N matrix is an N by M matrix such that the element of $A(I,J)$ of the original matrix A, becomes the elements $B(J,I)$ of the transposed matrix, B. Thus the matrix

$$A = \begin{pmatrix} 1 & 2 & 3 \\ 4 & 5 & 6 \end{pmatrix}$$

when transposed becomes

$$B = \begin{pmatrix} 1 & 4 \\ 2 & 5 \\ 3 & 6 \end{pmatrix}$$

Note that the element of $A(2,3)$ of the original matrix is in the second row, third column, and is thus 6. The element $B(3,2)$ of the transposed matrix is in the third row, second column, and must also be 6.

We now see why the transpose of a column vector is a row vector: If we call

$$A = \begin{pmatrix} 3 \\ 2 \\ -4 \end{pmatrix}$$

then $A(1,1)=3$, $A(2,1)=2$, and $A(3,1)=-4$. Therefore if D is the name of the transposed matrix, then $D(1,1)=3$, $D(1,2)=2$, and $D(1,3)=-4$. We thus get a matrix that has one row and 3 columns. It is $D = (3 \quad 2 \quad -4)$.

There is one special matrix we have not discussed: it is the identity matrix. It is a square matrix, and in BASIC it is written as IDN. If it is a 3 by 3 matrix, it looks like

$$\begin{pmatrix} 100 \\ 010 \\ 001 \end{pmatrix}$$

It has ones on the diagonal which goes from the upper left to the lower right corner of the matrix and zeros elsewhere. If we wanted to set the matrix B equal to the identity matrix, we would write 20   MAT B=IDN and dimension B in a DIM statement. Some properties of the identity matrix are as follows:

1. If you multiply a matrix A by the identity matrix, you obtain A as the answer.
2. If you multiply a square matrix by its inverse, you obtain the identity matrix.

We now list and explain all the matrix operations and special matrices in the following table. The table displays examples of the form you must follow when writing these statements. It also gives all the possible dimensioning options available on any system.

MATRIX Statement	Function

10   MAT READ A
       or
10   MAT READ A(L,M)
  The subscripts may be numbers, variables, or an expression.
 	
Other examples:
20   MAT READ A,B,C
30   MAT READ A(L,M),B,C(I,K)
	Reads data into elements of matrix row by row from left to right.
	  If both dimensions of A are smaller than 11, and A has not been dimensioned in a DIM statement, it must be dimensioned in the MAT READ. If A has been dimensioned in the DIM statement, the dimension may be reduced for a smaller-sized matrix in the MAT READ.

20 MAT PRINT A, or 20 MAT PRINT A 30 MAT PRINT A; Other examples: 20 MAT PRINT A,B;C 30 MAT PRINT A;B,C;	When a comma or no no punctuation at all follows a matrix, the computer prints the elements of A, one row per line; the elements are printed starting in columns 1, 16, 31, 46, etc. When a semicolon follows a matrix, the computer prints the elements of A closer together and, again, one row per line. A cannot be dimensioned in MAT PRINT. It must have been dimensioned previously.
10 MAT C=A+B	Adds elements of A to corresponding elements of B, giving the elements of C. Both A and B must have the same dimension and must be defined and dimensioned previously. They determine the dimensions of C.*
20 MAT C=A−B	Elements of B subtracted from the corresponding elements of A, giving elements of C. Both A and B must have the same dimensions and must have been previously defined and dimensioned. They determine the dimensions of C.*
30 MAT C=A∗B	Matrices multiplied. Dimensions of the matrices are related by C(L,N)=A(L,M)∗ B(M,N). Thus the number of columns in A must equal the number of rows in B. The number of rows in C equals the number of rows in A. The numbers of columns in C equals the number of columns in B. A and B must have been previously defined and dimensioned. The dimensions of C * are determined by the matrix product.

    * On some systems C does not have to be dimensioned; however, on other systems, C must be previously dimensioned.

(Continued)

Table (*Continued*)

MATRIX Statement	Function
25 MAT C = TRN(A)	C is the transpose of A. The transpose of a M by N matrix is an N by M matrix such that the element A(I,J) of the original matrix A, becomes the element B(J,I) of the transpose matrix. A must have been previously defined and dimensioned.*
20 MAT C = INV(A)	C is the inverse of A, i.e., C*A equals the identity matrix. The matrix A must be a square matrix and previously defined and dimensioned. The matrix C has the same dimensions * as A.
20 MAT C = (Scalar)*A	Scalar multiplication of a matrix A. All the elements of the matrix A are multiplied by the same scalar, which appears in parentheses. The scalar may be a constant, a variable, or an expression involving a calculation. The matrix A must be previously defined and dimensioned.*
10 MAT C = A	Matrix equivalence. The matrix C is equated to A. A must be previously defined and dimensioned.*
20 MAT INPUT A or 20 MAT INPUT A(L,M) The subscripts can be numbers, variables, or expressions	Same as MAT READ except that numbers are typed in during the execution of the program, one row at a time. For each row required, the computer prints a question mark.

    * On some systems C does not have to be dimensioned; however, on other systems, C must be previously dimensioned.

Special matrices

Name	Basic symbol		Use in statement	Form	Comments
Zero	ZER	10	MAT X=ZER(3,4)	$\begin{pmatrix} 0000 \\ 0000 \\ 0000 \end{pmatrix}$	All elements are zero
			or		
		5	DIM X(3,4)		
		10	MAT X=ZER		
Constant	CON	10	MAT X=CON(2,3)	$\begin{pmatrix} 111 \\ 111 \end{pmatrix}$	All elements are ones
			or		
		5	DIM X(2,3)		
		10	MAT X=CON		
Identity	IDN	5	MAT X=IDN(4,4)	$\begin{pmatrix} 1000 \\ 0100 \\ 0010 \\ 0001 \end{pmatrix}$	Square matrix which has zeros everywhere except on a diagonal line, going from the upper left to lower right; on the diagonal, the elements are all ones
			or		
		5	DIM X(4,4)		
		10	MAT X=IDN		

PROBLEMS

1. The inventory of different types of cans of soups for four stores, is given by the following table

Store No.	Mushroom	Tomato	Celery
1	6	10	20
2	17	18	4
3	3	19	10
4	64	30	4

   If you used the matrix C to represent this table what would the value of the following elements of C be? C(1,1), C(2,2), C(3,2), C(2,3), C(4,1), C(4,3).

2. Using the MAT ZER statement, write the statement that would assign zeros to the five counters:

   R(1), R(2), R(3), R(4), R(5)

3. Given the doubly dimensioned variable A, whose elements are given by

$$\begin{pmatrix} 6 & 9 & 4 & 3 \\ 3 & 1 & 6 & 4 \\ 2 & 1 & 7 & 2 \end{pmatrix}$$

   and using nested FOR–NEXT loops write a program that reads these elements in from the DATA statement 10   DATA 6,9,4,3,3,1,6,4,2,1,7,2 row by row.

4. Write a program that using a MAT READ, a DATA, and a MAT PRINT statement, produces the following matrix:

$$\begin{pmatrix} 1 & 2 \\ 3 & 4 \\ 5 & 6 \end{pmatrix}$$

5. What changes would you have to make in the program of problem 4 so that it produces the matrix

$$\begin{pmatrix} 1 & 2 & 3 \\ 4 & 5 & 6 \end{pmatrix}$$

6. What is wrong with the following program whose aim is to produce the matrix

$$\begin{pmatrix} 1 & 2 \\ 3 & 4 \end{pmatrix}$$

```
10    DIM A(2,2)
20    FOR I=1 TO 2
30    FOR J=1 TO 2
40    MAT READ A(I,J)
50    NEXT J
60    NEXT I
70    FOR L=1 TO 2
80    FOR K=1 TO 2
90    MAT PRINT A(I,J)
100   NEXT K
110   NEXT I
120   END
```

7. Which of the following matrix multiplications are allowed?

a. $\begin{pmatrix} 1 & 2 & 3 \\ 4 & 5 & 6 \\ 7 & 8 & 9 \end{pmatrix} \begin{pmatrix} 1 \\ 2 \\ 3 \\ 4 \end{pmatrix}$

b. $\begin{pmatrix} 1 & 1 & 2 & 3 \\ 3 & 1 & 2 & 1 \\ 4 & 1 & 3 & 6 \end{pmatrix} \begin{pmatrix} 3 \\ 2 \\ 1 \end{pmatrix}$

c. $\begin{pmatrix} 1 & 2 \\ 3 & 4 \end{pmatrix} \begin{pmatrix} 4 \\ 6 \end{pmatrix}$

d. $(1 \quad 6 \quad 3) \begin{pmatrix} 3 \\ 2 \\ 2 \end{pmatrix}$

e. $\begin{pmatrix} 1 & 6 & 3 \\ 3 & 6 & 1 \end{pmatrix} \begin{pmatrix} 2 \\ 3 \\ 4 \end{pmatrix}$

8. Write a program to multiply the following two matrices

$$\begin{pmatrix} 3 & 6 & 7 \\ 4 & 2 & 1 \end{pmatrix} \begin{pmatrix} 3 \\ 4 \\ 1 \end{pmatrix}$$

9. The following set of simultaneous equations

$$6 = 3X + Y$$
$$8 = 2X - 3Y$$

can be solved by using the following matrix equation

$$\begin{pmatrix} 6 \\ 8 \end{pmatrix} = \begin{pmatrix} 3 & 1 \\ 2 & -3 \end{pmatrix} \begin{pmatrix} X \\ Y \end{pmatrix}$$

Write a program which will solve this matrix equation for the values of X and Y.

10. For which of the following matrices could you find the inverse?

$$\overset{\text{A}}{\begin{pmatrix} 6 & 7 & 4 \\ 3 & 1 & 2 \end{pmatrix}} \qquad \overset{\text{B}}{(4)} \qquad \overset{\text{C}}{\begin{pmatrix} 3 & 2 \\ 1 & 6 \end{pmatrix}} \qquad \overset{\text{D}}{\begin{pmatrix} 1 \\ 2 \end{pmatrix}}$$

11. Write a program that will produce the following matrix using the CON matrix.

$$\begin{pmatrix} 6 & 6 \\ 6 & 6 \\ 6 & 6 \\ 6 & 6 \end{pmatrix}$$

12. Write a program that will produce the following using the CON and IDN matrices.

$$\begin{pmatrix} 4 & 2 & 2 \\ 2 & 4 & 2 \\ 2 & 2 & 4 \end{pmatrix}$$

13. The cosine of the angle θ between two vectors $\mathbf{A}$ and $\mathbf{B}$ is given by $\cos \theta = \dfrac{\mathbf{A} \cdot \mathbf{B}}{|A| \times |B|}$ where $|A|$, the absolute value of the vector $\mathbf{A}$, is given by $|A|^2 = \mathbf{A} \cdot \mathbf{A}$. The value of $|B|$ is given by $|B|^2 = \mathbf{B} \cdot \mathbf{B}$. Write a program which will find the angle between the following vectors $\mathbf{A}$ and $\mathbf{B}$: $\mathbf{A} = 2\mathbf{i} + 2\mathbf{j} + 2\mathbf{k}$, $\mathbf{B} = 2\mathbf{i} + 3\mathbf{j} + 4\mathbf{k}$.

14. Write a program that will multiply the following two matrices

$$\begin{matrix} & A & \\ \begin{pmatrix} 4 & 3 & 2 \\ 1 & 2 & 6 \end{pmatrix} \end{matrix} \begin{matrix} & B & \\ \begin{pmatrix} 3 & 2 & 4 \\ 6 & 7 & 1 \\ 1 & 1 & 1 \end{pmatrix} \end{matrix}$$

15. Write a program that will print the results of adding and then subtracting the following two matrices

$$\begin{matrix} & A & \\ \begin{pmatrix} 4 & 6 & 3 \\ 7 & 1 & 2 \end{pmatrix} \end{matrix} \begin{matrix} & B & \\ \begin{pmatrix} 6 & 1 & 1 \\ 2 & 0 & 4 \end{pmatrix} \end{matrix}$$

16. Given $A = \begin{pmatrix} 4 & 6 & 3 \\ 7 & 1 & 2 \\ 4 & 7 & 2 \end{pmatrix}$

Write a program that will find the inverse of A and will then show that $A*\mathrm{INV}(A)$ equals a matrix which, were it not for the approximations used in calculating $\mathrm{INV}(A)$, equals the identity matrix

$$\begin{pmatrix} 1 & 0 & 0 \\ 0 & 1 & 0 \\ 0 & 0 & 1 \end{pmatrix}$$

10

PRINT USING and Files

10.1. Image Printing: Using the `PRINT USING` Statement

Until now we had to rely on commas, semicolons, and the `TAB` function for positioning our results on the teletypewriter page. We now introduce a method that will enable us to instruct the computer to print our results—strings and numbers—as an exact image of the way we specify them in our program. We can do this by using the `PRINT USING` statement in conjunction with the `IMAGE` statement.*

In the `PRINT USING` statement, we specify the variables, numbers, expressions, and strings that we want printed. An example is `40  PRINT USING 60,L$,F$,A,W`. The number that immediately follows the word `USING` refers to the number of the statement in which we specify how we want these items printed. This statement—which we will explain in more detail in the next paragraph—is called an `IMAGE` statement. On most systems, the word `IMAGE` is not used in the program. The form of the `IMAGE` statement on your system may vary slightly from what we describe here. We suggest that you consult your computer manual for details.

In the program of Fig. 10.1a, we demonstrate the use of the `PRINT USING` statement and the `IMAGE` statement. This program reads the last name, first name, age, and weight of a person, then prints them in tabular form. In this program we use the statement

```
40 PRINT USING 60,L$,F$,A,W
```

to instruct the computer to print the variables `L$` , `F$`, `A`, and `W` (in that order) in a way we specify in the `IMAGE` statement

```
60:#########,  ####    ###   ##.#
```

Each of the groups of number signs, #, in the `IMAGE` statement indicates where and how we want the characters assigned to the corresponding item in the `PRINT USING` statement printed—the position of the # indicates in which columns we want the computer to print the characters. The space occupied in the results by these columns is called a field. The groups of #s in the `IMAGE` statement are called field specifications. The first field specification (nine #s) indicates that we want the computer to print the characters assigned to `L$`, in a field

---

*The instructions we describe here are used on the IBM CALL OS, IBM VM/370, and the XEROX Sigma 5–9 systems. These instructions are used in a slightly modified form on most other systems.

THE PRINT USING AND IMAGE STATEMENTS

```
10 REM THE PRINT USING STATEMENT
20 FOR I=1 TO 3
30 READ L$,F$,A,W
40 PRINT USING 60,L$,F$,A,W
50 NEXT I
60:#########,  ####     ###    ##.#
70 DATA JONES,TOM,10,84.28
80 DATA CONRAD,JOSEPH,6,96.74
90 DATA SMITH,JOHN,12,111.4
100 END
```

Figure 10.1a. Anything that appears in the IMAGE statement (line 60), except for the #, is printed in the results. Each group of #s—called a field specification—corresponds to a variable, number, or string in the PRINT USING statement (line 40). The field specification determines how a number or a string will be printed. The space occupied by the printed number or string is called a field.

nine columns wide. The second field specification (four #s) indicates that we want the characters that were assigned to F$, printed in a field four columns wide, etc. Anything that appears in the IMAGE statement after the colon (with the exception of the #s and, as we shall see, the !s) is printed in the results. For instance, if a comma, a semicolon, quotation mark, or a blank appear in an IMAGE statement, they will be printed in the results. Thus the comma in line 60 will be printed, as we see in each line of the results in Fig. 10.1b. We will now examine the effect of the IMAGE statement in line 60 the first time the PRINT USING statement in line 40 is executed.

Since there are no blanks in line 60 between the colon and the first field specification ######## the computer prints the string assigned to L$; namely, JONES, starting in the first column. It then prints a comma in the column corresponding to where the comma appears in the IMAGE statement. It then skips to the column on the teletypewriter page corresponding to the one in which the second field specification #### begins and prints the string TOM starting there. Strings are always printed starting from the left of the field. In both cases, the number of #s in the IMAGE statement turned out to be more than the number of characters in the string; this is allowed.

The computer next skips to the column corresponding to where the third field specification ### begins. It prints 10, the number assigned to A, starting from the right of the field, and thus leaves the leftmost column of this field blank. Thus when a field specification does not include a decimal point, integers are printed starting from the right of the field.

The computer then skips to the column corresponding to where the fourth field specification ##.# begins—this field specification has a decimal point in it. The computer aligns the decimal point in 84.28 (the number assigned to W) in a column corresponding to the one in which the decimal point appears in the IMAGE statement. It prints the digits to the left of the decimal point in the number, in the columns to the left of the decimal point in the field. It then prints the decimal point. It finally prints the digits to the right of the decimal point. If there are not enough columns in the field to accommodate the digits to the right of the decimal point, the computer rounds the number. In our case it prints the number as 84.3. If this field specification were written as ###, and thus did not contain a decimal point, the computer would print only those digits in 84.3 to the left of the decimal point in the number, namely 84. It would print these digits starting from the right of the field.

If there are more #s to the right of the decimal point in the field specification than are needed, the computer places zeros there. Thus if 84.28 were to be printed according to the field specification ##.###, it would be printed as 84.280.

We now return to the execution of the program. The next time line 40 is executed, the computer prints CONRAD, the comma, and then prints JOSE starting in the leftmost column of the second field. Since there is no room specified in this field to accommodate PH—the last two letters in JOSEPH—the computer does not print them. It then prints the value of A, which is 6, in the last column of the third field. Finally it rounds 96.74, the value of W, to 96.7 and prints it in the fourth field.

The third time the PRINT USING statement is executed, everything proceeds as we have just explained expect for the printing of 111.4 (the value of W). The field specification for this, ##.#, can only accommodate two digits to the left of the decimal point; however, there are 3 such digits in 111.4. In order to avoid the possibility of misleading you if it printed 11.4, the computer prints asterisks in this field. All of these results are shown in Fig. 10.1b.

```
RUN
JONES       ,   TOM         10    84.3
CONRAD      ,   JOSE         6    96.7
SMITH       ,   JOHN        12    ****
READY
```

Figure 10.1b. Strings are printed starting from the left of the field; integers starting from the right. A noninteger is printed so that its decimal point lines up with the one in the field specification, e.g., ##.#. The commas appear in the results because they appear in the IMAGE statement (line 60). The last number printed is too large for its field, so it is printed as ****.

The program in Fig. 10.2a is the same as that in Fig 10.1a except that we now label the results with the IMAGE statement in line 70. We can assure that the labels are in the correct columns by writing the second IMAGE statement directly after—and therefore under—the first one

```
70:    LAST NAME    "FIRST NAME"              AGE    WEIGHT
80:    #########,    ####                     ###    ###.#
```

and centering the fields under the corresponding labels. If we use quotation marks by mistake in the IMAGE statement, as we have done in line 70 for FIRST NAME, the quotation marks will be printed. We see this when the program is run, as shown in Fig. 10.2b.

In 20   PRINT USING 70 we show an example of how a PRINT USING statement can be used to instruct the computer to type an IMAGE statement—in this case line 70—which has no field specifications (#s) but consists only of strings. Note the number 70 in this PRINT USING statement is not followed by any items.

The IMAGE statement is a non-executable statement and can thus be placed anywhere in the program. It is only used when the associated PRINT USING statement is executed.

PRINT USING

> The form of the PRINT USING statement is: line number; followed by PRINT USING; followed by the line number of the IMAGE statement; the statement may end here or this last item is followed by a comma; followed by a variable, expression involving a mathematical operation, number, or string. If there are more than one of these items, they must be separated by commas. Examples:
>
> ```
> 30    PRINT USING 70
> 40    PRINT USING 80,"THINK",1.23,A$,A+B*C
> ```

IMAGE

> The form of the IMAGE statement is: line number, followed by a colon, followed by any characters you want printed and/or field specifications. A comma or quotation marks used in the IMAGE statement will be printed. Example:
>
> ```
> 70:    ANYTHING ##,# ####.#.
> ```

THE PRINT USING AND IMAGE STATEMENTS USED TO PRODUCE A TABLE

```
10  REM THE PRINT USING STATEMENT USED FOR
15  REM PRODUCING TABLES
20  PRINT USING 70
30  FOR I=1 TO 3
40  READ L$,F$,A,W
50  PRINT USING 80,L$,F$,A,W
60  NEXT I
70:    LAST NAME    "FIRST NAME"              AGE    WEIGHT
80:    #########,    ####                     ###    ###.#
90  DATA JONES,TOM,10,84.28
100 DATA CONRAD,JOSEPH,6,96.74
110 DATA SMITH,JOHN,12,111.4
120 END
```

Figure 10.2a. Same as Fig. 10.1a except that line 70 labels the columns produced by line 80. In order to print just what appears in the IMAGE (e.g., line 70), we type 20 PRINT USING 70. IMAGE statements are not executed they are only referred to when the associated PRINT USING statement is executed. They can therefore be placed anywhere in the program.

```
RUN
LAST NAME      "FIRST NAME"             AGE    WEIGHT
JONES      ,     TOM                    10      84.3
CONRAD     ,     JOSE                     6      96.7
SMITH      ,     JOHN                    12     111.4
READY
```

Figure 10.2b. Since quotation marks appear in the IMAGE in line 70, they also appear in the results.

In Fig. 10.3a we show how we can instruct the computer to print a number in exponential form by using an IMAGE statement. In order to do this, we must place four !s at the end of a group* of #s. For example

```
20:  FIRST PRODUCT IS #.###!!!!,SECOND IS ###.#!!!!
```

On some systems this group of #s must include a decimal point. On other systems, one may exclude the decimal point. The #s indicate how many digits one wishes to have in the non-exponential part of the number. On some systems, no matter where we place the decimal point in the field specification, it will always be printed after the first digit in the field. This is shown when the second number in the results is printed. The four exclamation points provide room for an E, a plus or minus sign, and a two-digit number indicating the power of ten.

In the PRINT USING statement in this program, we perform two calculations: 10   PRINT USING 20,2*3*4*5*6*7*8, 3*4*5*6*7*8. The results are shown in Fig. 10.3b

```
FIRST PRODUCT IS 4.032E+04,SECOND IS 2.016E+04
```

If there are fewer than four !s or more than four !s following a group of #s, as in

```
20:  ##.##!!        ##.##!!!!!!
```

of Fig. 10.4a, the number whose form is described by the first field specification (which has fewer than four !s) will be printed in nonexponential form. The two !s would be printed as though they were any other symbol, as is shown in Fig. 10.4b. The number whose form is described by the second field specification (which has six !s) will be printed in exponential form (because of the first four !s) and will be followed by two !s as is shown in Fig. 10.4b.

---

* On many systems the ↑ is used instead of ! in exponential field specifications.

EXPONENTIAL FIELD SPECIFICATION

```
10 PRINT USING 20,2*3*4*5*6*7*8,3*4*5*6*7*8
20: FIRST PRODUCT IS #.###!!!!,SECOND IS ###.#!!!!
30 END
```

Figure 10.3a. If we want a number printed in exponential form, we append four !s to the field specification. On some systems, the field specification must have a decimal point in it here.

```
RUN
FIRST PRODUCT IS 4.032E+04,SECOND IS 2.016E+04
READY
```

Figure 10.3b. For the system on which we ran this program, we see that no matter where we place the decimal point in the field specification, the decimal point is placed after the first digit in the field.

```
10 PRINT USING 20,30.3,   30123.4
20: ##.##!!      ##.##!!!!!!
30 END
```

Figure 10.4a. Shows what happens when we append fewer than four or more than four !s to the field specification.

```
RUN
30.30!!      3.012E+04!!
READY
```

Figure 10.4b. If there are fewer than four !s in the field specification, the number is printed in nonexponential form and is followed by !s. If there are more than four !s, the number is printed in exponential form and the extra !s are also printed.

If a plus sign precedes a field specification, as in $+\#\#.\#\#$, the number printed in the designated field will be preceded with a plus sign if it is positive, and with a minus sign if it is negative. On the other hand, if a minus sign precedes a field specification, as in $-\#\#.\#\#$, the number printed in the designated field will be preceded by a minus sign if it is negative, and by a blank if it is positive. All of this is shown in Figs. 10.5a and 10.5b.

If no sign precedes the field specification and the number to be printed in the designated field is negative, the computer will do one of two things depending on the version of BASIC you are using. It will either print the number with a minus sign preceding it or it will print a minus sign in the first column of the field and print asterisks in the remaining columns of the field.

CONTROLLING THE SIGN OF THE OUTPUT

```
10 PRINT USING 20,"SIGNS",+13.1,-16.2,+13.1,-16.2
20: #####  +##.##  +##.##   -##.##   -##.##
30 END
```

Figure 10.5a. If a plus sign precedes the field specification for a given number, the computer will print not only the number, but its sign as well. If a minus sign precedes the field specification for a given number, the computer will print the number, but will print the sign only if it is negative.

```
RUN
SIGNS +13.10 -16.20    13.10  -16.20
READY
```

Figure 10.5b. Running the program of Fig. 10.5a. The string SIGNS is printed in the first field.

If the number of field specifications in the IMAGE, e.g., 20:   FIRST ##.## SEC-OND ##.## END, exceeds the number of items in the PRINT USING statement, e.g., 10   PRINT USING 20,11.1 the computer uses the IMAGE statement up to the point of the first field specification which is not needed; then it stops. Thus when the program of Fig. 10.6a is executed, the computer only prints

FIRST 11.10   SECOND

since the string SECOND is followed by the first field specification that is not needed. Thus the string END is not printed. This is shown in Fig. 10.6b. If the number of items in the PRINT USING statement, e.g., 10   PRINT USING 20,11.1,22.2,33.3, exceeds the number of field specifications in the IMAGE statement, e.g., FIRST ##.## SECOND ##.## END, as is shown in Fig. 10.7a, the computer first prints the items for which there are field specifications. This is shown in the first line of Fig. 10.7b:

FIRST 11.10   SECOND 22.20 END

It then prints the remaining items in the PRINT USING statement—in this case 33.3—using the IMAGE statement as though it had not yet been used and thus prints a second line of results. This is shown in the second line of Fig. 10.7b.

FIRST 33.30   SECOND

We see that, as we expect, the computer uses the IMAGE statement only up to the first field specification that is not needed.

MORE FIELD SPECIFICATIONS THAN ITEMS IN PRINT USING

```
10 PRINT USING 20,11.1
20: FIRST ##.##   SECOND ##.## END
30 END
```

Figure 10.6a. Program in which there are more field specifications in the IMAGE statement than items in the PRINT USING statement.

```
RUN
FIRST 11.10   SECOND
READY
```

Figure 10.6b. The computer prints only that part of the IMAGE statement up to the first field specification that is not needed.

FEWER FIELD SPECIFICATIONS THAN ITEMS IN PRINT USING

```
10 PRINT USING 20,11.1,22.2,33.3
20: FIRST ##.##   SECOND ##.## END
30 END
```

Figure 10.7a. Program in which there are more items in the PRINT USING statement than corresponding field specifications in the IMAGE statement.

```
RUN
FIRST 11.10   SECOND 22.20 END
FIRST 33.30   SECOND
READY
```

Figure 10.7b. After the computer uses the IMAGE statement for the first two items in the PRINT USING statement, it uses it again for the third item, but this time only up to the first field specification that is not needed.

10.2. Data Files

In the course of writing programs, you will find it necessary to use the same set of data many times. For instance, you may write several versions of a program that will in all probability use the same data; or, on the other hand, you may write different programs that require the same data. Because of situations like these, it is very convenient to be able to save in the computer's memory the data for a given program, separate from the program itself. When data are saved in this way, the group of data is called a data file.

On some systems there are two types of data files available: (1) teletypewriter (sequential) files; (2) binary (random access) files.

On a teletypewriter file, the information is saved in a form (called the Binary Coded Decimal or BCD) that enables one to list the file simply by using the system command LIST. Thus when the characters on the file are printed, they appear in the same form as they would have if you had typed them on the teletypewriter; hence the name teletypewriter file. Another characteristic of a teletypewriter file is that, in order to obtain the tenth number stored on the file, you have to instruct the computer to read the first nine numbers. In other words, the computer must read the information written on the file in sequential order, hence this type of file is also called a sequential file.

On a binary file the information is stored in binary form, that is, all characters are written in a representation equivalent to zeros and ones. Binary files have two advantages over teletypewriter files. The computer can read a binary file faster than it can a teletypwriter file. Also, on many systems, the computer does not have to read the first nine pieces of data in order to obtain the tenth; for this reason, binary files are also called random-access files. It seems that each manufacturer uses a different form of file instructions in its version of BASIC. We have therefore chosen to describe the form that—except for minor modifications—is the one most commonly used. Also, in order to unify the treatment of both types of files (teletypewriter and binary), we will present the programs to be used with teletypewriter files so that, with a minor modifications, they can be used with binary files as well. On the version* of BASIC we will describe, the instructions INPUT # and PRINT # are used, respectivey, to read and write teletypewriter files; READ # and WRITE # are used, respectively, to read and write binary files.

Before you can write on a file, you must instruct the computer to make room for it in the computer's memory. This is called creating a file. We now describe the procedure for creating a teletypewriter file. This is done by first naming the file. After we type NEW, the computer requests the file's name by typing NEW PROGRAM NAME--, as is shown in Fig. 10.8a. We respond by typing the name we have decided to call the file: SAL. On most systems the file name can consist of up to 6 characters. Although we have not written anything on the file yet, we can save it by typing SAVE. This saves room in the memory for the file.

---

* We describe a modified Dartmouth version.

CREATING A TELETYPEWRITER FILE

```
NEW
NEW PROGRAM NAME-SAL
READY
SAVE
READY
```

Figure 10.8a. A teletypewriter file is used to save data. Before you can write on a file, you must make room for it in the computer's memory. This is done by first naming the file and then giving the instruction SAVE.

In Fig. 10.8b we present a program that writes a salesman's number and his salary for 2 weeks on the file SAL. SAL is an abbreviation for SALary. Before we can use a file in the program, we must use a statement that informs the computer that we will use the file SAL. This is done in

```
20   FILES SAL
```

After we type the salary information requested in line 30, the computer prints this information on the file SAL in

```
50   PRINT #1:N,S1,S2
```

This is similar to the ordinary print statement except that here we must inform the computer which file to write on (as we shall see in some programs we will use more than one file). The #1 informs the computer that we wish to write on the first file that appears after the word FILES in the FILES statement. In our case, it is SAL.

We type 5 sets of information in response to

```
40   INPUT N,S1,S2
```

as is shown in Fig. 10.8c. This information is written on the file in a way similar to what is depicted in Fig. 10.8d, i.e., in the order in which we type it. When the program is finished the computer places a mark on the file after the last number is written. This mark indicates that there are no more data on the file; i.e., the file is finished. It is called an end of file—abbreviated EOF.

FILES

> The form of the FILES statement is: line number; followed by FILES; followed by a list of files used in the program. If there is more than one file, the file names must be separated by commas. Example:
>
> ```
> 10   FILES A,B,C
> ```

PRINT FILE

> The form of the PRINT file statement is: line number, followed by PRINT # followed by a number, variable, or expression that corresponds to the position of the desired file name in the FILES statement. Thus 2 would correspond to the second file name in the FILES statement. This is followed by a colon—on some systems* by a semicolon. This is in turn followed by the list of the variables or expressions that will be printed on the file. If there is more than one variable in the list, the variables must be separated by commas. Examples:
>
> ```
> 10   PRINT #3:A,B,C(I)
> 10   PRINT #L:A,B(K+2),R$
> 20   PRINT #L+2:C$(3),A+2
> ```

The program we have presented in Fig. 10.8b can be used to write information on a binary file if the PRINT # statement is replaced with a WRITE # and the appropriate procedure is used to create the file. These instructions for writing on files may assume different forms on different systems.

* This is the case on the HP 2000C; however, only binary files are available. On this system READ # is used to read a binary file and PRINT # is used to write on a binary file.

WRITING ON A FILE

```
10    REM WRITING ON A FILE
20    FILES SAL
30    PRINT "TYPE:NUMBER,SALARY WEEK1,SALARY WEEK2"
40    INPUT N,S1,S2
50    PRINT #1:N,S1,S2
60    IF N <> 5 THEN 40
70    PRINT "THANK YOU "
80    END
```

Figure 10.8b. Writing information on the file SAL. In the FILES statement the computer assigns the number 1 to SAL, the first file in the FILE statement, so that you may refer to it in the program. Thus 50   PRINT #1:N,S1,S2 prints information on file SAL.

```
RUN
TYPE:NUMBER,SALARY WEEK1,SALARY WEEK2
?1,240.72,381.63
?2,256.91,325.70
?3,461.72,395.82
?4,371.64,287.20
?5,301.62,300.71
THANK YOU
READY
```

Figure 10.8c. Typing the information that will appear on the file SAL.

SAL	1	240.72	381.63	2	256.91	325.70	3	461.72	395.82	5	301.62	301.71	EOF

Figure 10.8d. How the information just written on the file SAL appears on it. When the program is finished, the computer places a mark on the file, indicating that the file is finished. This mark is called an end of file (EOF).

In Fig. 10.9a, we present a program that first reads the file SAL and then prints the information that is on the file. The statement

20   FILES SAL

again assigns the number 1 to SAL, so that in

40   INPUT #1:N,S1,S2

the computer reads the appropriate information from the file SAL. The first time this statement is executed, the computer reads the file SAL starting at its beginning. The data that is on this file was shown in Fig. 10.8d. Thus N is assigned the value 1; S1, the value 240.72; and S2, 381.63 as is shown in the first line of the table for Fig. 10.9a:

Time executed	N	S1	S2
1st	1	240.72	381.63

These values are then printed on the teletypewriter when

50   PRINT N,S1,S2

is executed. The second time line 40 is executed, the computer reads the information from SAL starting with the first piece of information it has not read (in other words from the point it left off). The values assigned to the variables at this point in the program are shown in the second line of the table for Fig. 10.9a:

Time executed	N	S1	S2
2nd	2	256.91	325.70

The variables N, S1, and S2 are therefore redefined. The computer then prints their values on the teletypewriter. When the program is run, as shown in Fig. 10.9b, we see that the computer successfully reads the file five times and prints the results. However, the sixth time it tries to read the file, an error message is printed

END-OF-FILE   IN LINE 40

We would have obtained a similar message if we had tried to read more information than was in a DATA statement. What actually happened here is that (as we previously explained) when the preceding program (Fig. 10.8b) had finished, the computer automatically placed an EOF on the file after the last number was printed. When the computer reads a file, this mark signals the computer that it has reached the end of the file. If the program tries to read any information passed the EOF, the computer produces an error message. In the next program we will show how to use an IF statement which will enable the program to recognize an EOF and thus transfer control to another part of the program; thus an EOF error message will not be produced.

The same procedure presented in Fig. 10.9a can be used to read the information from a binary file, if READ # is used instead of INPUT #. Again, these instructions may assume different forms on different systems.

PRINTING THE CONTENTS OF A FILE

```
10    REM PRINTING CONTENTS OF A FILE
20    FILES SAL
30    PRINT "SALESMAN","FIRST WEEK","2ND WEEK"
40    INPUT #1:N,S1,S2
50    PRINT N,S1,S2
60    GOTO 40
70    END
```

Figure 10.9a. Printing the information which is on file SAL. Because of the FILES statement, the INPUT #1 statement reads the information from SAL.

Time executed	N	S1	S2
1st	1	240.72	381.63
2nd	2	256.91	325.70
3rd	3	461.72	395.82
4th	4	371.64	287.20
5th	5	301.62	300.71

Table for Fig. 10.9a. How the variables on the file SAL are assigned to the variables in the program as the file is read in line 40.

```
RUN
SALESMAN         FIRST WEEK      2ND WEEK
   1                240.72        381.63
   2                256.91        325.7
   3                461.72        395.82
   4                371.64        287.2
   5                301.62        300.71
END-OF-FILE  IN LINE 40
READY
```

Figure 10.9b. Because an attempt is made to read the file for a sixth time, the computer encounters the EOF. Thus an error message is printed.

INPUT FILE

The form of the INPUT file statement is: line number, followed by INPUT #; followed by a number, variable, or expression that corresponds to the position of the desired file name in the FILES statement; followed by a colon—on some systems, a semicolon. This in turn is followed by the list of variables that we want read from the file. If there is more than one variable in the list, the variables must be separated by commas. Examples:

```
10    INPUT #3:A,B,C,(I)
20    INPUT #L:A,B(K+2),R$
30    INPUT #L+2:C$(3),A
```

We now present a program, shown in Fig. 10.10a, that uses two files. It takes the three pieces of data—a salesman number and his salary for two given weeks—from file SAL, adds a piece of data you type in—the third week salary—and writes all three on a new file called NEWSAL. NEWSAL is an abbreviation for NEW SALARY. In the beginning of the figure we show how we create the file NEWSAL. Then the statement

```
30    FILES SAL,NEWSAL
```

assigns the numbers 1 and 2 to SAL and NEWSAL, respectively. Thus

```
50    INPUT #1:N,S1,S2
```

reads the information from SAL and

```
90    PRINT #2:N,S1,S2,S3
```

prints this and the value of the salary S3 on NEWSAL as is shown in Fig. 10.10b.

In order to avoid the error message produced when the computer reaches an EOF, we have included in the program the statement

```
40    IF END #1 THEN 110
```

This transfers control to line 110 when the computer reaches the EOF on file SAL. If the computer does not encounter the EOF, the condition END #1 is false. Thus line 50 is executed next. Because of the FILES statement, the #1 in the IF statement refers to the file SAL.

The same procedure presented in Fig. 10.10a can be applied to binary files as well, if the correct statements are used. On some systems, the IF END # statement can be used to detect an end of file on binary files.

IF END

The form of the IF END statement is: IF; followed by END #; followed by a variable, number, or expression indicating the file number; followed by THEN; followed by the line number the computer is to branch to if it encounters an EOF on the indicated file. Examples:

```
10    IF END #2 THEN 30
30    IF END #N THEN 15
```

MERGING INFORMATION FROM A FILE AND THE TELETYPEWRITER ONTO A NEW FILE

```
NEW
NEW PROGRAM NAME--NEWSAL
READY
SAVE
READY
10    REM MERGING NEW DATA WITH FILE SAL
20    REM PRODUCING FILE NEW SAL
30    FILES SAL,NEWSAL
40    IF   END #1 THEN 110
50    INPUT #1:N,S1,S2
60    PRINT "WHAT IS SALARY FOR WEEK 3";
70    PRINT "FOR SALESMAN #";N;
80    INPUT S3
90    PRINT #2:N,S1,S2,S3
100    GOTO 40
110    PRINT "PROGRAM FINISHED"
120    END
```

Figure 10.10a. Takes data from SAL and new data—S3—that you type in and writes them on the file NEWSAL. Because of line 30, the computer assigns 1 to SAL and 2 to NEWSAL. Thus INPUT #1 refers to SAL and PRINT #2, to NEWSAL. The IF statement transfers control to line 110, when the end of file (EOF) is encountered; otherwise line 50 is executed.

```
RUN
WHAT  IS  SALARY  FOR  WEEK  3FOR  SALESMAN  #  1        ?314.26
WHAT  IS  SALARY  FOR  WEEK  3FOR  SALESMAN  #  2        ?284.11
WHAT  IS  SALARY  FOR  WEEK  3FOR  SALESMAN  #  3        ?311.16
WHAT  IS  SALARY  FOR  WEEK  3FOR  SALESMAN  #  4        ?319.61
WHAT  IS  SALARY  FOR  WEEK  3FOR  SALESMAN  #  5        ?386.17
PROGRAM  FINISHED
READY
```

Figure 10.10b. We type in the third week's salary for each salesman in response to the computer's question printed by lines 60 and 70. This information, plus the information from SAL, is printed on NEWSAL.

NEWSAL	1	240.72	381.63	314.26	2	256.91	325.70	384.11

Figure 10.10c. How the information appears on the file NEWSAL.

We now introduce a statement that will enable the computer to read a file more than once. It is the RESET # statement. It serves the same purpose for files that RESTORE serves for DATA statements. In fact, in some versions of BASIC, the instruction RESTORE # is used in place of RESET #. When the RESET # instruction is executed, it restores the situation in the specified file to where it was at the beginning of the program.* This enables the computer to read the entire file from its beginning more than once. In the program shown in Fig. 10.11a, the file NEWSAL is printed twice. Let us now investigate how the program works.

The IF statement in line 50 tests whether the computer has encountered an end of file on NEWSAL. If it has not, then the condition END #1 in line 50 is false. Thus the next statement executed is

        60   INPUT #1:N,S1,S2,S3

and the computer reads the desired information from NEWSAL. It then prints this information when

        70   PRINT N,S1,S2,S3

is executed. On the other hand, if the computer encounters an end of file, then the condition END #1 in line 50 is true. The computer then executes

        90   RESET #1

next. This now enables the computer to read the file again from the beginning when the statements in the I loop are executed for the second time. We see that when the program is run, as shown in Fig. 10.11b, the contents of the file are printed twice.

If the INPUT # statement is replaced by the specified form of the binary READ for your system, this program would print the contents of a binary file twice.

---

* On the HP 2000C, the instruction which does this for file # N is READ # N, 1.

USING THE RESET STATEMENT

```
10    REM PRINTS A FILE TWICE
20    FILES NEWSAL
30    FOR I=1 TO 2
40    PRINT "SALESMAN#","1ST WEEK","2ND WEEK","3RD WEEK"
50    IF  END #1 THEN 90
60    INPUT #1:N,S1,S2,S3
70    PRINT N,S1,S2,S3
80    GOTO 50
90    RESET #1
100   NEXT I
110   END
```

Figure 10.11a. The program prints the information stored on NEWSAL twice. Now NEWSAL is designated as file #1. The RESET # statement restores the situation in file #1 (NEWSAL) to the point where it was at the beginning of the program. This enables the computer to read the file again.

```
RUN
SALESMAN#        1ST WEEK        2ND WEEK        3RD WEEK
   1              240.72          381.63          314.26
   2              256.91          325.7           284.11
   3              461.72          395.82          311.16
   4              371.64          287.2           319.61
   5              301.62          300.71          386.17
SALESMAN#        1ST WEEK        2ND WEEK        3RD WEEK
   1              240.72          381.63          314.26
   2              256.91          325.7           284.11
   3              461.72          395.82          311.16
   4              371.64          287.2           319.61
   5              301.62          300.71          386.17
READY
```

Figure 10.11b. We see that the contents of NEWSAL are listed twice. The program can do this because of the presence of the RESET # statement in the program.

We now discuss two procedures that can be used only for teletypewriter files. In the first procedure, we show how we can list a teletypewriter file simply by using the system command LIST. In the second, we show how we can create a file without writing a program.

As we remember, the command LIST instructs the computer to list what is in the working area. In order to get the file NEWSAL in the working area, we use the system command OLD, as shown in Fig. 10.12a. The computer responds by typing

OLD PROGRAM NAME--

It is in fact asking for either the name of the program or the name of the file we want placed in the working area. We type NEWSAL. The computer brings this file into the working area and then types READY. We then type LIST and obtain the listing of the file as shown in Fig. 10.12a.

We can, without writing a program, create a teletypewriter file in the following way. First we name the file. In Fig. 10.12b, we see that we named the file ABC. We can then simply type each line of data. In our case, we have typed only two lines of data

100 1 240.72 381.63 314.26
200 2 256.91 325.70 284.11

You are required to begin each line of data with a line number when you create a file like this. We have used the numbers 100 and 200 for this purpose. Once we have saved the file ABC, it can be read by any program.

On most systems, when we read files created like this, we must also read the line numbers of each line of data we typed into the file. Thus assuming that ABC was file #1 in a given program, we would read what corresponds to each line of data on the file, by using a statement like

20   READ #1:L,N,S1,S2

The variable L would correspond to the line number, and the variables N, S1 and S2 would correspond to the data on each line.

LISTING A TELETYPEWRITER FILE

```
OLD
OLD PROGRAM NAME--NEWSAL
READY
LIST
1 240.72 381.63 314.26
2 256.91 325.70 284.11
3 461.72 395.82 311.16
4 371.64 287.20 319.16
5 301.62 300.71 386.17
READY
```

Figure 10.12a. By using the command OLD, we can obtain the file NEWSAL from the storage area. Since it is a teletypewriter file, we can use the system command LIST to print it. You cannot use LIST to print the contents of a binary file. You must write a program to do that.

```
NEW
NEW PROGRAM NAME--ABC
READY
100 1 240.72 381.63 314.26
200 2 256.91 325.70 284.11
SAVE
READY
```

Figure 10.12b. A teletypewriter file can be created without using a program, by simply typing each line of data after you name the file—here called: ABC. Each line of data must begin with a line number. The command SAVE, then saves the file.

We now discuss a situation that we can program much more efficiently if we use a binary file rather than a teletypewriter file. When you wish to change an item on a file—be it a teletypewriter or a binary file—all you have to do is write the new item in the original one's place. However, on a teletypewriter file, in order to reach the item on the file you wish to change, you have first to read all the preceding items on the file. On the other hand, on a binary file once you have specified the position on the file of the item you want, you can then either read this item or write another item in its place without reading all the preceding information on the file. For example, it is convenient to be able to position a file in a particular place if you wish to correct a given week's salary on the file NEWSAL. We could have created this file as a binary file, if we had wished to do so, by using a program similar to the one in Fig. 10.8b. However for didactic reasons, we will use the teletypewriter file we created in Fig. 10.10a and copy it onto the binary file BINSAL. We do this in Fig. 10.13a.

On some systems you save space in the computer's memory for a binary file by using the command CREATE. Thus the first thing we type* in Fig. 10.13a is CREATE BINSAL. The FILES statement

> 20 FILES NEWSAL,BINSAL

assigns the number 1 to NEWSAL and the number 2 to BINSAL. Therefore the statement

> 30 INPUT#1:N,S1,S2,S3

reads the salary information from NEWSAL and

> 50 WRITE#2:N,S1,S2,S3

writes this same information on the binary file BINSAL. We remember that INPUT # and PRINT # are the instructions for reading and writing teletypewriter files; READ # and WRITE # are the instructions for reading and writing binary files. Because of

> 40 IF END#1 THEN 70

When the computer encounters the end of file on NEWSAL, it executes line 70 and prints

> THE BINARY FILE BINSAL IS COMPLETE

as shown in Fig.10.13b. When the program is finished, it automatically places an EOF (end of file) at the end of BINSAL.

---

* On the HP 2000C we would type OPEN—BINSAL,1. The number 1 indicates that the file has one record (subdivision).

WRITING ON A BINARY FILE

```
CREATE BINSAL
10 REM COPYING A TELETYPE FILE TO A BINARY FILE
20 FILES NEWSAL,BINSAL
30 INPUT#1:N,S1,S2,S3
40 IF END#1 THEN 70
50 WRITE#2:N,S1,S2,S3
60 GO TO 30
70 PRINT"THE BINARY FILE BINSAL IS COMPLETE"
80 END
```

Figure 10.13a. We use the command CREATE to reserve space in the computer's memory for the binary file BINSAL. We then copy the teletypewriter file NEWSAL onto the binary file BINSAL. The #1 refers to NEWSAL and #2 to BINSAL. The WRITE # instruction prints information on a binary file.

```
RUN
THE BINARY FILE BINSAL IS COMPLETE
READY
```

Figure 10.13b. Running the program of Fig. 10.13a.

We now study a program that will change a given week's salary for a particular salesman on the file BINSAL. The program is shown in Fig. 10.14a. In order to position the file at the appropriate place for changing a particular salary, we use an extension of the RESET # instruction. As you might expect, in the extension of this instruction, we have to instruct the computer where to position the file. We specify this position by placing a colon after this instruction and then writing a number, variable, or an expression involving a mathematical operation whose value equals the number of items preceding the one we want. We now explain this in detail.

If we wanted to reposition file #1 so that we could read the first item on the file, or write something in its place, we would write RESET #1:0. We have written 0 here, since there are zero items preceding the first one. The instruction RESET #1:4, would instruct the computer to position the file so that it could read the fifth item on the file or write something in its place. Let us now discuss how the RESET instruction is used in the program.

The program in 40   INPUT N,M requests the salesman number—which is assigned to N—and then the number of the week for which you wish to correct the salary. This number is assigned to M. We type these two numbers in when the program is run, as is shown in Fig. 10.14b. The program then requests the corrected salary and we type it in. It is assigned to S. Since there are four numbers on the file for each salesman (corresponding to their salesman number and weekly salary for three weeks), there are $4*(N-1)$ numbers preceding the information for the salesman whose salesman number we just typed in. For example, if the value of N is 2, there are $4*(2-1)$ or 4 numbers on the file preceding the information for the second salesman. We must add $M+1$ to $4*(N-1)$, where M is the number of the week for which we wish to change the salary. We thus obtain $4*(N-1)+M+1$. But since we wish to position the file immediately before this item, we must subtract 1 from this last expression. We thus write the RESET statement as: 70   RESET # 1:4*(N-1)+M, as is shown in Fig. 10.14a.

When the program is run, we type 2 (salesman #) and 3 (week #) for the numbers we wish to be assigned to N and M, respectively. We will presently see that this means we wish to change the eighth item on the file.

The computer now interprets line 70 as

$$70 \quad \text{RESET } \#1:4*(2-1)+3$$

or 70   RESET #1:7. This means we are instructing the computer to position the file so that we can read or change the item which is preceded by the first seven items on the file; i.e., we want the eighth item on it. After the computer has positioned the file at the correct point, it then writes the corrected salary at this point on the file. It does this when 80   PRINT #1:S, is executed. We then have the option of changing more items on the file or having the computer list the contents of the file and then ending the program. We opt for the latter. Thus when the computer prints TYPE Y FOR MORE ;ELSE N. ?, we type N. The next statement executed, 120   RESET #1, instructs the computer to position the file to its beginning. When the I loop is executed the contents of the corrected file are printed on the teletype.

CORRECTING A BINARY FILE

```
10  REM CORRECTS A BINARY FILE
20  FILES BINSAL
30  PRINT "SALESMAN#, WEEK# YOU WANT CORRECTED";
40  INPUT N,M
50  PRINT "CORRECTED SALARY";
60  INPUT S
70  RESET#1:4*(N-1)+M
80  PRINT#1:S
90  PRINT "TYPE Y FOR MORE ELSE; N.";
100 INPUT A$
110 IF A$="Y" THEN 30
120 RESET #1
130 PRINT "CORRECTED SALARY"
140 PRINT "SALESMAN#","1ST WEEK","2ND WEEK","3RD WEEK"
150 FOR I=1 TO 5
160 READ #1:N,S1,S2,S3
170 PRINT N,S1,S2,S3
180 NEXT I
190 END
```

Figure 10.14a. By using an extension of the RESET # statement, we can instruct the computer where we want it to position a file. The value of the expression following the colon in this statement specifies how many items on the file precede the item we want. This program corrects a particular weekly salary for a given salesman on BINSAL. The READ # instruction reads information from a binary file.

```
RUN
SALESMAN#, WEEK# YOU WANT CORRECTED?2,3
CORRECTED SALARY?346.21
TYPE Y FOR MORE ELSE;N.?N
CORRECTED SALARY
SALESMAN#        1ST WEEK        2ND WEEK        3RD WEEK
   1              240.72          381.63          314.26
   2              256.91          325.7           346.21
   3              461.72          395.82          311.16
   4              371.64          287.2           319.61
   5              301.62          300.71          386.17
READY
```

Figure 10.14b. After we have corrected the third week's salary for salesman number 2, the program lists the contents of BINSAL. We see that here the correction is included.

On some systems, there are two functions that can be used with binary files. They are named LOC(I) and LOF(I), where the value of I is the number of the file in question.

The value of the first, LOC(I), is the number of items preceding the point on the file where the file is currently positioned. Thus, if the value of LOC(2) is 4, then file number 2 has been positioned so that the fifth item will be the next one processed.

The value of LOF(I) is the total number of items on the file. Thus if file number 3 has 40 items on it, the value of LOF(3) would be 40. Using these two functions, we could instruct the computer to go to line 80 upon reaching an EOF on file number 1 by writing

```
30   IF LOC(1) = LOF(1) THEN 80
```

PROBLEMS

1. What will be printed by the following program?

```
10    FOR I=1 TO 3
20    READ A,B$,C$
30    PRINT USING 50,A,B$
40    DATA 1,ST,RED,2,ND,WHITE,3,RD,BLUE
50: MY #,## CHOICE IS ####
60    NEXT I
70    END
```

2. What will be printed by the program in problem 1, if line 50 is changed to

```
50:MY#"##" CHOICE IS "####"
```

3. What is printed by the following program?

```
10      PRINT USING 20, 1, 2, 3
20      ONE #.#, TWO #.#, THREE #.# FOUR #.#, FIVE
30      END
```

4. What is printed by the following program?

```
10    PRINT USING 20,"ONE",1,"TWO",2,THREE
20: NUMBER ### ###
30    END
```

5. What is printed by the following program?

```
10    PRINT USING 20,19,ONE,2*3*4*5*6,1*2*3*4
20: ##.# ↑↑↑↑,###↑↑↑,#.#↑↑ #.###↑↑↑↑↑
30    END
```

6. Write a program which for the integers from 1 to 10 will print the number, the number squared, and the number cubed. Print the results in column form so that they are centered under the proper label.

7. Given the file ABC which contains five numbers in the following order

122.3	96.41	17.2	29.62	27.6	END OF FILE

   i.e., 122.3 is first and 27.6 is last:
   a. write a program that will copy this file onto another file called DEF.
   b. Write a program that will change the 17.2 on file ABC to 396.4, but will leave the rest of the file unchanged.
   c. Write a program that will read the numbers on file ABC and then write these numbers in ascending order on a new file called SORT.

8. Create a file called MARKS and place on it 20 student's marks. Then write another program that will read MARKS and will produce a histogram of the marks. The histogram should cover the following intervals:
   a. below 60
   b. between 70 and 79
   c. betwen 80 and 89
   d. between 90 and 100

9. Create a binary file called BINAR and write 20 random numbers on it. Copy that file onto a teletypewriter file called TEL. Print the contents of TEL by using the command LIST.

10. Create a file INCOM1 on which you place the salary of 20 men. Create another file INCOM2 on which you place the salaries of 20 women. Then write a program which will read the information on these two files and place it on a third file called MERGE. The salary for each woman should be preceded by the number 1 and the salary for each man should be preceded by the number 2, so that when you read MERGE you should be able to distinguish between a man's salary and a woman's salary.

11. Read the file MERGE created in problem 10 and make a histogram of
    a. women's salaries
    b. men's salaries
    c. combined salaries

Subject Index